Eve Of Apocalypse

The Valley Of Achor, A Door Of Hope

Rita De Masi Kelley

EVE OF APOCALYPSE
Rita De Masi Kelley

Published By:
KPG Book Publishers
(a division of Kingdom Publishing Group, Inc.)
P.O. Box 3272, Richmond, VA 23228
www.kingdompublishing.org

Library of Congress
©2010 by Rita De Masi Kelley

ISBN 13: 978-0-9826370-6-7

Cover design: Matthew Williams, Sr.

Dedicated to my son, David, and my most
cherished friends, Blanch and Irving Rotberg

ACKNOWLEDGMENTS

All Hebrew (Old Testament) Scripture quotations and references are taken from the ARTSCROLL Series of the Tanach, the Stone Edition. They include: The Torah/Prophets/Writings, The twenty-four Books of the Bible Newly Translated and Annotated. Published Copyright 1996 by Mesorah Publications, Ltd., 4401 Second Avenue, Brooklyn, New York 11232.

All New Testament Scripture Quotations identifies the "Delitzsch" a Hebrew/English Translation of the King James Version (KJV). Presented to the Jewish Nation by Hope of Israel Publications, P.O. Box 1700, Powder Springs, Ga. 30127.

To archeologists everywhere, I extend a deep, heartfelt thanks for making the results of their published works available to the public. My gratitude goes out to them in unlimited measure.

My thanks to archeologist, James Woods of ABR (Archeology Biblical Review), for his assistance in recommending Westminster Seminary's Library as a resource for archeological research in trying to locate the site of the Valley of Achor. ABR is in search of the Biblical cities of Bethel and Ai. The Valley of Achor lies somewhere between or near these locations.

Special thanks go to the Research Newsletter which ended my ten year search for the location of the Valley of Achor.

Special thanks also goes to Willamstown, New Jersey's Monroe Township's research librarian, for assisting me with obtaining many resource books.

In addition I would also like to acknowledge, The Tuttleman Library of Gratz College, The Harry Stern Family Institute for Israel Studies, located in Melrose Park, Pa. for permission to use their library in my quest for more knowledge of Jewish culture, religion and history, as well as other topics relating to the Jewish people.

A special thanks to Eastern Baptist Theological Seminary for the use of their library for my research.

This book also profits from the assistance of many persons whose names do not appear in this acknowledgment. That is because some people who were patients of mine in the hospital at the time I worked as a Registered Nurse that were discharged before I had the opportunity to keep a record. One of the persons I do recall was a chemical physicist from Rutgers University in Camden, N.J. The other person, an everyday citizen who was so well read that he was able to share his knowledge on the fact that there were cities other than Rome which stood on "Seven Hills" (Revelation 17:9).

The bibliography of this book I tried to insure that it would be accurate and complete, however, having read to date over one-hundred and fifty books, or more, I may have missed giving credit where credit was due. A human failing in covering thirty years of research. I therefore humbly acknowledge my debt of gratitude for every book, magazine, and scrap of material which assisted me in this composition, rich in biblical prophecy set against a fictional, fact based story line.

For permission to reprint copyright materials, grateful acknowledgment is made to all of the publishers, authors and agents in the Bibliography.

Not to be forgotten, my home church, Bethel Christian Assembly, my pastors, my Women's Proverbs Group and church members.

And special thanks to my immediate family and friends.

PREFACE

Norm Rorer of Christian Writers Guild once said, "Words bless, words kill, words inspire and words corrupt." It is also true, I believe, that words can be true and false at the same time. When semantics of words are misused, they prove to be deceptive and deadly. Aldous Huxley once commented, "Thanks to words, we have been able to rise above the brutes and thanks to words, we have often sunk to the level of demons."

I have had my own battle with words and its struggles with the mind. It happened during a time in my past when I was caught up in a religious cult. At the time, I lived in the polarized world of this religious cult. I lived in a state of continual fear and social isolation. Fear controlled my everyday thinking. I was full of fear that terrorized me to the point that my whole body trembled whenever I heard the name of Jesus.

My doctrinal beliefs were based on fear. Fear of believing any other doctrine than those of the religious cult. Fear that the end of the world was imminent. Fear that even if I did survive Armageddon I would be destroyed forever in an instant, if I made one mistake or committed one sin. So that no matter how good or sincere I was in the past or whatever good deeds I did do for God, even if they were done sincerely with a pure motive, it would not count!

Each and every moment of each and every day I lived in this nightmare in abject terror. "They," the religious leaders of the cult, were masters of deception. Masters of deception with twisted minds and twisted words. "They," those who remained nameless, ran the gambit of semantics in their published teachings.

I also faced fear of failure, not as a way to seek God's mercy and grace, but fearful of rejection and destruction by Him. This meant that I would be faced without mercy or forgiveness for any human transgressions. Thus, "They," committed the sin of omission by failing to teach that Jesus Christ died for our sins and the sins of the whole world. The weight was too much. The burden was unbearable. The reason "They" gave for omitting the name of each leader and author of all of their teachings published in their books, magazines, articles or tracts was explained under the guise of false humility, i.e., "In their organization they wanted none of their writers or the authors of their publications to be given undue honor or praise for their written works." "They," as they would refer to themselves (their leaders) and their anonymous writers who never revealed their writer's names or identified who composed and authored their religious books, magazine articles or tracts remained hidden. The real reason and only true motives were failure to take journalistic leadership, responsibility or accountability. This anonymity came in handy especially since their numerous predictions about the date for the "End of the World," had more than once failed to materialize. Date after date was changed on a whim and their followers were told to accept all their dates and their predictions without question.

"They" used linguistics, semantics and brainwashing techniques. This was done without the knowledge of their followers. "They" used these phenomena in and of itself wrapped up in a self-deception, creating a distortion between words and their real meanings, and using faulty language, forming abstract concepts in the interior world of words, in the minds of their followers that were not true.

It was after being deprogrammed that I completely erased from my mind all of the lies which "They" taught me, along with the subsequent concepts, which had formed my erroneous beliefs. When I came out from under the clutches of this religious cult I found out I had the rare ability to unravel my own misconceptions, perceptions, presumptions and assumptions, entering the stark, sobering world of "reality." In real time I discovered who the real Jesus Christ is, was and ever will be! The Holy Spirit is given to all who believe in Jesus Christ. I was finally able to face the "real truth." Set free from the chains of false beliefs and the misuse of words, I no longer was brainwashed.

In time, my mind went through a convulsive and colossal revolution, then on into a stunning transformation. I went from living in constant dread and fear, with a false sense of peace into a real faith and true peace, one which Jesus Christ Himself promised to those who follow Him. He said, "Peace I leave you. My peace I give unto you: not as the world giveth, give I unto you. Let not your heart be troubled, neither let it be afraid" (John 14:27).

A profound level of conscious self-awareness grew within me. I found I was now able to distinguish and discern between a variety of layers of my thoughts. I became increasingly more aware of the difference between objective and subjective thought. I began to understand the sin of omission used by most cults and that like most cults, they exhibit the telltale sign—use some truth mixed in with lies. Knowing the real truth created a tremendous healing in my thought life. No longer sad or frightened, I began to feel extremely happy. I found that now, no matter what the circumstances were, if they were "good" or "bad," I could function in the world around me like I never had before.

Nevertheless, during this transition, I did at one point feel like Eliza Doolittle did in the Broadway hit play, "Pygmalion," better known as, "My Fair Lady." In the story she was taken from a life of poverty off the streets of London and instructed by her rescuer, Professor Higgins on how to speak perfect English. Although she worked very hard to get all her words right, and after speaking perfect English correctly at a party held among the upper-class, she received no reward for her efforts. Not even a kind word from her teacher, Professor Higgins. Disillusioned, she sang over and over in song, "Words, words, words, I am so sick of words!" That is exactly how I felt. Words, I felt at times, were too often spoken without real meaning or bringing any true satisfaction. Despite my disillusionment, I can say with a grateful heart that I am happy that I did not give up my search for God and the real meaning of life. I did decide however, to find out who God was, who I was, why I was here on earth and where I was going once I died. So, I said to myself, "I am sick and tired of everyone telling me what to believe! I am going to sit down with my Bible and ask God to reveal Himself to me!"

It was then that I decided to give up and reject all I had ever learned or been taught about religious doctrine and all previous interpretation of the Bible's meaning taught to me by others. I began by praying for God's guidance and direction as I read and studied the Bible daily, exploring the inner meaning which lay behind the words and to help me reject and avoid falling into the vicious quicksand of heresy. During this same period of time, my husband, Albert, and I decided to join a Bible believing church.

Over the course of time, as I continued to learn Holy Scripture I began to understand myself, the world I lived in, and the people, family and friends I had. But the monumental experience of all was getting to understand and know God. It was deep and it was awesome.

The results of this search for the truth and its meaning gave me assurance and a sense of security and peace that were both miraculously wonderful and incredible. It was beyond my wildest dreams. I thought to myself, "Here I am, just an ordinary person who has met the extraordinary and invincible universal God!" Today, most religious groups and organizations would scoff, ridicule me or say that because of this "Theophany" or some would call a "Christophany," they would in unbelief reject my experience and call me psychotic and say, "No one can have this experience today." Yet the Bible in the so called "Old Testament," gives many references of Theophanies, i.e., God walking on the ground, the earth, appearing and speaking to men and to the seventy men who were with Moses on the Mount, during the Jews' Exodus from Egypt. Yet, the proof is that this "Theophany" paved the way for me to attain a higher thought life, improve my character and increase my social skills, all which led me to lead a more happy, positive and joyful life.

Soon I was able to clear my mind of the past, forgive and forget any and all hurts. I was now able to think more clearly. I felt that I had been given a fresh start. It was a new beginning for me, a paradigm shift, or you could say I had a wonderful "born again" experience. This was the beginning of a walk with Christ and led to my life as a Christian "mystic." An experience between myself and God. I believe this happened because of God's rich grace, mercy and love towards a woman who was an emotional cripple.

I believe it also happened because I did my part, by being willing to forego all prior religious beliefs I had held up until that time. I would call this experience, a "psychological self emptying," which I believe the Apostle Paul speaks about in Philippians 2:3–8. According to my understanding of these verses an act of humility is required before we can learn the truth.

Advancing in the knowledge of God through my daily Bible reading and study, I learned more about the historical experiences that occurred between the Living God and the Jews, both as a nation and as individuals. Eventually I found myself becoming more involved with the lives of the people around me.

A strong intellectual awareness developed in me, one that I believe I always had, but that apparently lay dormant, while it sat among the rusting chains in the prison of my own self-centeredness, self-righteousness and delivered from the more insidious self-pity and the more serious self-deception. The spectacular transformation which occurred in my mind started with my everyday life, and subsequently my daily life began to improve. The change was so dramatic that when I looked into the mirror, I could hardly recognize myself. I no longer suffered from depression. I felt more and more that I fit in with people who crossed my path each and every ordinary and extraordinary day. It was wonderful! So wonderful, a sense of relief and freedom flooded my heart and soul. I was free! I was transformed from living life as an emotional cripple. Delivered and no longer bound to the abstract world of a man-made religion. Instead I went on into the intoxicating and breathtaking world of an encounter with the Living and True God, my Maker and Creator!

So, with God's help I escaped the darkness and entered into His marvelous light. The chains that held my heart and mind captive were broken.

No longer living life wrapped up in the bondage of self-centeredness and ignorance, I felt whole, full of joy and excited about the future and the possibilities that were up ahead of me.

Because I was now able to make the transition from understanding spiritual matters in a mentally abstract way to understanding them within the context of a real and vibrant Christian "mystical" experience, I could say that I truly understood the meaning of Jesus' words, "You shall know the truth and the truth shall set you free" (John 8:32).

Free mentally, emotionally and spiritually. With my perceptions changed and renewed I no longer sought to escape the stark realities of life. I now looked at life's realities from a new and clear viewpoint. Reality blossomed into lessons to learn for growth and development of character and in a closer walk with God. I could now face my problems, learning how to confront them with God's love, care and discipline, going through them and the subsequent pain in a positive way. The results led to my making better decisions, securing the core of my being as I journeyed through this once in a lifetime trip in real time.

It was during this time that I also made a career change. Upon graduation from high school, I entered a career as a bookkeeper. Then through a series of unusual events I left that field and became a Licensed Practical Nurse (LPN). Later I would continue on in this career as a Registered Nurse (RN).

Upon graduating as an LPN, I entered the field of private duty nursing. The majority of my clients were Jewish professionals.

Taking care of the Jewish people created in my heart and mind a new awareness and a deep love and appreciation for these wonderful, dynamic people.

As I continued with my Biblical studies, I rapidly came out from under my ignorance about these special people, their culture and their profound history as a nation, at times with God and at times without God. A special love developed between me and the Jews I cared for. I must say this was one of the happiest periods of my life! And so I came to love the Jews of the Bible and the Jews of today, learning more about them through the Hebrew Scriptures and by living and working with them each day. I felt inspired by the believing Jews and their extraordinary relationship with the Omnipotent, Omniscient, Omnipresent God of the Universe as recorded in the Holy Bible. My lament was the fact that some of these wonderful Jewish people had become atheistic, if not openly, then by the way they lived their daily life, vacant, without God.

Early on in my career as a nurse, I had the privilege of taking care of a Jewish client by the name of Blanche Rotburg. Blanche had undergone surgery for a radical left mastectomy the year before and now one year later when I came to care for her she had a right radical mastectomy.

I can look back and remember that day as if it were only yesterday. It was my first day on duty with Blanche. I entered the hospital room and introduced myself. Blanche was lying down in the hospital bed. When she saw me enter the room she pulled herself up and sat in an upright position and pulling up her hospital gown she proceeded to show me the surgical stitches across her chest. She said to me, "How do you like my signature?" And sure enough the stitches zigzagged, looking like a John Hancock scrolled across her chest. We both laughed; that broke the ice. Blanche had a wonderful way of making me feel comfortable and at ease.

The next day Blanche did not disappoint me. In her awesome way with social skills always her priority, she said to me, "I want to go home by Saturday." (This was now Wednesday. Only her first post-op day.) Then she repeated, "I need to go home by Saturday because I am having a party and I need to make my hors d'oeuvres." Tell me, how can you forget a person like that?

Over the course of the next ten years I continued to take care of Blanche, mostly in winter months. By that time I had become like one of the family to her and her husband, Irving. To me they had become my second set of parents.

It was during those years that I met Blanche's husband, Irving, and many members of her family and friends. No one could be as devoted a husband as Irving was to Blanche. It was a real delight to witness, both the devotion and attention he gave Blanche.

The concept and subtitle for this book came out of this burgeoning love for these two very special Jewish people.

The focus of this novel is centered on the Jewish people, the Nation of Israel and a special place located in the land of Israel, once known in the Bible as the "Valley of Achor," the sub-title of this novel, "Eve of Apocalypse." Today this location is known as the "Wadi Qumran." Our Creator personally designated this place for the Jewish nation. This action on their behalf signified God's love and desire to give them a good measure of hope. Speaking directly to them, He said, "But I will court her again, (speaking to Israel) and bring her into the wilderness, and speak to her tenderly there. There will I give back her vineyards to her, and transform her Valley of Troubles into a Door of Hope" (Hosea 2:15–17). A hope that will carry them through a future time of "great trouble." The irony being that the name of this location, "The Valley of Achor" actually means "The Valley of Trouble." Hitherto God in the future will transform this Valley into "The Valley of Hope."

This verse of scripture for all intended purposes is for the future of the Jew. When I refer to Holy Scripture in this novel my focus will

X

be on the Bible and some of the Jews' religious, political, geographical and archeological conflicts. It will reveal some of their past, present and future experiences as Jews and their relationship with God, written on the pages of human history. To the non-Jewish reader I would like to say, we Gentiles are instructed by the words of God to, "Pray for the peace of Jerusalem" (Psalm 122:6). Although I acknowledge those who do have a genuine Jewish faith, I must also acknowledge my responsibility and role as a Christian who loves the Jews and the Jewish Nation. I will combat any anti-Semitism by the Church through these pages. I also wish to raise awareness, moral and spiritual support for Israel and the Jewish people, and to let them know there is a deeper and a more profound knowledge of God which can be obtained by knowing His Son, Jesus Christ. Yes the Jew is the repository of the Hebrew Scriptures, wherein lies a depth in understanding God which was made clear in the unmistakable words which Jesus Christ uttered and that are recorded in the Delitzsh (Hebrew/English New Testament).

Richard Wumbrand, a natural born Jew and himself a convert to Christianity, once stated, "Anti-Semitism (in the Church) is one of the many weaknesses it has, but on the other hand," he said, "It has its diametric opposite—Jewish chauvinism and contempt for Christian people and for Christian Jews."

Today, this observation could not be more true. We find that at the present time in our own generation that there are Jews who are born Jews by Jewish parents who have converted to Christianity, who become "completed Jews" as they call themselves. They are also known as "Messianic Jews," along with another group who are known as "Jews for Jesus." These groups do not join the traditional churches of Christianity. They instead worship and fellowship as independent groups in their own right, incorporating their Christianity with much if not all of their Jewish culture. In Israel they are however, not recognized by the Jewish State and there are currently laws pending to make it a "crime to convert or evangelize Jews."

It is my hope and my prayer that the Jews will increase their hunger for Jesus Christ and will no longer take offense at our attempts to lead them into a deeper relationship with God. Also, I wish to help them understand and acknowledge our one and only true motive; our desire to unlock the secrets which lie buried in the Bible. I acknowledge the spiritual treasures that I have received in my reading and study from them. I am therefore inviting them to take a look from an insider vantage point by exploring, analyzing, inquiring and delving into the brilliant biblical conceptions predicted in their Hebrew Scriptures by their prophets concerning His identity and their glorious future once they respond to it.

It has been said, "When you write, you prevail. Only a born writer can endure the labor of becoming one. Writers are born and then made better."

Because I am a nova writer I cannot and would not compare myself and what I wrote in this novel to what other great saints, philosophers, prophets and visionaries have written or interpreted about end-time prophesies. Sir Isaac Newton once said, "If I see so far, then it is because I stood on the shoulders of other giants." Since I cannot compare myself to his genius, I can only say that I hope what I have written will help the reader catch even just a flicker of light. I therefore ask the reader to keep in mind that this is a fictional novel and not a theological work. It is not a position or a scholarly treatise. Therefore part of the story is based on true fact, while others are based on possible scenarios as well as conjecture. All characters are fictitious. This novel is a fictional work. It does not in anyway reflect on the history making fictional novel, "The Protocols of Zion," which was released to the public on approximately February 1921. This book depicts what many at the time interpreted erroneously. They accused the Jews of "Hatching a plan to take over the world." When the "Protocols" were at that time of their release sent to the Russian government. The Czar examined them and rejected them as a cause for Jews to conquer the world. Incredibly, Hitler believed that they were true and authentic. He did not want the Jews running the world. He therefore used the Protocols as a death warrant to exterminate and eliminate all Jews.

But, according to Biblical prophesy, let it be known that God has chosen the Jew to lead the "Ultimate World Order" and not the Jews in and of themselves. Neither will it be by Jewish political power, but by the "Anointing" and the "Anointed One," Jesus Christ who will come. He will bring this about.

There are also times in this novel that I will call on the natural world and at other times using imaginary landscapes in fictional forms. My goal, I felt, was to help others see that speculations about prophesy are not harmful, unless you make it "Dogma." Instead I invite the reader into the world of discovery. It is my desire to help the reader to sharpen their God given gift of intuition, when considering the Bible's prophesies, without confusing the reader of the profound truth about God and the human character. Perhaps this fictional novel will cause the reader to look at "Biblical prophesy" through differing viewpoints while at the same time avoiding "heresy." Hopefully it will unravel some obscure perceptions, insights and analysis of the world's current events. Another goal of this novel is to assist the Christian community to learn some of the dangers of falling away from the faith. It is here I wish all to repeat daily, the heartfelt prayer of the blessed martyr, St. Justin, "... grant us ... to avoid all deceptions of error, and to become steadfast in faith. Amen." In that light, I would also like to make it clear that what I have written here is not "set in stone." All that I am suggesting is that as the story unfolds in this novel, it will reveal some new insights into old interpretations of end-time "Biblical Prophesies." It is my hope that the reader will be encouraged to stop, take a look and listen, letting the story speak for itself.

I am also asking them to take a look back on the factual and counterfactual. After all, what has been left to us in the entire book of "The Revelation" is only an "outline" of future events.

TABLE OF CONTENTS

In the Holy Bible, also referred to as Holy Scripture, we find written in Genesis the 15th chapter, the "Title Deed" given by God to Israel. Its writing reveals Israel's original territory with the geographical boundaries, deeded to them by God, the Creator, owner and proprietor of all things. He alone owns the "Title Deed" of the entire universe and especially this globe, our earth. Documented in Psalm 24:1 is the written endorsement, as follows: "THE EARTH BELONGS TO GOD!" And since He owns the Title Deed, He can give it to whomever He wants to!

Former Prime Minister of Israel, Benjamin Netanyahu in his book, "A Place among the Nations," offers support for the startling assertion that it was not the Jews who usurped the land from the Arabs, but the Arabs who usurped the land from the Jews. Some believe the Deed given to Israel by God includes all the land from the Euphrates River to the Nile River. This would include practically all of Syria, all of Jordan, about one-half of Iraq, all of Palestine, Lebanon, the Sinai Peninsula, and all of Egypt.

Documentation claiming Israel's historical rights to all of this territory by divine decree of the royal land grant is found in the following Biblical Scriptures: Genesis 15:7–8, 15:13–16, Deuteronomy chapters 28–30, Jeremiah chapters 30–31, and Ezekiel chapter 36. Descriptions of its borders and geographical boundaries are also found in Genesis 15:18–21 (Abrahamic), "… Unto thy seed have I given this land, from the river of Egypt unto the great river, the river Euphrates" (Exodus 23:24–31). (General) Numbers 34:1–14, (Mosaic) Joshua 1:3 (at the Jordan River), Ezekiel 47:13 (during the coming millennium). Isaiah chapters 59 and 60 tell us that the Jews are to experience world and international political supremacy. It is not that the Jew is worse or better than other men. Why then? For the welfare of all nations. Genesis 12:3, "In thee shall all the families of the earth be blessed."

As for the Arab Nations, their view of who owns the land of Palestine, is that Ishmael was Abraham's firstborn son and so the birthright belongs to them. Holy Scripture however records that the promise was to Isaac, not Ishmael, the full legitimate son of Abraham through marriage, but was by Abraham, conceived by Sarah's handmaid.

I will also echo what William E. Blackstone wrote in his book, "Jesus is Coming." He said, "The Title Deed to Palestine is recorded, not once in the 6,666 sentences of the Koran, nor in the Mohammedan Gerai of Jerusalem, nor the Serglio of Constantinople, but in the hundreds of Bibles now extant in more than three hundred languages of earth. Therefore this property along with its property rights belongs to the Jew by Divine Decree." As a matter of fact, Mike Evens states in his book, "Jerusalem Betrayed," that "Muhammad never actually set foot in Jerusalem."

1

And to conclude, "Not by the British, the United Nations, the Ottoman Turks, the Christian Crusades, nor the Islamic forces can change these birthrights." The Bible is therefore a Jewish Mandate.

Chapter 1

The Beginning Of The End Of The Last Days

"The choice is not peace or street riots, not even peace or war, but peace or annihilation."
~Michael Drosnin, Bible Code II

"The end of a matter is better than its beginning."
~Ecclesiastes 7:8

It was May 4th, the Jerusalem Day celebration. The celebration had begun a week after Passover's "Yon Hashooecha," Holocaust Remembrance Day. I, Felix Sebastian Fox, newly elected Prime Minister of Israel, was in my condominium at the King David Hotel, when at the stroke of midnight I woke out of a deep sleep to the ring of the telephone. I knew this was precipitating a national crisis. I fastened my eyes upon the telephone's pulsing red light. My hands trembled as I hit the emergency button, picked up the receiver, clutching it against my cheek. Breathless I answered, it, "Prime Minister Fox."

On the other end of the line, his voice quivering, he said, "Felix, this is Benny." It was my Minister of Defense, Benny Stein.

I said, "Yes, I am listening."

"Felix, we're facing a national crisis. Intelligence (The Mossad) has received an urgent document. A message has been decoded. It tells us that Iraq has a new leader, the Dictator, Ahmet Humrabi. And as president of Iraq he has broken our seven-year peace treaty. He's dismantled Iraq's Democracy and re-established a dictatorship, along with a coalition of ten Arab nations backed by its allies, China. Together they have taken over Jordan, wiping out all of Jordan's Royal Air Force, killing all of the Royal Family and set up government headquarters in Amon, the city on Seven Hills. What the hell does he want with Jordan," Benny said, and hesitated several seconds.

"Well, go on Benny! What is it," I asked? I said, "Why this is preposterous!" With my stomach turning, and sweat dripping from my body, I said, "I'll fix that stoned, diabolical drug addict, drug dealing piece of trash!"

Benny, answering in a deep halting voice said, "Felix, you'd better sit down for this one."

Boiling inside I braced myself and in a staccato tone of voice, I barked, "Benny, what about Operation Achor? Does Ahnet and his new government know about it?"

Benny replied, "Felix, word has leaked out about Operation Achor. Ahmet knows you have had to break the code contained in the treasure map recorded on the Copper Scroll and that you have discovered where all of the hidden treasures consisting of thirty-five tons of gold, the sixty-five tons of silver, along with all of the lost second Temple treasures."

I asked Benny, "Who is the traitor that caused the leak?"

Benny replied, "Intelligence is working on it as we speak, Felix."

"Benny, do they know where the treasures are located?"

Benny replied, "No. All they know, Felix, is that its buried in Jordan, somewhere in the Valley of Achor on land that was once originally ours and was up until now under Jordan's military zone. Ahmet, has taken control over Jordan."

"Benny," I belched out, "They know that the land is legally ours. For God's sake every Bible in the world documents that Israel legally holds the original 'Title Deed' to this territory. They will not get away with it. I'll see to that."

Benny replied, "Yes, Felix, that is our problem."

Thoughts whirled through my mind; one that I hoped would bring me some peace. I asked Benny about it. "Benny, do they know about Operation Chondriana?"

"No, thank God," Benny replied.

Relieved about his reply, I quickly informed Benny, "I'll issue an immediate directive, putting the military on full battle alert and institute a civilian nuclear attack evacuation plan. I'll call for an emergency session of the Knesset to convene. Start immediate mass production of the Chondriana. And Benny, make sure the 'Rizadh' (Arabs Secret Service) does not get word of it."

Benny hung up and immediately complied with my directive.

After I hung up with Benny, I alerted all government departments, ready to meet with them, when I heard what sounded like gun shots! Expecting to face another crisis, I rose from my bed as fast as my tired body would let me. Just as I reached the bay window in the living room, the source of the sounds, my bodyguards bolted into the room. Against their wishes, I cautiously opened the vertical blinds. I looked out the window and up into the night sky. What sounded like gun shots turned out to be an unexpected meteor shower. Grateful it was not a bomb, I watched as earth-grazers fell into a kaleidoscope of bright white, pink, silver and red flashes of tiny meteorites cascading with their hot cinders as they evaporated into dust on their downward dance, spiraling towards the earth. Seeing this was not a crisis, my bodyguards, Sam and Jeffrey, returned to their posts. I glanced at my watch, six o'clock Monday morning. I informed my bodyguards to expect two Mossed Agents and for them to be prepared to make a quick exit.

War was imminent. I, for one, had no time to lose. In a state of satisfaction, Benny, my father, Fillmore and I were ready to begin production of an army of 200 million human clones! Any fears or doubts which may have flooded my mind about using the Chondriana as a cloned army, but Israel had the right to defend itself. Would I be the one blamed for starting this war? Or was Ahmet the one who would become classified as notorious as one who started the war to end all wars? With just the push of a button would all be "said and done?" Would it turn out to be global nuclear war? Would it mean the end of civilization as we now know it? Would this be the beginning of the end? Would this mean the end of human existence, Armageddon? Would 95% of mankind die? Would they be the first humans to ever see their own extinction? Would it be a permanent extinction? My thoughts were interrupted by the sound of my pager. I picked it up and answered it. "Felix here."

"Mr. Prime Minister, the two Mossed Agents have arrived," my bodyguard spoke in a monotone voice.

"Let them in," I said. I unlocked the entrance door to my apartment, swinging the doors wide open. My two bodyguards stepped aside and let the secret service agents enter.

"Come in, gentlemen, come on in. Take a seat," I said. I recognized Sid as one of them.

In a grim tone of voice they said, "Good morning, Mr. Prime Minister."

Then, handing me a Top Secret envelope, Sid said, "You know me, Mr. Prime Minister, and this is Larry Birenbaum."

"Yes, good morning to you too, gentlemen," I greeted them both.

Both men sat down, looking as stunned as I did over the developing crisis. Placing the envelope on the top of my marbled desk, I pulled the documents out and read them. My hands began to tremble, causing the pages to shake as the reality of my decision to fight for the rights of Israel set in.

Breaking out into a cold sweat, a stygian darkness fell over me. I felt like someone had just hit me over the head with a hammer. I searched into my back pocket and pulled out my handkerchief, wiping my face and hands. When I finished reading the documents I put them down onto my desk and signed the directives declaring a state of war against Iraq, and all ten Arab nations of confederates. I then placed the Military Intelligence Unit (AMAM) and Israeli Defense Forces (IDF) along with our Navel Intelligence Reconnaissance Commandos, The Sayret Matcal on full military alert.

Sid said, "Mr. Prime Minister, The Institute (The Mossed) has followed all of your orders and has put all of our secret service agents in their target countries on full war alert according to Operation Daylight (Israel's highest state of alert), along with the plans for a mass evacuation plan for all citizens, except essential services. Then I contacted the Chairman of the Knesset, the state Attorney General, Larry Heim, and the Knesset's Law Committee Chairman, Jack Cohen along with the Minister of Judicial Affairs, the Deputy Commander of the police Investigation Division and the Commander General of Security to inform them of my actions in response to this crisis and the emergency session I called for all members of our government."

Sid, in turn, said, "The Institute has already followed all National Emergency Plans and Policies. They've already alerted the Shin Bet, our Internal Intelligence and the Shasack, our Internal Security Police. In turn they have also contacted the Magen David Adon (Israel's Red Cross)."

Then, hesitating, Sid asked Felix, "Do you want to activate the Kidon, our Assassination Unit?"

"Yes, but only as a last minute action," I replied.

"Well gentlemen, this concludes our meeting. I will keep you briefed on all succeeding developments. I will be leaving momentarily to attend the emergency session of Parliament. So, if that is all for you, good day."

Sid and Larry said in unison "Good-day, Mr. Prime Minister," and left the apartment.

Focused on the moment, I searched my jacket pocket and pulled out one of my Camel's. It was a habit I was determined to give up, but not right now. Picking up a lighter from off of my beloved Hemingway desk, I lit up my cigarette. Taking in a long, slow drag, I watched as the swirling smoke spiraled upward, filling the room with the rancid smell of tobacco and waited for Sam, my limo driver. While I was waiting I held no fears of being outnumbered by that Iraqi Dictator, Ahmet, or his newly formed coalition. In fact, I was exhilarated. We now had a secret weapon, the Chondriana. They were not mere Drones. They were not robots, but an army of cloned human beings. Those damn terrorists are going to get the shock of their lives! It would bring Israel out on top of the world's future. And no one would ever know the profound joy I had in unlocking the code of the Copper Scroll's treasure map, leading to my discovery of its enormous treasures and great wealth there in the Valley of Achor. We would enjoy the financial independence our people had longed for, but had been denied. No longer would Israel be humbled by relying on aid from other nations. This would make it easy to fund the mass production of Operation Chondriana. Knowing that we had added the gene Delta thirty-two, given to each of them along with other immune genes making them completely disease free! Who or what could mirror this intense and overwhelming complete my sense of security? For a moment in spite of the crisis, I felt we, our nation to be almost invincible!

As usual the ring of the telephone interrupted my thoughts. Annoyed I picked up the receiver and answered, "Hello, Prime Minister Fox here."

After a few seconds of unremitting silence the other party said, "Hello Felix, this is Dan Wingate."

Well, I thought, it does not take long for the press to seize the moment of crisis. Dan was from Asure Magazine. I knew Dan and his father, Orde Wingate, the father of the IDF, Israeli Defense Force. Originally the IDF was called the Haganah. The Haganah had our early roots in our informal Jewish efforts at self defense in the early days of WWI.

"Of course you no doubt have many questions about our current crisis with Iraq and its new Dictator Ahmet and what has happened to Jordan."

"Yes," Dan said.

"Yes, and we are next," I retorted!

"Listen Dan, I have scheduled an emergency session of the Knesset to convene at nine o'clock. When I call on the Press after the opening session, you can have the first question."

Dan said, "Thanks Prime Minister Fox, see you then," and hung up.

Speaking with Dan triggered memories of earlier days when Dan and I were in college for several years in the Mossed. It brought back pleasant memories of our frequent evening dinners Dan and Orde spent with my father, Fillmore, and my mother, Sarah, at our house. Those were the days, unlike today; days of intrigue and suspense spent deciphering codes, both becoming accomplished cryptographers. We enjoyed unlocking the toughest secret codes, learning from the writings of the profound master of code breakers, Edgar Allen Poe. Still today, the military will not need to break codes like AdFXGH that were used to beat the Germans in WWI, nor the Japanese PURPLE,JN25 cipher in WWII, because of our modern day advance in using applied algebraic geometry for coding theory as well as physics and computation, procedures that would leave even Poe in the dust!

Fond memories of my mother Sarah flashed across my mind. How well I remember her saying to me, "Felix, you will not be satisfied until you know the whole Ganesh migilah." She was an Orthodox, Jewish believer and a natural born Israeli with a big heart. After raising me as an Orthodox Jewish believer, she felt let down when I left the God of my fathers and became a secular Jew. I regret that I could never enter her life of faith.

She also had a superb intellect, often called a Blue Stocking. The title stood for women with strong intellectual ability and literary interests from the blue stockings worn by members of 18th century London's Literary Society. She had met my father Fillmore in London.

They married in Tel Aviv at the height of the 1929 United States Depression. He was born in London, but to a Jewish mother and a British father whose mother was Jewish, but whose father was Goyem or Gentile, hence my father was named, Fillmore Sebastian Fox.

I can remember it all so clearly. It was 1939. I was nine years old when my parents decided to leave Israel to escape the persecution of the Jews by Hitler and migrated to the United States. They set up housekeeping in Brooklyn, New York, on the lower east side, mixing in with other Eastern European Jewish Immigrants, where they along with the thriving Jewish Community who were known as the downtown Jews. Known as the tiny, Blue Socking with twinkling blue eyes, my mother took care of the poorest of the poor. Many times she would keep more than one immigrant couple for months at a time, some with new born babies and small children. Yet she always kept a low profile to Fillmore, whom she encouraged me to follow, because she said, he knew the whole "Ganese migilah."

The phone rang. Once again interrupting my thoughts.

I answered the call, "Felix here."

In his British accent I heard my father ask me, "Felix, how are you getting along? Are you going to implement the Chondriana as a war weapon?"

In an exasperated huff, I tersely replied, "Fillmore, you will find out soon enough! I've called for an emergency session of the Knesset to begin at nine o'clock this morning. I'll see you and you can hear the answer then."

My father retorted, "Now my boy, don't be so hard on me. I am in your corner. I want you to know that I will stand by you, whatever it takes to get the job done."

Exasperated, I said, "Fillmore, you always set my nerves on the edge with this boy stuff! Am I not the Prime Minister of Israel? When are you going to stop being a rascal?"

"Now Felix, this is no time to start haranguing me. I'll see you in your office before the session begins."

"Okay," I bellowed into Fillmore's ear, "See you then, but keep your shirt on, everything has already been taken care of. I have everything under my control, and that is it! Goodbye for now Fillmore!"

I pulled a Camel cigarette out of my pocket. Puffing incessantly always gave me relief from the tensions between me and my father.

Yet, even though my father was an austere and abrasive man, we had bonded in such an extraordinary way while I was growing up. That bonding took place through his deep insights and intellectual ability. With great wit and vivid descriptions he was able to take the

9

abstract historical events he had witnessed, making them so vivid, that I was able to feel like I had personally witnessed them myself. He was a good story teller.

I was proud of Fillmore's British descent. Born in the nineteenth century, at the same time of the Chinese Boxer Rebellion (the fight of China against Europe) and anarchist's King Umberto of Italy had made history. He never tired of telling me of his excitement when British General Allenby had ordered over one hundred planes to fly over Jerusalem and how they took over the city without firing one shot!

Even though Fillmore was now always a "thorn in my flesh," I held great respect for him and his noble dual heritage. After all, it gave me both an aristocratic, British Orthodox and a Jewish Orthodox education. And I could never complain for having followed him into the fields of physics and archeology, graduating from Hebrew University.

I recalled how deliriously happy I was when after WWII my father had made plans to return to Israel. I was seventeen when we returned to our homeland. It was exhilarating when together both of my parents and I watched Israel on May 15, 1948 become an independent nation. And I could never be more proud than when my father was appointed British Ambassador for the State of Israel.

Always a history buff and an avid listener, my father gave me an eye witness account of events he'd witnessed, both as a member of the elite scientific community created by Niles Bore the Danish physicist in Copenhagen. I felt like I was right there with Fillmore as he watched the development in the burgeoning fields of science and physics known as "Thirty Years That Shook the World," which had occurred in the early part of the 20th century, the most critical moments of his scientific discovery. (I always referred to my father by his first name, Fillmore, and rarely did I ever address him as father.) He was able to retell history so clearly and I was able to visualize the extraordinary marvels and milestones which had transpired in the "Age of Transitions." Skillfully he presented the momentous events that ushered in the "Industrial Revolution" from oil, electricity, to machines, the railroad, the automobile, the remarkable introduction of the telegraph, developing radio, the telephone, and the genius of Albert Einstein's brilliant conception of the equation of E=mc square.

But nothing could match the unparalleled state of excitement I felt when together, both of us witnessed the world take its incredible leap by soaring into the "Information Age," as television, the computer, mass media communications, the Internet, the cell phone, the atom chip replaced the silicone chip, forever changing the course of history and the world of the future.

I treasured the thrilling, inimitable eyewitness developments that Fillmore and I shared. It kept both of us abreast of the most exciting events in all the history of the world, forming, in spite of ourselves, an unbreakable bond between us.

All of the knowledge gained in the Age of Electricity, the "Age of the Automobile, the Aviation Age," the Electronic Age, the Technological Age, the Atomic Age, the Nuclear Age, the Scientific and Cosmic Age, the Computer or Space Age all linked to the Information Age took place in one generation as compared to all the discoveries in all of the accumulated past laid a broad and eclectic, multifarious foundation in mind. Fillmore was responsible for it all and I eagerly followed his footsteps. I even entered the service of the Mossed. Together we joined in with the international "Jet Set." We established ties to the world bankers, the Rothschild's and the Pitchley Park Foundation originally setup in Britain in 1935. And the International Powerhouse formed the German Mars hall Fund, known as the "Bilderberg Group" formed in 1940.

However, I was never more at home than when I was in the political theater. It all began in 1948 when the United Nations, the body of nations formerly known as the "League of Nations," established the Nation of Israel, making it an independent state.

In all fairness, the U.N. at that time did offer the Arabs the same opportunity. The Jews were willing, but the Arabs did not take up the option.

Yet, I remember so clearly, the victory of the six-day-war in 1967. Jordan had control of Jerusalem. Pressured by Egypt, Syria and Iraq to attack us. We won. My days in the Zahal troops and the IDF were triumphant.

With a superior and highly organized military, we, that is the troops, the IDF shouted the victory in the Hebrew words, "Har beyait beyadenu," "The Temple Mount is in our hands."

Yet, despite this victory, putting an end to the nineteen year division of the city into separate Arab and Jewish sectors, tearing the wall down which separated us, serious psychological barriers remained, leaving the entire region of the Jordanian military zone. And this wall was replaced in the twenty-first century, giving the West Bank to the Palestinians.

It was during my days when I attended the Hebrew University, earning my degree in bio-medical engineering that I first conceived of any army of human clones and developed the name Chondriana for them. The term I felt was fitting since the biological action is that the Chondriana, the pre-cursor of the Mitochondria, the powerhouse of the cell.

11

When I presented this scientific breakthrough to Fillmore he thought it was splendiferous!

Although human cloning provoked bans and protests worldwide by ethicists, politicians and genetic engineers was anathema and forbidden, it never deterred Fillmore, Benny nor I. Our first plan was to guarantee that mass production and mobilization of 200-million Chondriana now would make our country able and ready to meet any national crisis. Our secondary plan was to use genetics in medicine in order to eradicate disease and even death!

Concealing this "Top-Secret" operation from public view was no shot in the dark!

This off-the-books, cloak and dagger deal was not put together in haste. It was fully thought out by the three of us (Benny, my father and I) with open knowledge of the consequences. Besides, Benny Stein was not only my "Minister of Defense," but was also a trained specialist in the fields of Genetic, Microbiology, and Biogenetic engineering.

I took the next step; one more intrepid than any of my experiences or education had fostered. I decided to explore my own "internal world." It was a step into the metaphysical world, and also into the world of an Archeological Mystic. It was more than just mere curiosity, I had always aspired to search out all the boundaries, the natural and the supernatural, the "subjective non-sensory" and the "objective sensory world." And in the process of such a colossal challenge, I had hopes to find "the life of the mind."

It was no easy task. My goal was to master all the stages of my mind. I began by maintaining strict and rigid discipline of my thoughts. I learned how to hold total control of my every thought. I wondered what it would be like if I could reach the very zenith of emotional intelligence and internal vision. To get there I felt I was graced with the ability to utilize the skills of visualization and intense concentration, focusing to the point that I was able to think through my interior comprehension by both reflection and shut out the noise of yesterday and the mind's projections of tomorrow. Having heard the saying, "You can only live one day at a time," I never grasped it until I experienced the practice by myself. I learned that this is one of the greatest psychological and spiritual "keys," which lead one to a successful life. In addition to practicing "how to live one day at a time," I also had to practice living in the present moment.

To reach that point, I had to slow my thinking down below a nanosecond. This practice also made me a more avid listener. Quieting myself and my self-centered thinking, I crossed the boundaries of human consciousness and stepped into the world of the super-conscious.

This lofty place must be where the ancient religious philosophers and mystics, Jewish, Christian, and Muslim once stood. Once I even tripped over the Pagan Mystic. It was incredible! When like the Mystics of old, I was able to cross the bridge of abstract thought. Suddenly, it made the sensory, objective world intelligible and real to the concrete world of my five senses. My passionate and determined pursuit of interior discipline gave me complete freedom from negative thinking that it freed me. immature emotional behaviors of "envy," "jealousy," "bitterness," "hatred," "petty grudge-holding," "and learning to forgive freely." This made room for me to accomplish the "virtue" of generosity of heart, mind and soul.

I was able to complete this psychological self-emptying by withholding all of my assumptions and presumptions. This included how to stop regurgitating the past. I discovered the truth spoken by a theologian who once wrote, "To those who think about the past all the time it is not because it is all they have, it is all they choose to have." And no longer permitting myself to project the future. This did not mean I could not think, all it meant was that these thoughts must stay in hold when I reason things. Gone too on the rubbish heap, was a critical spirit. Refusing to criticize or censure others too quickly. I also found it necessary to stop being judgmental and condemning others. Then total freedom came when I put on hold all of my preconceived ideas and opinions, putting them on hold until I was sure they were valid to use.

However, the most profound benefit was great peace and bliss. It was a place located somewhere once described by the late Tilehard DeChardin, that "existed in the deep recesses of the mind where ... he was able to perceive and decipher itself ... a place which exists in the minds of all creative thinkers." But, I wondered if I could maintain myself in this realm of thought when faced with political pressures. After all, I may manage to have an uncluttered mind, but what about an uncluttered heart? I would just have to wait to see.

So, it was with a clear mind I entered the position as Prime Minister of Israel. My first move paved the way for the United States Embassy to move its relocation from Tel Aviv to Jerusalem and the United Nations to relocate its headquarters from New York to Jerusalem, making Jerusalem the capital. I strongly believed in the United Nations Charter and its multi-lateral procedures. This made it possible for me to then internationalize Jerusalem under its autonomy. Thus giving the national rights of access to all the holy places to Jews, Christians and Muslims. This includes granting them all the rights to world citizenship.

I also managed to keep NATO's new doctrine of humanitarian intervention and transformation in the same month that the former

13

Soviet Union satellite's joined NATO. ("NATO was itself transformed from a defensive military grouping into an institution prepared to improve its values by force.") However, I was keenly aware that some members of the Israeli Parliament who especially stood out were the four members of the National Religious Party (NRP) and its party leader, Murray Andrews. They were opposed to implementing my policies.

But, they worried me none. Murray had a widely known reputation and was often called "A rock head!" He always made it known to everyone that crossed his path that he viewed me as a "political extremist." Not satisfied with smearing my name to other party members, he made it public that he was suspicious of my involvement with the secret political club know as the "Bilderbergs." Worst of all he considered me a war-monger and a believer of Global war, and freely stated that I was "more dangerous to Israel than all of its outside enemies." And one thing he always made sure that I knew how he felt about me.

Now, I felt it was time to obtain an independent intelligence source. The name, Daura Ameen immediately came to mind. Daura was a natural born Iraqi, a Bedouin, yet he was always pro-Israel. He was a reputable Mole. His family was Marxist. But despite growing up in Russia's closed society and being raised as a "Faker" which is a devout ascetic Muslim, he successfully became a Russian spy, never fearing the twilight zone of a life without God or Karl Marx. And no matter where he worked he always returned to his home, down one of the narrow streets of Jerusalem.

Religion never came between us, despite the fact that he regarded Israelis as "Kifers" (unbelievers) and "Frajis" (infidels) because he was not past making a fast buck from any Jew. He was someone I felt I could trust as a privately paid spy. He was a master at obtaining "top secret intelligence."

When it came to obtaining what the Iraqis were up to, and if anyone could travel incognito, it was Daura. So I contacted our Internal Security and requested they dispatch him immediately to my condominium. I then paged my bodyguard, Sid, who was standing guard outside the doors of my condo.

Sid answered the page, "Sid here, Mr. Prime Minister."

"Sid," I said, "I am expecting a visit from Daura Ameen. He should be here within the hour. Let him in when he arrives."

Sid replied, "Yes, Mr. Prime Minister, will do."

No sooner had I hung up, I glanced out of my back porch window and saw Daura get out of his beat-up old Chevy. Two Mossad agents escorted him to the back door of the hotel.

It was Daura all right. I could smell his pungent, throat-choking stench of burning tobacco. The smell was overpowering, permeating through the cracks of the condo doors. The stench irritated my already seared nostrils, even though I was a damned good heavy smoker myself.

My bodyguard, Sid, let him into the condo, while the Mossad Agents waited in the Chevy.

I said, "Hello, Daura, my friend, so good to see you. Here, let me have your coat. Take a seat."

"Good morning, Mr. Prime Minister," he said with his bushy black hair falling down over his bushy eyebrows, no doubt one of his disguises. After taking his oversized coat, I saw that it had concealed his long blue-stripped galob (robe.)

Leaving his usually concealed Kalasnikov (rifle) with the Mossad parked outside the back of the hotel. Wearing a salt and pepper mustache and heavy beard completed his incognito look. At one time he was a member of the Desert Police (The Shuitat Bidzah), along the Arnon Bagdad Highway. Now a super secret, independent, private agent, known as a "Bagman," who was always on the look-out for a black-bag job. A name created by a former U.S.A.'s President, Richard M. Nixon, when he referred to anyone who pays bribes for information, who also were ever ready to commit burglaries. Daura was the one mole who made it his business to find intelligence, many times even before our own Israeli Mossad.

Daura took a seat, shook my hand with his rough hands. They could be as rough as he himself was. He said, "It's good to see you too, Mr. Prime Minister. How did you weather last nights meteor shower?"

I replied, "It was not as severe as the largest one in all of recorded history, the Leonid Comet in 1095. Heck that one blasted over 150,000 meteorites."

Daura commented, "Well it certainly did not beat out the Mere/Shoemaker Mission to the Asteroid, Eros!"

Daura said, "Enough of this NEO chit-chat. What brings me to this occasion?"

Facing him I said, "We've received classified information of an unusual development occurring right now in Iraq. Measures taken by Israeli engineers have discovered that Iraq is drying up the Euphrates River. I need for you to find out what they are up to."

Daura said, "I have MI5 (British Intelligence) located at Ein Gedi, and secured its intelligence. They're working on it. However, it's the first time they've used this technique. They have in the past dried up other rives. At that time their reason was to drive out the guerillas hidden in the wetlands. But, the real reason: they forced their own people to leave their homes and their livelihood, thus forcing them into collective towns where they could control them. When I receive more information, I'll get back to you as quickly as possible."

I asked Daura outright, "Why the Euphrates? And, why now?"

Daura replied, "What has Intelligence given you so far?"

I gave Daura a wry smile and said, "They intend to come after us! But, we are ready for them! We have something so superior it will make them lie down in the dust. You will hear about it soon. But, for now, I am going to leave it up to you to find the real story. Get back to me and we'll make it worth your while. By the way, see if you can find out what's happened to that woman, Felixovna."

Daura's eyebrows shot up and his beady eyes would pop out of their sockets.

Daura said, under his breath, "She can be a snake and a spy with ambition for 'Gynaary,' government by a woman."

Yet, he was wise enough not to ask for the reason for trying to locate her.

I ignored Daura's sly underhanded remark. After all I was the one pining over a lost romance.

Daura just as quickly changed the subject. "Well, I must be on my way. Call you soon, Mr. Prime Minister. Goodbye."

I said, "Good-day then Daura."

Daura replied, "Will do, Mr. Prime Minister, will that be all sir?"

Handing Daura an envelope, I said, "This should take care of your immediate expenses. Your living quarters have been set up with a fully operational office and secret entrance and exit located in the underground living quarters of the Residence. I handed him a map and said, "You and I are the only ones with a copy of this map. It includes several escape routes in a tunnel underground of the Residence. It will give you a safe and easy way to come and go." Then I handed him a secured cell phone and said, "This phone is a secure line and it is programmed to reach me 24-7. I've also left instructions with my bodyguards and staff at the Residence to give you anything you might need, along with a portable notebook. When making a request giving intelligence, use the code name Achor."

As I escorted Daura to the door, I said, "Anything you need, just let the staff know."

Daura said, "Thanks, Mr. Prime Minister. I'll contact you as soon as I find out what is going on."

"Thank you Daura, I'll hear from you then. Our agents out back will escort you to the Residence. As you leave me, bypass the lobby and exit through the back door of the hotel."

With a handshake between us, Daura placed the envelope inside the pocket of his coat.

As Daura left the hotel, I paged Ben, the driver.

I said, "Ben, this is Prime Minister Fox. Please escort Daura to the Residence. Show him to his living quarters and keep yourself ready to escort him whenever he requests it."

Everything around me grew quiet. A great hush filled my room. I felt I was in "sturgeon" darkness. Doubts, one by one, entered my mind, ready to slaughter my resolve and confidence.

I held the "key to life!" Totally self absorbed, I wondered would this change the death rate? Was it true that something so good would last? Would my decision to unleash a cloned army of perfect men prove the words of that mindless Murray Andrews leveled against me be true? That I was, "More dangerous to Israel than all of its enemies." Would the world view me as a political extremist with an eccentric, radical off the books operation, possibly a threat to world peace? Was the barometer of surrealistic events to spiral down quickly and end the world? Just as quickly I answered the questions of my own self-doubts, somewhere, deep in the recesses of my own mind, I faced these doubts.

I knew that I had a power which would rid Israel of its enemies. No one would ever dare come against us again. The cloak and dagger deal I knew would create great controversy, but I had the strength, I felt to meet the challenge.

Burgeoning courage and curiosity started to flow. All at once I felt fearless and an unpremeditated sense of courage welled up from deep within. I felt light and free. The darkness fled. In relinquishing my doubts and letting go of my fears I succumbed a sudden insight, so instantaneous that it did not even have time to form or cease in the subconscious of my mind. Was what I felt really a raw courage? Was this the unseen and unknown driving me into an explosion of action like the seed planted in me, which must die first before it can bear fruit?

I was released from the shackles of my own humanity. In one peon of time I released, it was a time, for me both profound, powerful and potent force, bound by man, "replication of life itself, at will." It was time, time for me to face the unknown. I would go it alone at first. I felt I now had control of the overwhelming passion I held for the nation's survival.

Then I recalled that "the faculty for spiritual perception is one which everyone possesses, but few use." In that split-second, I was able to use that rare faculty of the intellect, the power of intuition, "knowing something with no logical reason for knowing it." In this dynamic exchange of inner power, I felt courage would be engraved upon my heart forever! This incredible attitude was now mine and no one could ever take it from me.

In that instant of time I was going to trust the invisible force I now felt so strongly upon me. This was my reward, a treasure only I could know.

By and large, I was aware of the fact that a thirty-three percent margin for error exists in the use of our intuition. I knew that putting all of my reasoning or rationalization abilities, I made up my mind, not the mind that we call "reason" or human thinking, but the mind that is moved by the heart, the emotions. The paradox being that even though the emotions "are the seat of intelligence, and they cannot in and of themselves verbalize themselves into spoken words, rather they conceive of a decision and move it into action, by way of the will." To assess what my emotions were "saying," was no easy task, but my decisions moved it into action by way of my will. It was difficult to achieve. It required a strict and constant discipline of my mind. It meant daily practice of all the moral virtues exercising my social skills with genuine care and developing a rich character. This meant I was always, moment by moment going upstream, while everyone else, it seemed, was floating at ease headed in the opposite direction, going downstream where there is hardly any struggle. As far as I was concerned it was very hard to change, but going backward "would be worse," and "standing still" would be far more deplorable. But, this was Israel's worse threat to its continued existence since its inception in 1948. And even though my decision to retaliate would be brutal, I felt the outcome would result in peace, world peace, permanent peace for all mankind.

Flanked by my two bodyguards we entered the Parliament building. My office being on the first floor and taking the back entrance gave me the privacy I needed and it made for a quick come and go virtually undetected.

Having been caught in a rainstorm on the way over to the Parliament, had soaked me and my clothes drenching wet.

I headed straight for the shower, removing my wet clothes and placed them in the dryer. I checked my watch for the time. Fillmore and Benny Stein, my Minister of Defense would not be here for another half-an-hour. I quickly showered and shaved and put on a clean dry set of clothes and a new pair of shoes for such an occasion. Looking in the mirror, I put a comb through my thick black wavy hair, which when in my youth I had bean teased by friend and foe alike that I looked like a girl! Now as an adult it proved to be one of my best attributes. My thoughts to me back to the time when I first met Benny Stein. He was at the time a Colonel in the IDF. Benny was brilliant and despite the disparity in our ages we bonded quickly. We had our differences of course, and despite having been brought up by believing Jewish parents, we made very different choices. Our parents were both bulwarks of steel during our growth and character development. We even shared the same education and love of politics. But it was Benny's intense interest and skills in the field of genetics that cemented our bond. √

It all started when in 1952, when Watson and Crick, both scientists, discovered the "key to all life," in DNA. The display clearly showed that DNA consisted of a complex protein of a high molecular weight, consisting of deoxyribose, phosphoric acid its four nucleic acids; two purines, adenine to guanine and two pyridines; thymine to cytosine, which was found to form the self-copying code of a DNA molecule, the scientific miracle of all time.

I recalled, as clearly as if it was yesterday how excited I felt when Fillmore and I, along with other top scientists witnessed their prototype.

It had all begun back in 1989 during the first "Human Genome Project" (mapping the complete gene sequencing created by the United States Government, once and for all time.)

To me, the human blueprint, the genetic script, gave molecular biologists a human directory and thanks to American biologists, James Watson and Frances Crick, scientists all over the globe now have a "whole encyclopedia!" For cracking the genetic code, thereby unlocking the genetic script, the human blueprint, they won the 1992 Noble prize for their discovery. The race was over so, I thought at that time, but now, this very day, we stood at the dawn of an incredible revolution in molecular biology.

Up until the genetic code was discovered, most scientists thought the discovery of the electron in 1897 was "a seminal event," but the DNA far exceeded that discovery.

The telephone rang, breaking off my nostalgia. I picked up the telephone receiver. "Yes, this is Prime Minister Fox speaking."

"This is Benny, Felix."

I felt secure having Benny Stein as my Minister of Defense. As colleagues, we share being at the top as Nuclear Physicists, Molecular Biologists and Genetic Engineers.

I said, "Benny, I'm in my office at the Parliament building. Come in now so that you can be briefed on the agenda. We must implement some action in our state of emergency."

"I'll be there in five minutes, Felix. See you then."

Placing the telephone receiver back into its cradle. Hearing and being with Benny always allayed any fears and anxieties I had. His tranquility was like feeling the soft breath under a breeze on a hot sunny day. I was more than grateful too for his eternal optimism. I needed that right now, for my mind was set to race over preparing for war. Having to face the stress too of binning the enormous production of a cloned army of 200 million.

Under a cloak of secrecy, Benny, Fillmore and I had already obtained the genetic profiles and the genetic fingerprints of the members of the Knesset (Israel's Parliament). For me, pooling of their genes was nothing short of fantastic, stimulating and reviling!

The fact that we had successfully been able to manipulate their gene pool into the Chondriana would reach titanic proportions in science. This selective, massive reproduction of men without the need for gestation by women reached the stratosphere of our scientific research and discovery.

Becoming a clone smith was going to be even more satisfying than sex. Not that I dismissed the practice. Neither had Fillmore and for that matter Benny always had a bevy of beauties surrounding him. Tall, dark and handsome, and with a sophisticated wit, he was thought of by most women and even some men as being charming and charismatic. Not the least of all having a body-builder look and massive black hair. You could say he was the equivalent of James Bond, both slick and suave at the same time. Besides at forty he was still an eligible bachelor. And what a fashion head! He always purchased his designer suits at the Hamdina Square. He knew how to work his electrifying life style. Yet he knew he would, no doubt always be known as an androgynous bachelor. He lived with his mother, Blanche. Both he and his mother were natural born Israelis, but his father was born in America in New York's East side.

His parents met in New York, but, after the war was over they migrated back to Israel and settled down in Tel Aviv. Not unlike me, Benny cherished the days he spent with his father ever ready to tell him many stories about the Jews who'd immigrated from Eastern Europe to the United States in order to escape Hitler's massacre of the Jews. How they lived, hoped and loved their time in America, but regrettably there were times full of pain and heavy heartedness because of those who hated the Jews, even in America. Those people were full of bitterness and persecuted them, denying them work, sometimes even stoning them or spitting on them. However, Levi never failed to lift Benny's spirits with words of encouragement and optimism of "better things to come."

Benny told me that his father, Levi, always an optimist, never failed to help Benny look at the "south side" of pain and suffering. He made sure that Benny knew "nothing was ever wasted" and that

20

included events of great evil. Levi would always take examples from the Jewish Bible that reflected on difficult situations. He would frequently ask Benny what could you learn from this pain and sorrow? This concrete and unique way of teaching Benny many of his own life experiences and the Torah remained embedded in Benny's mind and heart. Many times he would single out historic figures for their philosophical various beliefs and practices. Benny told me one character he would never forget was Joseph. From the Torah his father would tell Benny that Jacob had twelve sons and the special one was Joseph. Benny said he would never forget the lessons of the virtue of forgiveness, love, humility, integrity, faith and faithfulness of Joseph to the God of our fathers. Murder! The pinnacle of jealously and hatred filled the hearts of his brothers against Joseph because of their father, Jacob's, favoritism toward him.

They plotted to kill Joseph but it failed. Divine Providence entered into the situation. And they instead sold Joseph to slave traders on their way to Egypt. Later, they told Jacob, their father, that Joseph was killed by a wild beast. Jacob believed them.

And Joseph met his own supposed misfortune of landing in an Egyptian jail for a crime he did not commit. But, when it looked like there was no hope to get out of jail, God not only released Joseph from jail, but raided him up to become Governor of all of Egypt, second only to the Pharaoh on the throne! Finally Joseph reunited with his father and brothers during a severe famine, reaching all the way from Egypt to Canaan where they dwelt in tents. But, when their father died, his brothers become fearful that Joseph will take revenge out on them for their crimes against him. But, Joseph told them, "You meant evil, but God meant it for good," to bring about that many including themselves to be alive for the famine was going to last for seven years. Benny's faith in Divine Providence came to the test when suddenly and unexpectedly his mother died. Benny in a maelstrom of fiery thoughts raced with pain asked me, "Felix, what good could possibly come from her premature death? She was only sixty years old."

Nagging doubts punched big holes in Benny's philosophy of life. Still, he did not give up on God. Benny always resided a waste of his mind and totally avoided harboring bitter emotions. His mother's brother, Uncle Moshe Rosen who attended the funeral, left him with more questions about death. Benny feared the terrors of death, he vividly recollected the seven days that they all had sat Shiva for his mother's funeral. He told me he asked his Uncle Moshe many of them.

He would tell me verbatim what they had discussed. His asked his Uncle Moshe, "Why did she have to die?"

"Benny," he replied, "The best words of comfort is to invite you to investigate the deeper things of God, for answers to that eternal question." Moshe pulled out from his jacket a small book. It was a Bible. He handed it to Benny and said, "Benny, son, read this verse from Psalm 36:10.

Benny, apprehensive at first, quietly read, "For with you is the source of life ..."

Uncle Moshe, said, "Benny I know of your terror of death and of your interest in knowing more about it. I know you belong to the Eternal Life Club. Think about what I have said and read all of this Bible. I am leaving for a few days. When I return from Hong Kong I'll call you and we can set up some time to go into some of your unanswered questions."

Benny said, "I know she was your sister too."

Benny's heart was aching. He had never once in all of his life felt such pain. He told me that he was grateful to his Uncle Moshe and looking forward to future discussion. He was anxious to try and put the puzzle of life and death together.

He said that his Uncle Moshe did not waste any time in getting started. When he boarded the plane headed for Hong Kong he penned a letter to Benny. He had me read it too. It read:

My Dear Benny, I know your grief and mine at this time of your mother's death. I can honestly say along with most people who have lost a loved one and ask the question, why must we die? Yet, still we can ask ourselves, is biological death the complete end of our existence? Will science make application of genetics and put an end to death?

The psalmist wrote, "Death shall consume them" (Psalm 49:14). So, we can say, along with other writings, that "death is the Shepherd of all mankind."

Benny, it is common knowledge that we cannot escape death. But, does this mean that we should abandon, discard or bury our dead without ever seeing them again? One cannot help but wonder, Is there another existence after biological death?

No doubt you and I are in a maelstrom of emotions over the loss of my sister and your mother, but you being an avid scientist with a specialty in genetics may wonder if genetics could offer us the possibility of eternal life. Is there any hope anywhere that indicates that there is a post mortal survival after the death of our bodies?

Was Arlo Gunthrie, Woodie Gunthrie's son, on target when he said, "The biggest genetic disaster of all is death?" Is it true or even possible that there is no cellular death? Can the BCLZ gene you told me about really stop cellular death and give everyone living eternal life? On the other hand is it true what some scientists believe and some teach that "matter never ceases?" Is it true when some scientists declare, "Nothing can be annihilated?"

Is it possible in the very near future, discoveries in the field of genetics could offer us "immortality?" Is it possible that the recently formed "Immortality Club" can make it possible to live in our present physical body and never die? What about the Torah? What have they written about death and life after death? Is there truly at the time of death a real separation of the mind from the body?

What about the people who have had NED, near death experience? Do they offer us a glimpse of death as passage or transition rather than termination? Is it true, son, I ask, that at physical death there is a gateway to another life? Is there any real proof that there is life after physical or organic death? Respected psychiatrist, Raymond Moody, offers any proofs of NDE from individuals he has written about and refers to life after death, but asks, "Is there life after death?"

I ask you, son, personally, is death the end of human consciousness? Or, is death a dreamless sleep that has no awakening? Or, is it true that we are mortal? Or have an immortal soul that leaves the body after its organic or biological death?

What is the true state of our beloved dead? Is there another time, another place? Is it a fact that time does not exist after death? Or is there nothing after physical death, like some atheist claim? Should we go about living carelessly, giving no thought to the hereafter? Should we then live selfishly, indulging in all kinds of pleasures and give no thought to our spiritual life?

No doubt, in the course of your scientific experience there are some questions I have written here that may have crossed your mind at one time or another and some of them you may not have pondered over, but if you are willing, we can spend some time to go over these and any other questions. Benny, through reading the daily papers, I learned of your interest in extending your life indefinitely. I know you thirst for answers to questions about life and death, so intently that you have joined the Immortality Club for the answers. But, son, the People Unlimited lay claim to but do not possess the Eternal Flame.

Benny, David Dempsey said, "It's better than I can," when he wrote in the New York Times Review, "The Bible is the epicenter of a literary earthquake." So, do not be surprised when we discuss it for the answers, its message may "shake" you up.

What I would suggest is during the few days I will be gone, it may be a good start to read the Bible, the one I left with you. It is a

Jewish copy of our Tanach, written in Hebrew and underlined in English (Old Testament). Along with that, is a copy of the Delitzsh, our English translation of the New Testament.

I recommend you read a few chapters of it every day. I would like to also suggest that before you begin, clear your mind of all of its prejudices, opinions and any preconceived ideas or concepts you may have about God, the Bible and our topics which you may have formed by your religious upbringing. Put on hold all of the opinions of others. Instead, go before the Father, the "God of our fathers" and ask Him to give you the meaning to what you are reading. In all humility praying along with the psalmist when he said, "... Make your way known to me. Hashemm teach me your paths. Lead me in your truth and teach me ..." (Psalm 25:4–5).

In addition take special note when you read the Tanach (Hebrew Bible) that your mother gave me and I am now giving you. It is the Stone Edition of Torah, published in 1996 by Mesorah. Read what it has to say about what was written by the prophet Isaiah in chapter fifty-two and fifty-three. It was and is used by Rabbis all over the world today. Read it along with its side by side English translation. You will see that they are identical.

The Tanach contains, you will find upon your own reading and investigation, innumerable prophesies about the "Messiah" who is the only one who can extend His free gift of eternal life to all who want to receive it. Some may come to you and argue that this entire chapter of Isaiah fifty-three means the "suffering servant" refers to the nation of Israel, but I ask you, "How I ask, can a nation die for a nation itself?" You may also come across some secular Jews, when once you begin to read the Bible in all true humility, who will say "You are in dangerous territory." Or, "Remember the Inquisition and the Pogroms." They may also say, "Remember the thing which has been done to the Jewish people in the name of Yeshua Ha Mashiach over the past two thousand years." However, I must ask you, is it God's fault that some of His kids give Him a black eye? Should we blame Yeshua Ha Mashiach, the Son of the living God for some of His bad kids? Should we stay prejudicial and miss out on the option of receiving His true offer of everlasting life?

He came from heaven to earth to show us the way. He gave the Apostle Peter the keys. Now not literal hand keys, but the psychological keys on how to live this life and maintain joy and happiness under all circumstances, either good or evil.

It has been written for all the world to read, "For God so loved the world, that he gave his only begotten Son, that ... believeth in him should not perish, but have eternal life" (John 3:16). Now I leave the word "whosoever" blank. Put your name there Benny and receive His free gift. All it takes is to believe in Him and His words. You do not have to work for it or pay for it! You can have it right now!

Now, you may or may not wonder if there is any proof to what I am writing to you.

Yes, there is. But, it takes your first step, to approach God in all humility and He will give you proof that Yeshua is not dead, but alive and He desires to communicate with you in a personal relationship. And there is another Jewish man named John who recorded what he heard Yeshua say, "I am the way the truth and the life" (John 14:6). This shows that He is the only God that you can have a personal relationship with. You cannot have a personal relationship with Buddha or any other god. To those who do believe in Him and what He had to say there is the promise, "Death is the last moment in time, but the first moment in eternity." This son, Benny is the true metaphysical nature of death. Remember, Yeshua is a Jew too!

In addition I would like to make mention of a lack of faith in the Kabbalist. My reason being that their belief is pantheistic and not monotheistic. Their concept is a subjective deception. They believe teachings that are not from our "fathers."

Later, when I get to see you I will explain more about deception and the human mind.

I am happy that you are open to discuss Yeshua and His teachings and His claims out rightly, forthrightly and frankly. You have much to gain. And I believe you always are one that always considers taking up the option. It is what you have been looking and longing for all of your life, possession of eternal life.

Looking forward to seeing you soon.

Sincerely and with much affection, Uncle Moshe

I put the letter down on the desk. Like Benny, I sat down, feeling stone cold. Benny picked up the letter, holding it so tightly he almost crumpled it up. Then he spoke and said, "I wonder if Uncle Moshe is a Messianic Jew? What would have caused him to convert? Was it old age that made him mentally unbalanced? Is he psychotic? Perhaps even a lunatic?"

Even though questioning Uncle Moshe's emotional and mental stability raced across our minds, it was clear to see that this had not reflected on Benny's personal views about Yeshua Himself. Unlike myself he had no bad feelings toward Yeshua or those Jews who had converted and believed in Him. After all Benny argued, Yeshua was a Jew too! I personally would never consider taking that path myself. However, I was unsure about Benny. Why if he did convert the consequences would be political and religious suicide. It would spell death to his multifarious career. Besides I knew Benny. He would never want to be disowned by his family and Jewish friends.

Benny left Felix. Regardless of his own doubts, fears and questions about the "truth" he remained curious and was actually looking forward to a further discussion and analysis with his Uncle Moshe on this topic.

Sometime later Benny went on to tell me exactly what had happened next.

He said, "I put in a call to my Uncle Moshe. He answered the phone and I said, 'Uncle Moshe I received your letter. It is quite a bombshell.'"

He questioned Uncle Moshe, "Uncle Moshe, are you a Messianic Jew?"

"Yes," Uncle Moshe responded. "Does that upset you?"

He replied, "Yes, but I want to show you I am willing to put aside all my prejudices, as well as my own personal opinions and concepts. You know, Uncle Moshe, that I was never narrow-minded. I want you to know that I am looking forward to seeing you. We'll sip some wine and you can share what in heaven's name has happened to you. How about coming over tonight, say around seven o'clock? We can have dinner together."

Excited and delighted, Uncle Moshe said, "Where shall we dine?"

"How about the King David Hotel," asked Benny?

"Sounds good to me," replied Uncle Moshe, "But what about the crowds attending the 'Jerusalem Day' celebration?"

Benny replied, "The crowds should dissipate by seven o'clock."

Uncle Moshe said, "Since I have just arrived home I have not had a chance to unpack, but I'll take a quick shower and change. I should make it in time."

Benny said, "Good, then after dinner we can have our discussion at my condo."

"See you then, Benny," said Uncle Moshe.

Benny said, "Okay, Uncle Moshe, see you then."

Meanwhile Benny showered, shaved and slipped into his silk striped, royal blue suit. Benny and Uncle Moshe arrived at the hotel at the same time. After dinner they headed to Benny's condo in Benny's stylish Fiat.

Moshe remained pensive during the ride. It would be his first visit after sitting "Shiva."

It was hard for him to hold back the tears as he pondered going to his sister's place and not seeing her there. It was so difficult to bury his sadness.

Benny was quiet too.

Reaching the apartment, the valet parked Benny's car and he and his Uncle took the elevator.

Benny unlocking the door said, "Come on in Uncle Moshe. I have a bottle of your favorite Manishevitz wine waiting for you."

"Thanks son," he rebounded.

Moshe entered the living room. The fragrance of lilacs filled the room. These were always his sister's favorite flower. But it made him feel the emptiness and loss of his sister more intensely. Tears, like liquid gold, rolled down his cheeks and down onto his beard. Memories flooded his mind as he thought back on the years they spent together growing up.

Dabbing his eyes and blowing his nose, he said, "Benny it is so hard to be here without your mother. The smell of fresh lilacs makes it even harder."

Benny said, "Uncle Moshe, you had better put those tears away before I let loose too." Chocking on his words and holding back his tears, Benny said, "It's a heartache for sure," he stammered. "But, I am keeping the lilacs she loved. I don't have the heart to remove them, at least not yet. Somehow, even though they are a sad reminder, they make me feel closer to her, like she's still here with us."

Moshe mumbled, "Yes, it sure does."

Benny took out two glasses and poured the wine into them.

Moshe could not help but notice how well lit the room was. It was like sunshine that always hugged her beloved chintz draperies. They bore her mark for sure and they were in Benny's taste too.

Moshe asked Benny outright, "Do you plan to stay here Benny?"

Benny replied, "I am not sure right now. I have to give it some thought before I make that decision."

After some more small talk, Benny said to himself, "This is it. Here we go, with God, religion and Yeshua are coming up." But, for some unknown reason he felt he was going to get to the bottom of it after all. He was used to hearing Bible stories that his father taught him when he was growing up.

Solemn, Benny said in a more gentle voice, "Here Uncle Moshe, sit down here on the overstuffed chair you always liked. You will be more comfortable in it."

27

Moshe said, "Thanks Benny." Then getting up and taking Benny's suggestion he went over and sat down on a stunning pale blue overstuffed chair. The cushions were so firm and comfortable. He hoped it would not lull him to sleep. He was quite tired from his day of travel and the heavy meal he had.

Benny poured them both another glass of wine. Clinking their glasses together, Benny made a toast and said, "To you and I, to our health and to our nation."

Uncle Moshe said, "Mazel Tov."

Benny, his heart still aching, chocking back the tears over his mother's death said, "Uncle Moshe, why do the good always die young and the wicked live on?"

Benny, not being his usual pompous self sounded to Moshe as being sincere like he was really searching for answers.

Moshe, somewhat pensive sensed a new found humility in Benny and so he proceeded to reach into his jacket pocket and pull out a Stone edition of the Hebrew-English Bible.

Moshe then asked Benny, "Are you ready to investigate the knowledge of God?"

Benny cleared his throat, took a few sips of wine and said, "Yes, I am ready, but go easy on me. I am not used to bearing my soul, or sharing my thoughts and feelings about God."

Moshe got up out of his comfortable chair and stood next to Benny. He said, "Son, let me now pray to the God of our fathers as we pursue the stark realities of 'life and death issues.'"

"Well, you see Uncle Moshe, in the past I have always avoided any open discussions about my personal views and I have never engaged in open prayer with anyone. However, I am willing to take the time with you. I know you are aware of my innate curiosity, so I'll take a leap of faith."

Moshe smiled and gently took hold of Benny's hand and started to pray. With his eyes closed he said out loud, "God of our Fathers, Abraham, Isaac and Jacob, today I ask you to lead and guide our thoughts, opinions and concepts about who you really are and to make it clear to us about your Son, Yeshua."

For a moment I stood astonished by my Uncle's address to God. I was waiting for him to pray to Yeshua.

Moshe continued praying, "You are not a God of the dead but of the living. Right now I ask you to reveal yourself to Benny. Lead and guide our discussion of life and death and all that comes in between. Remove all of Benny's fears and every thought that would stand in the way of his learning the truth. The truth about You, if he had any conflict that may be going on inside of his heart and mind right now. Help him come to know You and serve You. Amen."

Benny looked at Uncle Moshe. He seemed to have such a peaceful glow about him.

"I hope I don't sound flippant, Uncle Moshe, but are you going to go over Philosophy 101?"

Moshe took the question with good humor and stride and let out a muffled laugh.

Uncle Moshe replied, "Why yes, Benny, it was designed to help us learn the truth. Do you have enough time for us to go over it?"

"Yes, I do. I have the entire evening."

"Okay, then let's put a time limit of one hour to go over the basics. Since there is so much to learn, how about if we meet once a week and continue our discussions on an ongoing basis?"

"That sounds good to me, Uncle Moshe."

Uncle Moshe said, "Let's start our discussion with the 'objective truth.' The things we can see, hear, taste, touch and feel. Then we can discuss the subjective truth, along with some theoretical ideas and how they are related to finding out the truth about God, man, life and death and all that might come up in the course of our discussions."

"But I have a question, Uncle Moshe. Are the five senses reliable enough? Is it possible for any two people, even two people who are open-minded, to interpret their perceptions of reality and reach one and the same conclusions? And what if one or both of those persons has a mental defect due to lack of insight or perhaps they are ignorant or suffer from faulty deliberation? Where, Uncle Moshe, would that leave the truth?"

With a gentle grin, Uncle Moshe said, "Since these discussions will be only between us, I think it is fair to say we will not have to consider those questions. I am sure that we both are of a sound mind. Should some questionable characters arise we can discuss them as they arise. Okay?"

"Your point is valid and well taken, Uncle Moshe."

"Thank you, Benny. However, God is not a God of confusion. Like all organized things there is protocol. And it is no different with God. His protocol begins when He knows we are ready and sincerely willing to approach Him. The first prerequisite of His protocol is an attitude and act of humility. The second prerequisite is to be sincere and genuine in our search for Him. We must be willing to clear or put on hold all of our arrogance, conceit, pride or pretentiousness. It means we must clear our minds of all its opinions, assumptions and presumptions, putting them temporally on hold. It means we start fresh."

"In order to do that, Benny, I am going to ask you to put away all secular and religious philosophy for now and go directly to the Word of God, the Holy Bible. We are instructed by the command of God that this is the first place which we are to look in search for Him and the truth about Him."

"But, won't that take years of study?"

Uncle Moshe replied, "We shall see, Benny." Then opening his Bible, Moshe turned to the first chapter of Joshua, verse eight. "Benny please read along with me."

Out loud, Moshe began to read, "This book of the law shall not depart out of thy mouth: but thou shalt meditate therein day and night, that thou mayest observe to do all that is written therein: for then thou shalt make thy way prosperous, then thou shall have good success."

Benny interrupted Moshe and said, "But that would take years to do. Only Rabbis and religious theologians and scholars have that kind of time."

"Now Benny, today we must go to the Holy Scriptures that were given to a band of Jews in the first century. They have additional insights and instructions left for us to know."

Moshe went on to read from the New Testament, the Dieltzsch, book of Hebrews, the first chapter.

"God who at sundry times and in divers manners spake in times past unto the fathers by the prophets, Hath in these last days spoken unto us by His Son, whom He hath appointed heir of all things, by whom he made the worlds: Who being the brightness of His glory, and the express image of his person, and upholding all things the word of his power, when he had by Him purged our sins, sat down on the right hand of the Majesty on high."

"It is plain to see from these words that Yeshua with the Father is the Creator and the Son of God who died for our sins."

Benny's mouth dropped. He was in shock. His hands trembled as he held the Bible in his hands.

"So, today we are commanded to listen and take instruction from Him. He was sent from heaven to earth to show the way."

Benny felt his knees grow weak. "Uncle Moshe, according to this, Yeshua is our Creator?"

"Yes, Benny. However. I will go over the details with you shortly."

"Benny, we are instructed by God's Word to keep His law. Now that has been summed up by Yeshua into two commandments." Turning to Mark 12:28–31, Moshe read out loud.

"And one of the scribes came and having heard them reasoning together, and perceiving that he had answered them well, asked him, Which is the first commandment of all? And Yeshua answered him, And thou shalt love the Lord thy God with all thy heart and all thy soul, and with all thy mind, and with all thy strength. This is the first commandment. And the second is like it, namely this: Thou shalt love thy neighbor as thyself. There is no greater commandment."

"Benny, can you see now how Yeshua summed up all the law? With love. For if you love God and your neighbor, you won't steal from him, or be jealous of him."

Moshe sensed Benny's emotional reactions. "Benny, can you see how these two great commandments are the answer to how to practice all the law. Strictly by love."

"Uncle Moshe, this is so profound. I need a few moments to absorb it all."

"Still, we are admonished to read the Word of God daily, just as we need to eat food daily. If we do not meditate on it daily, we will end up with a weak spirit. And just like not eating every day can lead to death, so too, now reading and meditating on God's Word daily, we will loose our relationship with Him. Read what Moses wrote and taught the Israelites in Deuteronomy 9:3. 'Man must not live by bread alone, but by every word that proceedeth out of the mouth of the Lord, doth man live.'"

"Benny, let me ask you, how many meals do you eat a day?"

"The usual three."

"What would happen if you stopped eating?"

"Well, I would not last long. I would eventually get sick and die."

"Can you see now how important it is for you as an individual to take responsibility for your relationship with God to stay alive spiritually?"

"Uncle Moshe, I think I am catching on to what you are saying. I can see now that I cannot leave my Holy Scriptures for just the Rabbi to read for me. I must start and dust it off and sit down and read it for myself, of course asking God to lead me and guide me. But, how can I know that Yeshua is real?"

"Well, you know that there are over three-hundred Jewish prophecies that Yeshua fulfilled. I have a list of them."

Moshe handed Benny the list and said, "Now you can go over these and you will see that there is no one then or since to this day that can meet these claims to perfection but Yeshua."

31

Benny started to sweat. Even his hands were sweating. Whenever that happened he removed his silk suit jacket and then wiped his brow with his handkerchief.

Moshe then summed up the discussion, "Now you can meet the two prerequisites so that now you will be able to begin your own independent search and learn about God, your own internal senses, your own perceptive intuition. Pray also for the guidance of the Holy Spirit."

"Who is the Holy Spirit, Uncle Moshe?"

"He is a person. He is the third person in the Godhead."

"Oh, the Trinity."

"Yes, but I will show you scriptures that show you their nature and that the 'one' God means 'united as one.' They all have the same nature. Just like when couples get married they are spoken of as being 'one.' But, they don't become one person, the are united as 'one.' They now live together, plan together and never do anything without the other."

"One more thing, Benny. It will take time to get used to using your intuition to discern things. However, there is a thirty-three percent margin for error. That is why God has given us in addition, the power of human reasoning. But, to be sure we are getting the truth, which is why we must go to the Holy Scriptures to clarify any conclusions of our concepts. Knowing what they say will establish genuine truth. And since you hold them in high esteem, we can then proceed to search."

Benny said, "But, Uncle Moshe should we not seek out the experts in matters of religion?"

Moshe replied, "I can answer that in more than one way. But suffice it to ask, who is the highest authority to go to but God Himself! Is not that what our fathers did? And what about Moses and the prophets? There was direct communication with man from the out set. And is it not true that even today the experts do not always agree? If we were to listen to every one of them, I ask, would the truth then no longer be the truth? So, I believe you will agree with me that the only option we have is to begin a dialogue through prayer. Implementing the correct protocol to approach Him and Him alone."

Bwnny began to mull over all of what his Uncle had been saying and concluded that he had a good point. But, he said, "Uncle Moshe, that is truly subjective. How can we test it to know that it is the truth?"

"Once you exhibit true trust and faith, God Himself will make it perfectly clear to you. Any doubts you may have He will reveal to you. Sometimes His revelation will take a period of time and sometimes it will be instantaneous. It will be through your insight and or intuition."

Turning to Matthew 17:20, Moshe read, "This verse shows that even the smallest amount of faith is enough, that is the size of a mustard seed. That is the smallest seed."

"Sometimes Benny, it is difficult for others to understand how the process of faith is to be exercised. I have an illustration of the mental mechanics of the process. Do you have enough time for me to continue?"

"Yes, I have the entire night. Go on, Uncle Moshe."

"This illustration exhibiting the mental process of faith takes place during a real event. It happened in the early part of the twentieth century. It took place in New York's side of the Niagara Falls. There were, at that time, a few men who were daredevils. They were known as the Equiblebust, or in laymen's terms, 'High Wire Tightrope walkers.' These men started the craze of walking on a tightrope crossing over the Niagara Falls. This event was so exciting that many people gathered to observe it. The press captured its suspense and thrills. The press had a field day! The story goes like this: There was one man who after walking across the entire length of the falls on a tightrope who approached the crowd of observers who had watched his daring high wire act. He made them a proposal. He asked the crowd of observers, 'How many of you gathered here today believe that I can cross this tightrope pushing a wheel barrel?' Almost everyone in the crowd enthusiastically replied, 'Yes, we do.' And so the tightrope walker proceeded to walk across the entire Niagara Falls, pushing a wheel barrel. The crowds went wild. In utter amazement and sheer terror, they thought the tightrope walker would slip and fall to his death. Instead he came through like a warm summer breeze. The crowd was ecstatic. Then the artist approached the stunned crowd and asked them, 'Now, do you believe I can cross the Falls on this tightrope pushing a wheel barrel with someone in it?' One of the onlookers commented, 'This is incredible.' Another said, 'Far-fetched.' One person huffed and said, 'I say it is impossible, unthinkable, unimaginable.' 'Far-fetched,' the artist yelled out. 'Are there any believers here who think I can do it?' Transfixed a great number of people said, 'Yes.' 'All right then, who will be the first one to get in?' A great silence fell over the crowd as one by one walked away. Now Benny, do you think you could put yourself into the barrel?"

But, before Benny could answer, Moshe went on, "You see when we trust the person we would get into the barrel. Well, that is the kind of faith we need. Utter trust that once we get in the barrel, God will go with us and we trust Him enough to believe He can keep us from falling whenever we step into the unknown. I encourage you to take up this option. Take that total risk. You have a lot to gain."

Cool, calm and collected, placing my arm around Uncle Moshe, Benny said, "Uncle Moshe, I am willing. Uncle Moshe, help me to believe."

A smile, a mile-wide crossed Moshe's face. He blushed and tears filled his eyes and rolled down his short cropped beard. He said, "Benny, you know what this decision will mean. You will face being ostracized by family and friends."

"I know, Uncle Moshe."

Moshe said, "I'll pick up from where we left off discussing the purely subjective experience with God."

Anxiously he asked, "Uncle Moshe, how can you be subjective when being objective requires visible evidence?"

Moshe responded, "I can answer that. I believe in the subjective experience of the reality of God. When we exercise faith in God by using our intuition and in addition searching the Scriptures to see if they both agree we can be sure that we are receiving Divine Revelation. However, few people use their intuition. That is because many do not have the required disciplined mind. To attain that we must follow the prerequisite established by God Himself, 'Be still and know that I am God.' So we must learn to keep a clear mind and a clean heart. In addition, one must have the 'mind set' to be willing to let go of some or all of our treasured opinions, presumptions and assumptions. Also, since there is a 33 percent margin for error when depending upon our intuition, the final litmus test is to compare what has been written in Holy Scripture on a topic, then through the use of our reasoning powers to reach final conclusions. Now some are not all black and white. There may be some things that will go unanswered, sometimes for short periods and sometimes for long periods and sometimes never. Trusting God, Benny, requires many times, patience. At times when using our reasoning powers we can find ourselves using a variety of opinions. Sometimes utilizing the pragmatic and other times using abstract theories."

"There is one form of this theory that comes to mind, Benny. Dewey proposed it. It is called 'Experience Verification.' This form can be used to test our experience abstract, metaphysical and theological beliefs throughout the history of man that can be verified by your experience with God and the things of God. Learning how to discern 'Divine Providence' does this. However, this is not written without a warning. I will repeat it. 'No theory of truth has been universally accepted by Philosophers.' Saying that, Benny, I am going to ask you to put aside any and all secular and theoretical, speculative and hypothetical philosophies. However, to be fair we can briefly go over religious philosophies which will be more relaxant to this discussion. Don't you agree?"

Running his fingers through his thick, black hair, then cupping his hands under his chin, he thought for a few seconds and said, "I agree. Let's put secular philosophy on hold for now and concentrate on the relevance of religious philosophy to gain knowledge of God."

"Uncle Moshe, when my father was alive he would frequently go over religion and religious philosophy. For that reason, I believe, I will be better able to absorb it."

Moshe said, "Okay, Benny, I'll begin, but I'll be as brief as possible."

"In short, there are three non-Jewish views, commonly known as the Christian philosophers. One is the 'Ontological' conceived of by St. Anslem who concluded that the fact that you can even conceive of God is proof that God exists, elsewhere would such a thought come from? The second one is called the 'Cosmological' and third the 'Teleological.' Both of these views were both put forth by St. Thomas Aquinas. In reference to the Cosmological view, he said, 'Of the reality of the existence of God, that if we were to look around the world and the universe, we can see things in motion, not by accident. The earth and the planets cannot move themselves. There had to be a first mover.' The Theological, i.e., 'Proof of a Divine Design.'" (*Philosophy, the Power of Ideas, by Noel and Kenneth Brunner. Mayfield Publications, 1249 Villa Street, Mountain View, California 84001, 1990.)

"I will paraphrase what Sir Isaac Newton once experienced by using a observable illustration with one of his students."

"One day Sir Isaac Newton had completed constructing a small model of the earth and the planets rotating in their true orbits. One particular day, one of his students, an awkward fellow, also with an avid thirst entered Sir Isaac Newton's laboratory. When he saw the small working model of our immediate universe, he exclaimed, 'Why this model is exquisite. Who has designed it? And how did they put it into such accurate motion?' Sir Isaac Newton answered the inquiry and said, 'Why, no one,' he exclaimed. The student replied, 'Oh, come now, professor, someone had to make it.' Sir Isaac Newton flinched and said, 'Young man, you believe someone made this replica, this model of the earth and the planets and yet you do not believe that someone made the real thing!' Startled by Sir Isaac Newton's statement, the students face flushed red, almost biting his tongue. Surprised by his own foolishness, it hit him hard. And from that day on he became a Believer."

Benny, tongue in cheek, so to speak, looked straight into Moshe's eyes. Oh, Moshe had given him a wink, and he noted all the creases around them, but something deep inside him looked eternally young.

Moshe then asked Benny, "Do you believe all that Moses and the Prophets wrote down were God's words and not their own?"

Benny replied, "Yes. My father instructed me in the writings and he and I shared the love of the writings of the 'Great Rambam Maimonidies.'"

"Good," said Uncle Moshe. "Now, let me read to you a reassuring comment by R.H. Pfeiffer, on his introduction to the so called Old Testament."

"And I quote, 'No book or collection of books, in the history of mankind has had a more attentive reading, a wider circulation or a more diligent investigation than the Old Testament.'"

Curiously, Benny asked Moshe, "But aren't you going to bring in the New Testament too?"

"Benny, this may sound cliché, but you never fail to amaze me. To answer your question, yes we will get to that, but first things first."

Moshe then pulled out of his black carrying case a copy of the Stone Edition of the Hebrew Scriptures. Although it was written in Hebrew, it had modern day English translation under each word.

Handing Benny a copy, he said, "Benny, this is a gift for you."

"Thanks, Uncle Moshe."

Benny was sitting on a lavish chintz chair. Moshe went over and sat next to him. "Benny," he said, "Turn to the book of Joshua. I want you to read out loud chapter one, verse eight."

Benny was a little hesitant. So, he took a few sips of wine, cleared his throat and began to read, "This book of the law shall not depart from thy mouth, but thou shalt meditate therein day and night, that thou mayest observe to do according to all that is written therein, for then thou shalt make thy way prosperous and then shalt thou have good success."

Benny holding the open Bible in his hand, turned to Moshe and said, "It's day and night, quite a bit I must say."

Moshe holding back the tears brimming in his eyes tenderly asked Benny, "What is always on the minds of people in love?"

Benny replied "Obviously, each other. But, are you telling me that is the kind of love that God desires from us?"

Moshe replied, "Let's go to Deuteronomy 8:3 for the answer. Read it out loud Benny."

Benny, letting out a sigh could not evade his Uncle's skillful handling of the Bible. Almost in defeat he turned to the verse and read it out loud, "Not by bread alone does man live, rather by everything that emanates out of the mouth of God does man live."

His nerves a little jumpy, Benny said, "Why, we just covered that in the New Testament."

Moshe said, "Benny, once you read the entire New Testament, you will see numerous Hebrew of so-called Old Testament verses repeated but done so in new insight. Be prepared for a huge paradigm shift."

Benny started to sweat. Oh, how he hated to sweat. Nothing could get on his nerves more than to perspire, ruining his clothing and creating an embarrassing offensive odor. Pulling out his handkerchief, he wiped his clean-shaven face and said, "It appears to read quite to the point, I would say, Uncle Moshe."

"Yes, Benny, there is no escaping it. Just like setting time aside to eat nourishing food on a daily basis, we need to read and meditate on God's Word daily."

Uncle Moshe said, "So far Benny, you have not missed the mark. You certainly are quick intellectually and I might add also very insightful."

Benny chuckled and quipped, "Watch out Uncle Moshe, that kind of flattery can get you everywhere!"

Moshe smiled and got back on track and said, "Once you are willing to put any prejudice, apprehension or fears to rest, you will get the full impact of a relationship with God." Moshe went on, "Now Benny, I want you to read what one Jewish man who witnessed all of what Yeshua said and did. That turned out to be the very Jewish, Apostle John. Another Jewish eyewitness was the tax collector, Matthew. In his writings you will find the only authentic, documented Jewish genealogy of the Jews up until the very birth of Yeshua. And the very fact that from the turn of the first half of the first century, no one that time until this very day can be identified, traced or singled out by birth to come from the tribe of Judah to fulfill the prophesied Ha Mashiach's authentic legitimate lineage."

Once again Benny began to sweat. He was so damned uncomfortable. But, he silenced himself out of respect for his Uncle.

Moshe said, "Do you recall your father teaching you that Moses prophesied that when He, the Ha Mashiach, would come that we were to listen to Him?"

Benny, somewhat exasperated replied, "That is very basic Judaism, Uncle Moshe."

Moshe replied, "Yes, but more insight is given into the nature of 'That Man' as many of us who at times refer to Him. Benny, He proved He had by His miracles and His words, proved that He was more than just 'a man.'"

Turning to the book of Hebrews, Moshe said, "I would like to read something to you." Reading from the first chapter, he read verses one, two and three, "God, who at sundry times, and in divers manner spake in times past unto the fathers by the prophets, Hath in these last days has spoken unto us by his Son, whom he hath appointed heir of all things, by whom also he made the worlds: Who being the brightness of his glory, and the express image of his person, upholding all things by the word of his power, when he had himself had purged our sins, sat down on the right hand of the Majesty on high."

Benny could hardly believe what Moshe had just read. These verses were plain enough. How could he ever escape their message?

Letting out a deep sigh, Benny stopped reading. He wondered if this was the end of the discussion, but knowing Uncle Moshe he knew it was not over.

Moshe asked Benny, "Who do these verses instruct us to listen to?"

He answered somewhat awkwardly, "The answer is obvious, Uncle Moshe. His Son."

Moshe smiled, his beard gleaming white. He said, "Benny, what you read makes it clear that His Son was with Him in creation. And that He is the Son who shed His blood to pay for our sins."

Benny was sweating buckets by now. Why, he had never heard such a profound message. Confused, he asked, "Uncle Moshe, where does that leave me?"

Moshe turned to the book of Deuteronomy 18:15 and said, "Let me read this to you for the answer to that question."

Turning the pages he found the verse and began to read Moses' instructions, "A prophet in your midst, your brethren, like me, shall Hashem, your God. To him shall you hearken."

Benny was ready to burst. But, instead he said, "Uncle Moshe, I am amazed by all you have shown me. I must say I have never heard a more lucid and very clear explanation about the identity and purpose of the Messiah. I have mixed emotions. I feel like I am ready to burst and yet, part of me is wanting to hear more. Especially about the free gift of eternal life."

Handing Benny a pocket size book, Moshe said, "This is a copy of the Delitzsch. It's a Hebrew/English translation of the New Testament. I want you to read it and get back to me with your comments and questions. However, let me suggest before you read it from cover to cover, that you go to prayer and ask the God of Abraham, Isaac and Jacob to lead and guide you. Asking Him to reveal the truth about the identity of Yeshua Ha Mashiach and if He is the one you should listen to."

"I'll read it tonight, Uncle Moshe."

Moshe grinned from ear to ear, his beard curling up as he smiled at Benny. Nothing could have made him more happy than when he saw Benny put the small New Testament into his jacket pocket.

Quietly, Moshe uttered a prayer for Benny not to receive any distractions that would hinder his reading it tonight. He felt he knew Benny well enough to know he would not lie to him.

With that in mind, Moshe said, "Well, how about if we meet on Friday and continue with our discussion?"

Benny said, "That would be fine, how about meeting here at seven o'clock?"

Moshe said, "Good. I'll see you then."

Benny pulled out the New Testament and started to read. Somehow he drifted off to sleep and was awakened early the next morning by a call from the Mossad. Intelligence briefed him on the pending threat of war.

Benny got on the hot line with Felix.

Felix informed Benny that he would be expecting the Mossad to shortly arrive with "top secret" documents.

After a quick shower and shave, he left to meet with Felix at his office in the Knesset.

Entering the building, he ascended the stairs to the third floor, ignoring the elevator. He was in no mood to bump into anyone else at the moment. Focused on the unprecedented "Operation Chondriana" he, Fillmore and Felix and soon the nation were about to embark upon. With no warning, he felt a strange sense of impending doom grip him like a vise. What was once impossible was now not only possible, but ready to hit the nations over the head like a sledgehammer. "Chondriana," the cloning and build-up of a man-made army was ready to create a biological Hiroshima. (*The Human Blueprint, by Robert Shapiro, St. Martin's Press, N.Y., N.Y. 10011, 1991.) One of unknown, unthinkable with indestructible strength. One that would make your hair "stand on end." Why? Because once you manage to kill them they can come back to life within three days! And for the world at large they would baffle description and stagger belief!

This "Chondriana Operation" was kept so secret by the "gene hunters," Felix, Fillmore and Benny that even the Lisa Le Kishrei Madu, (LAKAM), Israel's Defense Ministries of Scientific Affairs Laison and Bbuena, the Rizadh (Arab Secret Service) had any knowledge of their breathtaking, epochal development.

Benny reached the top of the stairs of the third floor. From that vantage point he could see Felix's door was closed. His shoes made a scuffling noise as he walked down the hall. Reaching Felix's door, he stepped up to it and gave it a gentle tap.

Felix bellowed, "Come in!"

He grabbed the door knob and turning it to the right, he slowly entered the office, closing the door behind him. Felix looked up from his desk and nodded for Benny to take a seat. Fillmore was present. He greeted Benny and said, "Good morning Benny."

Benny said, "Good morning, Fillmore, Felix."

Grimacing, Felix said, "I wish it was a good morning."

Benny quickly sat down onto a comfortable leather chair, feeling the soft silk suit brush against his body. He glanced at his watch. It was exactly eight o'clock. An air of silence and tension permeated the office. Silence prevailed until Felix broke it.

Without hesitation, Felix blurted out and said, "Benny, Fillmore, you know we are faced with a grave and very critical situation. Iraq's new leader, Ahmet Hussein, has made the threat and his newly formed ten nations Arab National Alliance. Also, Russia, all the countries of the near and far east, including China have become their allies. Their treaty is to abolish our nation. Ahmet has already captured our newly built Temple. He has slaughtered all of our priests! This means that the "Chondriana Operation" will have to be implemented for our nation's security. Therefore it will no longer be considered an experiment or kept secret any longer."

Benny's heart started to pound faster like a drum roll. He felt the blood rushing to his face, his nerves on edge, he shouted, "That imbecile. We were finally rid of Saddam Hussein, now this!"

Then, his voice shaking, Felix turned towards Benny and asked him, "How many Chondriana can we replicate in one day?"

He cleared his throat and looked Felix straight in the eye and with a stone face he answered Felix in a brisk voice. "One every thirty seconds and up to two-hundred million in a twenty-four hour day!"

Felix then asked Benny, "What is the margin for error?"

"None," replied Benny in an unexpected state of shock. Even as the words left Benny's lips he could hardly believe that they were ready to begin mass-production of a cloned army.

Abruptly, Felix said, "We need a force of 200 million."

Benny felt like he had a pack of marbles in his mouth. He could hardly speak, but finally managed to say, "Well we are right on target. All the gene pools of our military geniuses are in place and they are without any foreseeable problems."

Elated, Felix said, "Wonderful, fantastic! Benny, I always knew you had what it takes to pull off an operation of this magnitude. This calls for a drink."

Several bottles of Brandy and Scotch sat on top of Felix's fashionable Hemingway desk.

Felix got three glasses out, filling them to the brim. Handing one to Fillmore and one to Benny he proposed a toast. Clicking their glasses together, Felix said, "To our victory! Mazel Tov!"

Putting his glass down, Felix, his hands shaking, handed Benny and Fillmore a copy of the Directive declaring war and the Directive to begin mass-production of the Chondriana or clones.

His voice trembling, Felix said, "Sign here."

Benny swiftly signed both documents and handed them back to Felix.

Fillmore, matter of fact penned his signature and handed them back to Felix.

Felix triumphantly said, "Now we are ready for Parliament!"

Felix looked at Benny, who had suddenly looked as if he had turned to stone. It was as if time stood still. He was frozen in the moment.

Felix broke the spell. Snapping Benny back into the reality of the moment, he then asked Benny, "How long will it take to begin mass-production?"

Still somewhat in a daze, Benny replied, "I can seal a control of this immensity in fifteen minutes!"

Felix gave Benny a casual approving smile. Patting Benny on the back he said, "Brilliant, Benny! Simply brilliant!"

Even though it was early in the morning, and usually not the time they would take in hard liquor, Felix poured another round of drinks. Taking in a hard swallow and said, "We are on our way gentlemen. Let's go!"

While Felix and Fillmore headed for the Parliament, Benny went to his office down the hall for a few minutes before the session was to begin.

On his way to his office, Benny started to entertain second thoughts and doubts about implementing Operation Chondriana. Should he continue? Have we fully explored all the pros and cons? Once we declare war there will be no turning back.

His thoughts traced back to the first time they had contemplated cloning a human army by mass-production. Oddly enough they devised this plan during the time they went to America. Joined by other world scientists, who attended The American Association for the Advancement of Science.

The main speaker was the famous Ian Wilmut, who made a special speech entitled, "The Right and Wrongs of Cloning." He was the leading scientist of the research team who cloned the fist lamb named "Dolly."

Dolly was created not by umbilical stem cells, but by cloning a donated egg fertilized with a sperm.

The three Gene Hunters, Benny, Fillmore and Felix perked up when they first heard that stem cells proved to have the ability to replicate whole body organs of the entire body. And that they actually had the ability to regrow limbs, critical for treating the wounded during times of war, or to those who may have suffered such a loss due to unforeseen accidents. They were informed that stem cells could regrow blood vessels in the heart, blocking blood vessels in tumors and produced the unbelievable ability to reset the primeval genetic clock that causes cells to age.

Upon hearing that there now existed a possibility that man could live forever, Benny was beside himself! He was totally interested in living forever. And he could not agree more with Arlo Guthrie's statement referring to death as being "the greatest genetic disorder of all!"

His desire was so intense he joined the newly formed Immortality Club. This group adheres to and believes in the mind bender doctrine, "All you have to do is think that you will not die, and you will not die."

We knew then that regardless of a ban on cloning humans, Felix, Fillmore and Benny planned then that we would clone a human army of men.

His thoughts scattered as Benny reached his lab. He could not begin such a task on behalf of Israel's defense. Someone once told him, "War is the final destination of hatred." Still, today Israel's bid for survival left them to respond without any other option. Or did it?

Chapter 2

The Mysterious Copper Scroll

It was a clear day in June. The bright rays of the sun glistened against the windows of the Hebrew University, making them sparkle. The students were busy going to and from classes, some headed for the library and others no doubt were cramming for the upcoming finals.

I entered the building and headed towards the Dean's office. I had come at the Dean's request, even though I questioned his motive. Still, this would be my last lecture before I campaigned for Prime Minister of Israel, so I decided I would make the best of it. I entered the Dean's office.

"Good morning," I greeted the secretary. "Ms. Goldstein is it?"

"Good morning, Mr. Fox. Just call me Goldy," she said.

"Fine then, Goldy," I replied.

She said, "Dean Freeman is in. I'll tell him you are here."

Dean Freeman, dressed in a drab brown suit and a skimpy looking tie, entered the room and said, "Good morning, Felix, come in."

"Good morning, Dean Freeman."

"Here, have a glass of lemonade. Take a seat," the Dean said as he filled the glass and passed one on to me. It had been rumored that Dean Freeman held a secret, deep jealousy of my rapid rise in politics.

"Felix," Dean Freeman said, "It is a pleasure to have you lecture today. The faculty and staff are anxious to hear what you have to say. So much has been going on. The revolution in archeology has more than tripled registrations over the past five years."

I said, "I am delighted to hear that."

Curiously Dean Freeman inquired, "Might I ask, have you made any new discoveries?"

I hesitated for a moment, took a sip of lemonade and placed the glass down on the desk. With a frown on my face, I looked up at the Dean and said, "I do have the honor of giving my alma mater a little tidbit of two outstanding discoveries."

The Dean's eyes lit up. He got up from his chair and walked swiftly over to the door and closed it. An agile man, the Dean stooped down at his desk, opening the bottom drawer and pulled out a bottle of brandy.

"Here Felix, this calls for a little celebration," he said as he poured me a glass.

"Thanks," I said. I always enjoyed a little liquor before a lecture. It makes my day. I had resigned myself to the fact that the very next words to come out of the Dean's mouth would be spinning on memories of our work together with the Mossad. And I wasn't disappointed. No sooner had this thought crossed my mind the Dean began.

As the Dean positioned himself in his chair, he put his feet up on the desk. "Felix," he said, "How is your father feeling?"

I said, "Quite spry and ornery as always."

"Felix," the Dean said, "It has been a couple of decades since we last worked together. I'll never forget how you, your father and I took part in Operation Gold in 1955 when tunnel digging under Berlin gave us the ability to tap into the Russian military telephone system. Seems like digging appeals to you Felix."

I gave the Dean a dirty look. The Dean let out a gasp, stunned by my remark. Quickly, he opened the drawer where he kept his stash of liquor. Glancing into the drawer where the Dean had pulled out his brandy, I caught the glint of the sun's ray through the window as it hit the rim of a .45 Magnum pistol.

The Dean noticed and quickly shut the drawer. He said, "Today is always full of surprises, nothing like being prepared is it?" I nodded as if to say "Yes," but his statement did not give me any reassurance. I decided to remain civil out of respect for his father.

"If you will excuse me Dean Freeman," I said, "I am ready to leave for the forum."

"Why sure Felix. You go on ahead and I'll be with you in a few moments."

As I walked towards the forum I wondered if the Dean had the gun focused on me. But, then again the fact that I would soon be running for election as Prime Minister I thought it wise to pack the PBK Walker, a British gun given to me by Fillmore.

Reaching the forum, I climbed the steps to the stage and sat down. Dean Freeman quickly followed behind me, climbed the steps, then walked over to the podium, adjusted the microphone and checked for the placement of a glass of water. There was a pitcher filled with ice and water and a glass all prepared for the speaker. Glancing around the forum I noticed several people with cameras and press badges racing towards the front seats of the auditorium.

The Dean's face was flushed red at the notion he was being an opportunist, but despite my face of disapproval, he didn't offer an apology for leaking my first publicly announced discoveries to the press. He straightened his tie and with a sly, self-satisfied grin on his face he got up and walked toward the podium.

Scuffing my feet and repositioning myself in my chair, I did a slow burn, unable now in the presence of the press and the students filling in the seats to reprimand Dean Freeman for his underhanded actions. In the front row, I noticed a knock out, tall, tanned blonde. She took a seat directly facing me. She gave me a shy grin. Smoothing her skirt, her hands fell against her hourglass figure. She crossed her legs, folding her hands across her knees.

45

Had I seen her before? She was older than the average student. As I thought back I did recall hearing about her. She was in the military, an officer I had met through one of my generals. Her reputation for being an unusual beauty had spread easily, but at the time I kept my distance because my focus was centered on my studies and research. I felt I did not need any interference. But, now the time was different. I had several months before election, although that would be demanding, it would still leave me some time for more personal interests. So, I decided to bate her. Soon all the seats in the forum were filled and it was time for me to begin my lecture.

The Dean stood up at the podium. There was piercing feedback from the speakers. He went on and said, "Good morning, ladies and gentlemen, all staff of Hebrew University and members of the press."

"Archeology," he said, "has been pursued by many in the areas of the middle-east. Some for personal gain in search of hidden treasures and some who look for the challenge of a lifetime. Tedious work, but rewarding beyond measure."

"Today it is my privilege to introduce to you a man you are all familiar with. His work in the field of archeology has been innovative and his research and discoveries have led the way into uncharted paths. An accomplished Terrestrial, Nautical, and at one time an Orthodox archeologist, I might add as an ambitious overachiever, he is also an omniferous specialist in the fields of geology, biology and microbiology with focused interest in genetics and nuclear physics, a subject too abstruse for most people, yet he maintains a humble attitude. Top scientists have sought him out for consultation and advice. It wasn't long before his fame as a protean genius spread worldwide. A new type of researcher, he has been liberated from the myopic of modern science, implementing the use of Psychic Archeology, a new and independent science as well as serology, the study of caves. This has led to the discovery of tunnels going from the temple mount through to the Dead Sea, an area now known today as "The Valley of Achor." This led to one of the discoveries he will reveal to you today. Influential and in demand as a speaker. Others would call him a Political Giant."

"James Freeman Clarke once said, 'A politician thinks of the next election; a statesman the next generation.' I now give you an archeological dilettante, outstanding statesman and the next possible Prime Minister of Israel, Felix Sebastian Fox!"

The audience stood up and gave rounds of applause. Rising from my seat I motioned with my hands quieting the crowd's applause. Glancing, intently towards the blonde seated before me, I said, "Good morning students, staff of Hebrew University and members of the press."

"Accustomed as I am to public speaking, I must say I hope your expectations of me will be met."

"In your studies, many of you have been made aware of one of the tremendous revolutions and controversies which swept through the scientific world in 1952, regarding the earth's interior continental shelf, its continental slope and plate tectonics. At that time much of the scientific community as well as myself became engrossed in Wegener's theory of 'continental drift, that all lands and continents of earth were at one time all connected together, existing in a state of Pangea, where earth's land masses stretched into one super-continent from pole to pole.' It was deep below its landscape that earth's churning powers and volcanos exerted their power by triggering earthquakes and tsunamis especially along the Pacific Rim. As a leading scientist, Wegener also came to the conclusion as did other scientists that these underground mountains and rocks contained trillions of tons of water. A precious commodity needed in the arid land of Israel. Today, it is my pleasure to reveal that plans are in their developmental stages to procure this valuable substance."

"We also know that Israel occupies the very center of the earth, which includes the area called Qumran. Qumran lies among the ruins, just fifteen miles from Jerusalem on the northwest shore of the Dead Sea. It is the southernmost and largest lake in Israel. It is some thirteen hundred feet below sea level, the lowest place on the earth's surface. The Dead Sea's surface area measures some 47 miles long and ten miles wide."

"Known also as the Arabah, east of the Jordan River over to the Dead Sea, below the slopes of Mount Pisgah to what is known as Cave number three. It is one of the many caves in Qumran where the 'Mysterious Copper Scroll' was discovered in 1952."

"At that time a survey of eleven caves in Qumran was begun, during a joint major archeological expedition, involving the French School, Ecole Biblique and the American School of Oriental Research (ACOR) under the direction of Jordan's Department of Antiquities and in a loose cooperation with the Amireh Bedouin, who knew the area best. I might add Jewish scholars were not permitted to become involved with this rare find."

I continued, "For those of you who have never seen the original Copper Scroll, you can now see it on display, housed in the Jordanian Archeological Museum, located on the Ammon Citadel in Jordan, the ancient capital that rises as a sharp hill in the middle of the modern city, also known as 'The City on Seven Hills.' Facts and Information about the Copper Scroll, prepared by Queen Noor of Jordan, is available for purchase on CD ROM."

47

"For many years very few people, other than scholars and archeologists knew about the existence of the Mysterious Copper Scroll and its detailed cryptic list of sixty-four locations, which tells of buried treasures, treasures beyond our wildest dreams. As time passed, information about the scroll spread more freely, allowing the Israeli Department of Antiquities and I the opportunity to examine it and to attempt to decipher its code. I believe once the code is cracked, it will disclose the location of the 2nd Temple treasures. This code consists of seven groups of two or three Greek letters, unknown and still a puzzle to many scholars. One place in the scroll indicates that once the 'Kalal,' the name of the vessel containing the ashes of the Red Heifer, is found that it would reveal another copy of the Copper Scroll, only this one would not be written in code but in simple, clear language. The second copy would reveal the landmarks in which one could find these profound treasures."

"However, my interests and the interests of the state of Israel are not only in the scroll's historical significance and its property rights, but also for the challenge of trying to uncover these hidden places. As Abraham Lincoln once said, so rings true for us, 'Will the catching end the pleasures of the chase?' How many of you here today are interested in the chase?"

The audience applauded loudly. "News reached the archeological community, most scholars, myself included, refused to believe that in addition to 2nd Temple treasures believed to be hidden by Jewish priests before Titus, the Roman Emperor, sacked Jerusalem in 70 A.D. that there existed other vast treasure, 65 tons of silver and 35 tons of gold. Today, we believe it to be imaginary. Since the original discovery, the quest has been on to find each of the 64 locations of these treasures. Archeologists in the field are using up to date equipment to help in their search, using such archeological tools, as remote sensing, satellite imaging, and Subterranean Interface Radar. The thermal infrared photogrammetry gives an X-ray of the ground, able to penetrate what the naked eye cannot see, hidden in the ground, in rocks, mountains and hills. However, our research has come to a halt due to Arab control and we are unable to pursue a further dig. Perhaps some time in the future one of you may prove to be successful in this endeavor. Now, do I have any questions from the audience?"

A tall, lanky young man stood up and asked, "Is it true that the Copper Scroll was especially rare since nothing else had ever been found written on copper before?"

I proceeded to answer, "Most find, as many of you here today are aware of, that most writings discovered in the past consisted of either papyrus or leather. The material of the Copper Scroll itself is considered very rare, in that it consists of two rolled strips of unusually pure copper containing about one percent tin, which some believe to have protected it from severe oxidation. Originally, it formed one scroll about eight feet long and eleven inches wide. At the time of its discovery the scroll was found to be too brittle to unroll and the decision to have it sawed into strips. This caused some of its contents to be lost. More can be read about this in an article written by P. Kyle McCarter, Jr. in the 1992 issue of Bible Review, titled 'The Mysterious Copper Scroll.'"

Another hand went up and a very attractive auburn haired woman stood up and asked, "Mr. Fox, what can you reveal about the text of the scroll?"

I replied, "As previously written and published, by P. Kyle McCarter and I quote, 'The text of the Copper Scroll is believed to be written in the Hebrew Mishnaic, a rabbinic text with peculiar spelling, assembled sometime about 200 C.E.' You can find out more on this in the same article."

An average looking student with disheveled mousy brown hair and thick glasses stood up and asked, "Mr. Fox, is the government of Israel going to pursue an active search for the locations of hidden treasures listed on the scrolls and will you take part in the search?"

I replied, "Not at this time. As regards the government, you can rule out any involvement by the Parliament."

"I would like to conclude," I said, "by letting you know that photographs of the Copper Scroll as well as its contents are on CD and are on sale at your Campus Bookstore. Thank you for your attention." Leaving the podium I sat down as the audience applauded the conclusion of my speech.

Dean Freeman approached the podium and said, "Thank you Mr. Fox. To those of you in the audience, this now concludes our session. If you have any further questions or inquiries, Mr. Fox has said he will be available for anyone including the press over the next fifteen minutes here in the auditorium."

The press stepped in flashing photos. I shook the dean's hand and stepped down the stairs, leaving the podium. The press surrounded me, along with a small group who stayed and approached me with their questions and inquiries. In the midst of all the commotion by the press, the tall, blonde approached me.

"Felix, do you remember me," she asked?

"I do believe we have met at one or two military functions. You're Felixovna, aren't you?"

49

"Yes, and I am pleased that you remembered my name. May I give you my card?"

"Why, I would be delighted to accept one."

Felixovna gently handed me her card.

I took it gracefully from her hand and placed it in my jacket pocket. Addressing the small crowd I said, "It was a pleasure to be here and to answer your questions. Should you have any others, feel free to call my secretary and I'll see what I can do to answer them for you."

Then taking a good hard look at Felixovna, I said, "I plan to step outside and have a smoke, would you like to join me?"

"Of course," she answered. And with that we both left the auditorium.

I felt excited about her, as we walked through the hall and out onto the grounds.

Finding a bench we sat down in a quiet secluded section of the campus. I offered Felixovna a Camel. I said, "Hope these are not too strong."

"Why no, I have been known to smoke the heavies and even cigars. I find them to be quite intoxicating."

Surprised by her answer, I looked into her eyes. They looked like pools of refreshing blue water. Striking my lighter I lit her cigarette, then mine. I told her, "This is the last lecture on my circuit. I am looking forward to some R&R."

She said, "What a coincidence. I am on leave up until August. I have a condo at Ein Gedi and I am hosting a party there tonight. Would you like to come? That is if you have no other engagements."

Thinking she may have a man of her own there, I said, "I would not like to impose upon you."

She responded, "Oh please do come. My father would be so happy to meet you. He is fond of your work and your research."

Relieved that her father would be present I had hoped she did not have anyone special that would be there too.

"Oh, and feel free to bring a guest with you," she said.

I said, "I don't have anyone special, so I will just bring myself." I hoped this response would leave the door open to establish a future relationship with her.

Felixovna then remarked, "I was always partial to the name Felix." And we both laughed.

Always a chain smoke, but now I got it down to a few. Enjoying the long slow drags made me relax.

She said, "Well then, I'll see you tonight, say about seven? Attire will be informal."

Smiling she said, "I have to go now, I have finals in arch to take."

She looked so gorgeous as I took her hand and gracefully planted a kiss.

"Till then," I said.

I watched her as she made her way back into the College. Then I paged my limo driver and said, "Max, I am outside Hebrew College. I'll be sitting on a bench in front of the library. Please come for me now."

Max said, "Be there in ten minutes, sir."

I began to think through preparation for tonight's engagement. Let me see, I'll send a basket of flowers. I'll have time to get in an order at the bakery and have them deliver a box of petit éclairs. Informal, let's see, I'll wear my black Armani pants, my silk, powder blue shirt and my black alligator shoes. As I was completing my thoughts about the night, Max pulled up.

"Good afternoon, Mr. Fox," greeted Max.

"Good afternoon to you Max," I said, "To the condo, Max."

"You're looking chipper," said Max, noticing the smile and glint in my eyes.

"Yes Max," I said, "I have had a very full day. By the way, I have an engagement to attend tonight at Ein Gedi. Order a basket of flowers to be sent to this address, along with an order of petit éclairs from the bakery." Handing Max her card I said, "Pick me up at 6:15. I am due to be there about seven."

"Sure, Mr. Fox," said Max, "Any special type of flowers?"

"Yes, have them deliver the most exotic, orchids, perhaps," I replied.

I sat back, relaxed and entered into some deep thoughts about the possibility of forming an intimate relationship with Felixovna.

"Here we are Mr. Fox," said Max.

Coming out of my self-imposed silence. Thinking about her made time sweep past like the wind.

"See you at 6:15 Max," Felix said. "Good day."

"See you then, sir," Max replied.

I entered the lobby of my hotel, nodding a few hellos to some of my neighbors. I entered the empty elevator. I felt secluded. I always liked that feeling, especially when my thoughts were in a state of expectation and excitement.

After entering my condo, I poured myself a brandy and sat down to reflect on what I would say to Felixovna. I was really smitten with her. I had managed to remain a bachelor with no special attachments. For as long as I could remember, my feelings had never reached this pinnacle. I knew her condo was located in a plush vacation area. I could picture spending time with her in that romantic atmosphere.

Removing my clothes, I laid them down on the hamper. I stepped into a hot shower. Showering, I thought that her eagerness to see me again so quickly could mean she felt attracted to me even though I was self-conscious about having a large stocky frame. She was unusual and beautiful. I couldn't wait to embrace her. As thoughts of her filled my mind and senses, I shaved. Excited, I dried myself, and then gently I patted on my Aramis after-shave. Combing my thick wavy hair into place. At least my hair was one of my best assets, full and in style. I felt it was one of the things that kept me looking young.

My pager rang. It was Max. "Felix," he said, "I am parked out back."

"I am ready," I said, "I'll be right down." I hurried out of my condo door, down the back stairs, out the back door of the hotel and stepped into my limo.

"Good evening," said Max.

"Good evening," I replied.

"Will you need me to pick you up sir," Max asked?

"No, I'll hail a taxi home, thanks," I said. Max was probably wondering why I was not my usual self. In all the twenty years he had been with me he had never seen me so emotional and animated. I guess he suspected I had an evening out with a special woman. After all, I very rarely went to such lengths on a date.

Filled with anticipation, I felt alive. The ride was pleasant. The countryside was barren, but lush, green and picturesque with expensive private homes lining the road leading up to Ein Gedi. We came to a stop in front of a two-story gray-stone mansion. It looked like it had about thirty or more rooms. Max pulled up to the driveway, parked and opened the door for me.

"Good night, sir, have a good one," said Max.

"Good night, Max, see you tomorrow," I replied.

I felt anxious, but I kept it in control. I didn't want to ruin my appearance by working up a sweat. I knocked on the door. A maid answered, opened the door and said, "Come in sir, come in, right this way." She led me into the living room. "There are hors d'oeuvres and the bar is open on your left. Feel free to help yourself. Dinner will be ready soon." I glanced around the large room. Its high ceilings decorated with wood columns and a stunning Italian Bisque chandelier. The room was crowded, with about twenty or so people, all engaged in conversation. I walked over to the table and picked up some ice-cold oysters then went over to the bar and ordered a brandy. The bar was elegant as well as the Damask covered furniture. The walls were lined with several paintings by Chagall, very tasteful I thought to myself. Then as I turned to glance at the archway leading to the dining room, I caught a glimpse of her. She looked even more beautiful than she did the first time I saw her. She caught my eye and motioned for me to approach her.

"Felix, I am so glad you're here," she said as she reached out for my hand. Her hands were so silky soft. I could hold them all night.

"Felixovna, how good to see you. You look lovely," I said.

"Why thank you, Felix," she said in a soft voice.

It was hard for me to think of her as a hardened virago soldier. Her whole demeanor now was totally feminine. I wondered how she could mix the two together and still come out so sweet and luscious. She had an appealing, non-pretentious earthiness about her.

"Felix," she said, "I would like you to meet my father." Taking me by the hand she led the way.

"Father," she said, "This is Felix Sebastian Fox, the researcher and physicist you always rave about. Felix, this is my father, Jack."

I said, "Happy to make your acquaintance. I believe you know my father, Fillmore, quite well."

"Oh, yes," Jack replied. "We completed a great deal of research together. He must be up in years by now."

"It's hard to believe it Jack, but he's reached 105, and doesn't look a day over 90," I said. "He's still physically spry, emotionally stable, and mentally astute and alert."

"How could I ever forget those bold icy-blue penetrating eyes," said Jack. "He was always every bit the British gentleman. When I knew him he was never one to skip a shave, always the consummate dresser. Never sparing any expense to don him, and in vogue at all times. Wearing designer suits with braces, a waist coat, and a pair of Oxford ties. Those were the glory days we shared together. We spent a great deal of time together with Orde Wingate, that Brit & father of the IDF, the Zahal."

"Yes, my father's stories showed he was a relentless visionary campaigner, a first world military force, who had become the envy of all the nations of the world."

The maid came out to the entrance of the living room interrupting their conversation and said, "Dinner is ready, please take your seats."

"We can continue our conversation at a later date perhaps," I said.

"Quite so, quite so," said Jack.

Taking their places, Felix was surprised to find himself sitting down next to Duara.

"Why, Daura. How good to see you," I said. What I wondered was a mole doing here?

Daura said, "Why Felix, fancy meeting you here tonight."

"I should say the same," I said. "How did you get your invitation?"

"Well, Jack and I have been close friends for over twenty years. His mother and my grandmother grew up together."

And Daura asked, "And how did your get your invitation Felix?"

"From Felixovna," I replied.

Daura commented, "Quite a liberated woman, isn't she?"

"Quite, if I may say so myself."

Daura let out a quick chuckle and said, "Watch out Felix, she can be a snake!"

I turned and glared at Daura, appalled that he would make a derogatory comment about such a beauty. I was so taken with her that I blindly ignored Daura's remark, giving it no consideration.

Daura was taken aback. He had never known me to let anything slip by. However, this was not the time or place to inquire about it. With that we commenced with eating dinner.

The smell of fresh lobster bisque filled the room. Whiffs of wine came from the kitchen. Whoever was cooking had to be good, I thought to myself. A maid entered the room and served codfish provincial with macaroni shells cooked in wine with fennel seeds. When she came to serve me I inquired, "Madam whom should I thank for such a heavenly meal?"

"Why your hostess, sir," she answered.

I looked over to where Felixovna was sitting. I caught her eye and gave her a smile and lifting my glass of wine I said, "A toast to a great hostess and cook."

Everyone agreed and toasted Felixovna.

Graciously she said, "It has been my pleasure to have you all here and to know that I have contributed to your gastronomical tastes."

Everyone smiled and said, "Bravo!"

Dessert was simple, cheesecakes of all varieties were served, i.e., cherry, chocolate-chip, almond among them. The maid told me Felixovna herself had made them in advance.

As people finished their meal, some of them gathered at the bar, others went out onto the veranda to smoke. I was among them. I pulled out my pack of Camels and lit up. Before I had time to even turn around, a strong fragrance of sandalwood permeated the air and Felixovna was standing next to me.

"Have you enjoyed the evening," she asked?

"Charming, delicious and exciting now that you're standing next to me," I said.

"I am delighted to know you were pleased," she said, "And thank you for the lovely flowers and the petit éclairs. The maid is putting them out right now."

"My pleasure for sure. Tell me, Felixovna," I asked her, "Where did you get your domestic skills?"

"From Mama," she said, "Before she passed away."

"My condolences," I replied.

"It has been ten years now, so I have adjusted and gratefully I have my domestic abilities to remember her by."

I gently put my hand under her chin and said, "You were wonderful. Can I see you soon?"

"Yes, I would like that. What did you have in mind?"

"Dinner at my condo and an evening at the opera house, say about seven tomorrow night. I can send my limo driver, Max, to pick you up at say six-thirty."

"Okay, 6:30 it'll be. Now excuse me while I mingle with some of the other guests."

I took her smooth soft hand in mine and gave her a gentle kiss. "You're adorable," I said.

She gave me a quick smile, her lips puckered up as if to kiss me and said, "See you then."

I was entranced. For the first time I felt like I could fall in love. I felt a warm flush come over me. Her fragrance lingered in the air. I was attracted to her beyond belief. She was so forthright. I didn't feel confused. I didn't have to be concerned, I thought, whether to go fast or slow with her. She had surrender written all over her. Our mutual attraction reminded me of how Fred Astaire and Ginger Rodgers made such beautiful music together. My hopes were high that she could be the one I had yearned for all of my bachelor years.

Dreamily I went to the bar, ordered a Brandy Alexander. Then I sat down in a plush Chinese armchair. The home was immaculate, yet it had a lived in feeling too. My tastes in decor were always contemporary, but that aside I liked being in her home. Conversations dissolved and several guests left for the evening.

"Felix, why don't you stay? It's getting late and we have several guest rooms. We would be happy to put you up for the night," Felixovna said.

"How thoughtful of you, thank you my dear, however I would like to make preparations for tomorrow evening. Rather than take a taxi as I planned, its late so I'll page my driver and he'll pick me up." With that said, I paged Max.

"Max, pick me up, I am ready to leave," I said.

"I'm on my way," said Max.

I hung up the phone and went over towards Felixovna's father. Reaching for his hand I shook it and said, "I have had the most delightful evening, sir."

"Call me Jack," he said.

"Jack, thank you for a wonderful evening."

"Tell me," Jack asked, "How are things developing with your quest for the treasures of the Copper Scroll?"

"Well," I said, "As I lectured at Hebrew College today, where I met Felixovna, I told the audience that I think it may be some time before we repossess the sacred center of our Jewish history. Sure the Temple Mount was in our hands, yet Muslims continue to administer the site. Perhaps some day things will change but for now the status quo stands."

"How dreadful," said Jack! "It would mean so much to the cause of the nation to find such bountiful treasures."

"I could not agree with you more," I said. All the while I was secretly progressing with the dig and had made a phenomenal breakthrough, one that I did not reveal to my audience that day. For this was all top secret now. The doorbell rang. It was Max. Seeing Max by the door, I said, "Goodnight Jack, and thanks Felixovna once again for a most enjoyable night."

Both of them said, "It was our pleasure. Goodnight Felix."

I was all a glow. When I stepped into the limo, Max noticed and said, "Quite an evening, sir."

"Definitely stimulating Max, definitely stimulating. By the way, I would like you to pick up Felixovna here at her home tomorrow evening say about six-thirty and bring her to my condo for dinner. We will need you after dinner. We have plans to attend the opera."

"Sure thing sir," replied Max.

When I arrived at my condo I anxiously started plans for the next night. I put in a rush order with the florist for fresh orchids.

Then I called my maid and said, "Mollie, be here tomorrow. I am having company for two. I'll have a menu ready for you in the morning so you can shop for whatever groceries you might need and order some champagne. Dinner is set for seven sharp. My guest and I will be leaving for the opera right after dinner. So clean up and then as soon as you are done you can leave."

"Yes, Mr. Fox. See you then."

Happy that all of those details were settled I went right to my wardrobe and picked out my formal wear, took a shower and then went to bed. It was hard for me to go to sleep. I tossed and turned the whole night, dreaming on and off about Felixovna. I wondered why she had not been hooked up with someone. I wondered, was it destiny that I had met her at all?

The next day I went through the day as if in a cantharis. I decided to buy her a gift. Nothing too expensive, she might refuse. I spent most of the afternoon shopping at the Kiker Hamdina Square, similar to New York's posh 5th Avenue. I finally decided on an adorable white teddy bear with a pink ribbon around its neck. I couldn't believe my own actions. I was acting like a high school kid in love for the first time. But this was my first time. All the years of studies including the intense studies for a Juri's Doctorate in International Law while at Harvard, left me no time for sensual pleasures.

Before I knew it, it was five o'clock. I left the office and took a cab and hurried home. I quickly showered and shaved, dabbed some Armani after-shave on, and checked with Mollie on the progress of dinner.

Mollie was in the kitchen. "Big date tonight, eh, Mr. Fox," she said.

"Never mind Mollie, keep your nose in the kitchen. Did you put out our best silverware?"

"Yes, Mr. Fox," Mollie said, exasperated as she wiped her brow. I made some last minute checks on the table settings, lit the candles and plugged in my best herbal essence potpourris, Sandalwood. I thought it would blend in well with her fragrance, of course hoping she had decided to wear the same perfume as the night before.

The doorbell rang. It was her. She looked ravishing in a soft silk, white, clinging skintight evening gown. It was decked with silver sequins. It draped across her well-endowed chest and wrapped around her waist in the shape of an 's.' Sheer and cool for the warm breeze that filled the air.

Her jewelry was conservative. Her makeup was unblemished. With her height I wondered why she chose the military instead of a more safe and lucrative career, such as modeling.

"Come in my dear, come in," I said, taking her hand and giving it a gentle kiss.

"Good evening Felix," she said as she leaned towards me and kissed me gently on the cheek. My pulse began to race.

I removed her mink stole. "You look sensational," I said as I glided my hand around her waist and led her to the dining room.

"Thank you, Felix," she said. "You look smashing yourself," as she glanced at me up and down with a coy smile on her face.

Regardless of my age and large frame, I was grateful to have black wavy hair, combed loose and deep set blue eyes kept me attractive and youthful looking.

A fresh corsage of orchids was on the table. I looked into the pool of her blue eyes and said, "May I?"

As she looked up at me, she said, "Thank you, Felix. What a lovely thought."

Gently I took the orchid out of the box.

"How about pinning it here," she suggested, pointing to the left side of her gown, where it draped around her shoulder. I started to shake inside, but I did not let on to her how nervous I was. I lifted my fingers under the top of her shoulder and pinned the orchid to her gown. How soft her skin is, I thought as my fingers touched her bare skin.

"I have something else for you, my dear," I said as I handed her a gift wrapped box.

"And I have one for you too," she grinned as she took a small gift wrapped package from her stylish pearl sequined purse.

"You first," I said.

Carefully she unwrapped the box and lifting the lid saw a small white teddy bear wrapped with a pink bow.

"Oh how sweet of you, Felix. Thank you," she said. "Should we name it," she asked?

"Why yes," replied Felix, "Why don't you name her."

"I think I will name her Anna," she said and left her on top of the curio as Felix pulled her chair out and helped her get seated.

I opened her gift. It was a black pen engraved with my initials. I said, "Thanks."

The food smelled delightful as it wafted from the kitchen through the dining room. It's savory aroma made anticipation of a splendid meal hopefully work into a splendid evening.

"Mollie," Felix shouted, "My dinner guest is here."

Mollie entered the room and said, "I know, I heard the doorbell."

"Mollie, this is Felixovna." Mollie made a muffled laugh at the name.

"Good evening, nice to make your acquaintance," said Felixovna. "And by the wonderful smell coming from the kitchen, I can tell something wonderful is being cooked up."

"Oh, I made some borsht, some Kasha and some roast chicken. My mothers' recipe from Russia," Mollie said.

"What a coincidence," said Felixovna, "My mother was from Russia too. She lived in St. Petersburg. Who knows they might have known each other."

"Excuse me while I attend to the dinner," Mollie said.

"Felix," Felixovna said, looking straight into my eyes, "Why not call me Winnie? Our names are so alike, twins perhaps? Not in public mind you, but in private maybe," she said.

She was getting so intimate so quickly; my heart was beating off the wall. Her laugh filling the air as we sipped our dinner wine.

She said, "Felix, I just love your elaborate modern decor. All of your mirrors surrounding me, they make me feel like a queen."

I was attentive and thrilled when she said being tall in frame made her feel somehow secure and protected. Something she said she was not accustomed to need.

She said, "Felix you're very appealing and I am so glad that our paths crossed yesterday." It was so much better than the brief, casual introductions they had months ago.

I pulled up a chair and sat down. All the while my legs felt weak and shaky. Mollie served dinner. I was so taken with her I could hardly eat, but to show his delight in being with her, he marshalled himself, keeping cool, calm and collected.

"Mollie is an excellent cook," said Felixovna. "The borscht was remarkable and the chicken & Kasha were exquisite.

"Yes, she does quite well," I said.

Molly overheard the praise. She quickly stepped into the room, removing the plates.

"Why thank you for your kind words Felixovna. Have a good time you too," she said.

"Thanks Mollie," we said in unison. I was curious about how she and her father had met Daura. After all he was a private spy. I couldn't resist it so I found myself blurting it out.

"Tell me, my dear Felixovna, how did you and your father meet Daura?"

"We, that is my father and I, met Daura at our permanent residence at Bali's in Key Biscayne, Florida. Jack, I call my father by his first name."

"Another coincidence," I said! "I call my father by his first name, Fillmore."

"Well, to continue, Jack and I always went for the exclusive touch and elegant quarters and with dial-up conveniences, we found the States very appealing. Jack needed to do business in the States and the warm weather was always ideal for me."

"Sounds like some place I would like to visit," I remarked.

"Then let me offer you an open invitation," said Felixovna.

"I'll take it," I said, thrilled that she would leave me such an open door.

"Call me," she said, "And we can synchronize our schedules. You have it Felix," she said, giving him a sweet puckered up smile.

It took all of my restraint not to let out a sigh and swoop down on her lips. I quickly gave myself an inner shrug and got back into our conversation.

"You and I seem to have a lot in common," I said. "When did your mother pass away?"

"She passed away when I was twenty. And your mother," she asked me, as tears glittered in the corners of her deep blue eyes. At that moment I could almost deny her nothing.

"Her name was Sarah," I replied. "She was a victim of a terrorist bombing. It happened on the eve of our nation's colossal birth. Our entire family had left New York, where we had stayed during the war with Germany. After the war was over we returned to Tel Aviv."

"Oh, Felix, how horrid. I do extend my sympathy."

"You're such a gracious woman, not unlike my mother. When she passed away, my father, Fillmore, exiled himself from women and would never marry again. Up to date he has held that resolve. I will never forget it," I said. "In my own way it's kept me a bachelor for too long and right now I am having second thoughts."

"If I am not being presumptuous, would that second thought refer to me?"

Staring at her beautiful face, I said, "Without being brash, I must say what I never thought I would say, yes, only you."

A warm feeling overtook Felixovna. She got up from her chair went over to Felix, took his hand into hers. I stood up and facing me she clutched my lapels with both of her hands and pulled me to herself and in a small giggle she said, "Felix, I am glad you saved yourself for me!"

Caught by surprise at her bold gesture, I was left speechless. Between the smell from the foods and the smell of her perfume, I felt bathed in ecstasy.

With our meal finished we went into the living room and Mollie served coffee and humintash, left over from the holiday.

A photo of Felix, Fillmore and his mother, Sarah, sat on top of the impeccably kept black, baby grand piano. Felixovna stood up, picked up the photo and remarked, "How youthful your father looks. And your appearance today is very youthful. Why you hardly look a day older than this photo. Tell me Felix, how do you do it? Is there some special formula that you both have?"

"To answer your question, yes, there are a few things I followed Fillmore's lead in gaining and maintaining a youthful appearance. We take several new-age medications. Medications that not only keep us youthful, but increase our longevity too. Are you interested for yourself," I asked her?

"Absolutely, and for Jack too," replied Felixovna. I then went over to my desk and picked out a business card and handed it to her.

I said, "This is the address and telephone number of the physician who monitors us, helping us maintain our youthfulness and longevity."

"What are some of the medications you are taking now," Felixovna asked?

"Some of them," I replied, "were originally intended to treat various diseases. For instance, Deprynl, used for Parkinson's and Exelor, used to prevent memory loss for sufferers' with onset or diagnosed Dementia or Alzheimer's."

Sipping her coffee, she nibbled on a cookie. Smiling she said, "All of this sounds very profound, continue on Felix."

I said, "Let's go out onto the terrace where I can light up, if you don't object."

"Of course," Felixovna said, rising from her chair, the folds of her dress unraveled around her body as she took Felix's outstretched hand. There was a slight chill in the air as they came out onto the terrace. The terrace itself was fashioned into a semi-lunar style, giving us privacy. It was twilight as we watched a brilliant sunset. Shuffling through my pocket, I took out a Camel and lit up. I was pleased that she did not object to my smoking because I enjoyed the relaxed feeling it gave me after eating such an elegant meal.

Feeling a chill in the air, I placed my arm around Felixovna's shoulder, enjoying the feel of her soft skin and the enchanting fragrance that smelled like sandalwood. It seemed to envelope her whole body. After taking several drags, I died it out in a brilliantly chromed portable stand filled with sand nestled in the corner of the terrace. Felixovna noted that Felix overlooked nothing to make his home beautiful, convenient, and comfortable all at the same time. Interrupting the romance of the moment, Felixovna said, "Felix, we still have some time before the opera, why not continue to clue me in on the rest of your health secrets?"

Such a beautiful woman, who could blame her for wanting to know how to keep it that way.

"Yes, of course," I said, "Aside from over the counter herbs and vitamins, taking them along with the popular use of Ginko Bilboa and Neuro-Sharp for increasing alertness and giving increased mental energy, we, that is Fillmore and I, took advantage of alternative medical use of intravenous Chelation Therapy."

"What did that consist of," asked Felixovna?

"Chelation Therapy is a treatment originally used for years for anyone with metal poisoning, mostly lead poisoning. It is a natural amino acid with no side effects other than a positive side effect later discovered to cleanse the body's blood vessels of plaque especially beneficial for the coronary arteries. Fillmore and I had weekly treatments for nine months, then for yearly maintenance, once every three to four months for one week."

"Astounding, Felix. Quite an amazing experience. It seems to show in the color of your face. Your skin has a healthy glow to it, and your cheeks are rosie. Tell me, what do you do for skin care?"

"Have you ever heard of SOD," I asked her?

"No I haven't. What is it," she asked?

"It is a topical cream, Superoxide Dismutase. It helps prevent oxidative damage to the cellular DNA. I also use Pseudocollegen Glycolipids and Evening Primrose Oil. Another treatment is hyper baric oxygen or HBO2. In the past and as for now, it has been used to facilitate recovery from a stroke, but Fillmore and I use it as a treatment to prevent the aging process."

"I am very interested, Felix. How would I go about obtaining such wonderful treatments and therapies?"

"You will find all of these treatments and therapies given by the physician whose name is on the business card I have given you. He does it all," I said.

"Sounds rather exciting. Women all over the globe will want to obtain it."

"Absolutely," I replied. "It will not be too long before it will be available to the general public."

Glancing at my watch I saw it was time to leave for the opera. "It's time to leave for the opera," I said. "I'll page Max, my driver, to pick us up."

"I'll freshen up," Felixovna said, as she walked off the terrace.

I paged Max.

He answered, "Max here."

"Max," I said. "We have finished dinner and are ready to leave for the opera."

"I'll be there in 10 minutes," said Max.

"Thanks," I said and then hung up.

Felixovna quickly powdered her nose, checked her hair and her hose, left the powder room and entered the hall where I was standing, holding her fur wrap. Graciously she slid her arms through the wrap and I planted a soft kiss on her neck.

"How enchanting," she said, as her eyes gave me an inviting, seductive look. All the while I had hopes of marriage. During the drive to the opera we carried with small talk. We both enjoyed "The Barber of Seville." Waiting for her to take the lead after the opera, I decided to bring her home instead of back to my condo. Arriving at her home, she invited me in for a nightcap.

"Shall I send Max home," I asked her?

"Yes," she said.

Felix dismissed Max. Secretly I was pleased. My heart swelled within me. It made me think that nothing was too good for my money to buy her.

"Felix, we have a guest room why not stay over?"

Every nerve in my body felt as if I was ready to explode. After what seemed like a long time, the room settled into silence. My hands trembled as I brushed her silky blonde hair away from her high set cheekbones. The moonlight seeped through the room. I could see the silhouette of her face etched in my mind. She was more than I could wish for. I pulled her close to me and gently kissed her. Her warmth and tenderness felt like a warm breeze filtered through the air.

If anyone had told me what being in love was like, I could never have imagined this moment. I never would have been able to comprehend it until now. Or was it infatuation?

What followed that night led to many nights we would spend together. We had wonderful excursions by the pools of Ein Gedi. But it all came to an end when she was called back into military duty. It was too soon I thought. I've grown accustomed to her. Perhaps we should marry sooner than we thought. With elections coming up I felt it might be wiser to wait until that was over and done with. So I said nothing of my intentions to delay the event to her. I did however give her a friendship ring and she in turn sent me a platinum male and female statue. A few weeks passed without hearing from Felixovna.

I was under a great deal of pressure from the election process and I was exhilarated with the victory of winning the election and becoming the nation's Prime Minister. However, my heart and body ached for her. I tried to locate her, but I was unsuccessful. I finally contacted Daura. If anyone knew where she was it would be him. But, even he had no idea. Finally he pressed one of his generals and they said she was missing in action while stationed in Lebanon. I was devastated.

I tried endlessly to find out if she was taken prisoner or worse yet, she could be dead. Even after a thorough search of the obituaries there was no word. I tried to reach her father, but Jack was on business in the States and I was unable to reach him. Unable to satisfy my hunger for her, I forged ahead and buried my pain in work with plans for "Operation ACHOR."

I called my father, Fillmore, and my close friend, Benny, to meet with me at my office at the Parliament. I was sitting at my desk when my friend and confidant, Benny, who had just returned from his bi-yearly brain spa, and his weekly trip to the Immortality Club, entered the office.

"Have you made yourself immortal yet," I asked Benny flipidly? Those who belong to the Immortality Club believe that if you sincerely believe it will transform your cells. You at the same time must reject the urge to age and die and if you do you will live forever.

Benny sat down, glaring at me and he gave a mute answer.

"Good morning Fillmore, " Benny and I said, both greeting him at the same time.

"Take a seat, Fillmore," I said. "Coffee, tea and biscuits are here."

The two men sat down, while I set out the cups.

"Tea, Fillmore," I asked?

"Yes, with two lumps, please," Fillmore replied.

"How about you, Benny? I can see you're feeling quite rested after all the pampering and personal treatment you received during your trip to the brain spa. Why you must be feeling a great surge of energy from eating all those veggie foods you had there."

Benny replied, "Well, I need a change. I'll have coffee and a biscuit please, Felix."

I then got up out of my chair, walked over to the door and locked it.

"Whoa, what is this all about Felix?"

"Gentlemen," I said, "I want you to be the first to know what I am about to share with you. This is top secret. I have discovered a new set of tunnels. These are not the ones the diggers have already uncovered under the Temple Mount."

"Incredible, my boy, incredible," said Fillmore.

"Astonishing, Felix," Benny said, "Tell me, how the h– did you do it?"

Pulling a map out from under the blotter on my desk I spread it open and said, "I deciphered the code of the Copper Scroll." Pointing to a spot on the map, I said, "Here is where I located a passageway approximately twenty-five feet high and one-hundred and forty-three feet wide. It leads to a smaller passage that the Copper Scroll describes as a very large chamber on a third level. It was there I saw a tremendous sight. All the treasures of the tabernacle were in one room, with lots of space. The walls were tiled, but part of the east side lay in crumbles. No doubt from an earlier earthquake."

"Stupendous, boy, stupendous," Fillmore interrupted.

"Fillmore, you're getting on my nerves now with this routine 'boy' stuff."

"As I was saying," I went on impatiently, "I also discovered while I was alone in this small room, none of the diggers were outside. This meant I would not be noticed entering or exiting the tunnels. Anyway, you won't believe what I found there." I relished the fact that I had Benny and Fillmore sitting on the edge of their seats.

Fillmore asked, "Well b– what, did you find? Go on!"

"I found the other copy of the Copper Scroll!"

Benny was beside himself. "When did all this happen," he asked me?

"Last night, when the diggers were all done. It was about 2 a.m. and the guards at their posts were sound asleep."

"My God, Felix," said Benny, "How the heck did you keep this all to yourself up until this morning?"

"My secret," I replied, "Like you right now, I could hardly believe my good fortune. I was in a state of awe and shock. It took up until you both arrived before I could come down from all the excitement I felt."

"Go on, boy, go on," said Fillmore.

"Father, it would be greatly appreciated if you could refer to me as Mr. Prime Minister, please."

"Don't be flustered, boy, don't be flustered," said Fillmore.

Ignoring Fillmore's last remark, I continued, "Early in April, my limo driver, Max, drove me to Ein Gedi on a personal excursion. Without my bodyguards, I decided to take a small back road, very isolated and not frequently traveled. Max, I said, take this back road, I believe it may be a shortcut."

"No sooner had we passed at the George Allenby Bridge and pulled onto the road, we blew a flat tire. While Max attended to it I saw something glitter in the moonlight behind some very heavy brushes. I decided I would go back the next night alone and check it out. That was what I did last night. On my own, bringing with me my hand held Spectra Precision Pipe (dirt) laser to explore the area. When I arrived in the area it was about two in the morning. I parked my car behind some trees. I pulled out my PBK Walker, the one you gave me Fillmore." Fillmore beamed and gave Felix a big grin. I knew Fillmore himself packed a Dan Weston Delila, a British gun, good in crowded areas and successfully silent with no bang!

"I was free to move on foot. No guards were around. So, I took my flashlight, quietly through the brushes. The glint turned out to be an empty bottle of gin. I went to take it and cast it aside when I saw a hole, the size of a man's hand. I placed my hand into the hole and the sand and rocks gave way, covering me in dirt and rocks, revealing a huge opening. I was pleased to find that I could make my way into what turned out to be a cave, leading into a wide corridor, large enough for me to walk through comfortably. To my amazement I was able to walk through a series of passageways, each measuring ten and a half feet long and ten and a half feet wide."

"Grateful I was alone, I slowly walked through the first tunnel, my shoes shuffling through rocks scattered all over the floor of the cave until I approached a set of seven steps. To my amazement I found it led to an even larger corridor that led to another passageway. All along this passageway the walls were tiled on one side and cracked and crumbled on the other side. This led to three more rooms, each being ten and a half feet square. This led to another set of seven steps. When I reached the top of the last set of steps I discovered a tunnel with a labyrinth of twists and turns. I placed rocks into position creating arrows all along the way, to make sure I could later find my way out."

"Suddenly, I approached a large room, which had four passageways, one going east, one going west, one going north and one going south. By the entrance in each direction there was a set of eight steps. I chose to climb the steps facing north. At the top of the eighth step I entered a long passageway, about ninety feet by forty feet that led to another room ten and a half feet square. On the ground to one side of the room I noticed what appeared to have been a series of shelves lying one on top of the other. Some were cracked, others were crumbled. The other side of the room was in good shape similar to the other rooms. On these shelves lie dust-encrusted layers of sediment. Brushing what I could aside I saw several trunks among the debris. One of them lay open. My eyes fell upon several items inside the trunk. There was very little dust or debris inside the trunk; apparently a small quake may have caused it to open. Inside the trunk was a square box about two feet long and one foot wide. Its appearance was stunning. The outside was made of pure emerald held together by gold hinges."

"Excited, I opened the box and found inside a silver scroll. I gently removed it sensing that something was in that box or in this room that would tell me where the sixty-five tons of silver and the thirty-five tons of gold were located that were listed in the Copper Scroll."

I took out a Camel, lit it up and slowly inhaled the smoke, able then to calm my excited emotions.

"As I looked more closely at this wonderful site, my focus centered on a book that was inside the box. It was covered in gold. I hesitated at first, and then decided to open it. Inside was a small papyrus scroll. I gently removed it. I placed the fragile scroll into my saddlebag and quickly exited the series of rooms, passageways and tunnels. When I arrived back to the entrance of this series of caves I managed to cover it with brush and rocks leaving a marker for my return. Using an old fiat, I usually kept for clandestine activities I headed for my condo, not knowing what lay ahead. Arriving home, I quickly showered and shaved, slept a few hours, then put in my call to you and Fillmore to come to the office at Parliament this morning for a briefing."

Benny spoke up and said, "Where are the items?"

I unlocked my safe and pulled out the most stunning find ever.

Fillmore said, "Well, my b—," then hesitated and said, "Well Mr. Prime Minister, do you believe there could be something here that will unlock other secret locations which could lead to the temple treasures, the vast amounts of silver and gold?"

I replied, "How ironic it is that we could not pursue a dig in the area of the Temple Mount, upon which the Dome of the Rock now stands, because of Arab control, and now we find a possible breakthrough in the Valley of Achor at the other end of the tunnels. And to answer your question Fillmore, the answer is yes."

Benny said, "Well Felix, what is your next move?"

Still exhilarated I said, "I am putting Operation Achor into motion. Fillmore, you can take this silver scroll and be responsible for deciphering it. No one else will be assigned to help you. Too much is at stake. This operation will be a sub-rosa, consisting of only the three of us. Benny," Felix continued, "I need you to assist me every night this week and help me to excavate the hidden room."

"What about your bodyguards," Benny asked?

"I've paid them to lay off me in the wee hours of the morning. They are used to my personal nightly excursions to visit Ein Gedi. We should not have any trouble with them."

Benny asked, "What time shall we meet and where shall we meet?"

I said, "Meet me at the President's Residence at midnight. Bring your tools and wear a set of work clothes. We'll drive the old Fiat."

"You have it. See you then. Good day," Benny said to Fillmore and I.

Fillmore blurted out, "Felix, I feel like I am ready to burst. How do you expect me to deliver the contents of this scroll without revealing it to other archeologists?"

I said, "Fillmore, right now I don't give a damn about any other archeologists! We need to keep a lid on this. Don't let me down on this! You can do this, not for me but for the greater good of our nation. That's it! I have lots to do now. Meet with Benny and me tomorrow morning at eight. Let me know between now and midnight if anything develops. Until then good day!"

"Good day then to you both."

****

Meanwhile, Murray left the Knesset, stepping out into the freezing rain. Mumbling to himself, he berated himself for forgetting his umbrella. Before long he was drenched. When he reached Ruppin Road he tried to hail a taxi, but to no avail. So, he had no choice but to continue walking. He had a five o'clock train to catch. Picking up his pace, walking past the President's Residence, the Theater through the Rose Garden, he crossed Emek Refain, then dashed quickly into the railway station. He was so soaking wet that his shoes began to squeak. He removed his hat, shaking off the excess rain water. It was four-thirty, enough time to get a hot cup of coffee before the five o'clock train left for Tel Aviv. He stopped at a little newsstand in the station and bought a cup of coffee.

Sitting down on a terminal bench, he sipped the warm brew. His body began to relax, taking the edge off of the chill in his body. Reaching into his coat pocket, Murray took out his handkerchief, wiping his face dry. Finishing the cup of coffee, he put the cup in the trash can and began walking towards the train. Turning a corner post, he noticed a small bearded man approaching him. When the man got closer to him, he grabbed hold of Murray's arm, as he was ready to pass him by. The old man smiling, spoke in an excited tone of voice, part English and part Hebrew.

"Murray, Murray Andrews. Murray, it's me. Don't you remember me, Moshe Rosen? Shalom. Man, Shlomkha."

At first, Murray did not recognize Moshe. It had been more than ten years since he last saw him. He may have forgotten what the old man looked like and considering the passage of time since they had last seen each other, naturally he had aged some, turning white. And looking a little shorter, probably from old age. But one thing Murray could never forget was the offense his parents felt when they found out Moshe left Judaism and converted to Christianity. Today, those Jews who leave Judaism and convert to Christianity are known as "Messianic Jews." Murray called them "traitors." Taking one good look at Moshe, although his beard was white, his face had a warm, peaceful glow about it, a somewhat divine radiance, a hesed (benevolent and kind) look. Murray felt somewhat confused by it.

Murray said, "Why yes, I recognize you now Moshe. I am on my way to Tel Aviv and the Great Synagogue."

With a happy look on his face and speaking in a joyful tone, Moshe said, "I am on my way there too, but first I need to check into my hotel."

Then once they boarded the train, the torrential rain came to a stop and the sun burst forth against a clear azure blue sky. Hiding his dislike for his conversion, curious, Murray said, "Moshe, you look so radiant, why except for your white beard I could hardly recognize you. Where are you coming from?"

"I've just spent some time at the Yad Vashem memorial on the Mount of Remembrance in Jerusalem," said Moshe.

Murray asked him outright, "Moshe, tell me what has happened to make you look so simchas (happy)?"

"Murray, it is a long story. I'll start by saying I am truly blessed to be alive." The train was quiet, not too many passengers were aboard. They both sat down next to each other. The train made a steady humming sound as its wheels touched the tracks. The sound eased Murray's tension, helping him to relax. Moshe removed his coat, carefully setting it down in the seat next to him. Murray had to hang his up, hoping it would dry some before they reached Tel Aviv.

"So, tell me Moshe, what is going on in your life right now?"

"Murray, I know you will have many questions by the time I get done talking. How about we go for a late dinner tonight, say about seven-thirty? I am staying at the Hilton Hotel, a few blocks from city hall and the zoo, right off of Arlosoroff Street. We can dine there, the food is exquisite. I'll bring you up to date about my past then."

Not wishing to offend the old man, Murray said, "Sounds good to me, we can meet after services."

As they engaged in small chatter, the train reached the station.

Upon their departure from the train, Moshe bid Murray, "Shalom (Good bye)."

Murray in turn bid Moshe, "Shalom Aleikhem (Good bye. Peace)." Leaving the station, he saw Moshe quickly hail a monit (taxi).

Entering the back seat of the taxi, he greeted the taxi driver, "Shalom Aleikhem. Hilton Hotel, please," said Moshe.

The taxi driver gave Moshe a smile, "Shalom. Nice day out, isn't it?"

Moshe grinned back to the driver and said, "When we reach the hotel please wait for me outside. As soon as I am done registering and send my bag up to my room, I want to leave for the Great Synagogue."

In the meantime, Murray entered the Great Synagogue apprehensive about meeting Moshe for dinner. He knew a discussion could lead to an argument over religion. However, he really liked Moshe. But, there was one thing that never left his memory. He remembered it all so clearly, as if it were only yesterday. His parents accused Moshe of being anthropomorphisitic. Moshe tried to convince Murray's parents that he was not an idolater. He had, "Proof," he said, "that Yeshua HaMashiach was GOD who became a man and not a man who became GOD."

Those were the last words Murray heard Moshe say to his mother and father. Despite their disputes, Murray's parents continued to keep their friendship with Moshe alive. Then, just as services were about to begin Murray saw Moshe arrive at the Great Synagogue, taking his seat, and glancing through the congregation as if looking for him.

Service began, but it wasn't until the congregation stood up for Kaddish (one of the five prayers recited during synagogue services that praise God's Holy Name) that Moshe caught Murray's eye.

Wishing he could avoid him, but as soon as the Alenu (prayer recited at the conclusion of every synagogue service) was completed, and the congregation began to exit the synagogue, Moshe scurried over toward Murray.

When they stepped outside, Moshe was ready to hail another monit. But, wishing to be polite, Murray said, "Moshe, I have my car parked up the next block. I usually leave it near my apartment and take the train back and forth to Jerusalem. Besides, it gives me time to read and avoid the stress of driving in heavy traffic."

Moshe, he was sure liked the idea of not having the expense of paying for another taxi. On their approach to the car, Murray's car, Moshe, always speaking out, said without hesitation, "Nice miklonit, Murray. Was it costly?"

Murray avoided the question. But he did take pride in owning a Saab. It was two years old, small, but since he had no wife or children it served him well. They arrived at the Hilton, just about seven-thirty. Murray parked in the hotel garage. Together they entered the hotel restaurant. The decor was very elegant, making Murray feel a little bit uncomfortable to be in such luxurious surroundings. He would never have suspected that Moshe had such sophisticated and expensive taste.

70

After being seated, the waiter handed them the menu.

"Would you care to have a drink," asked the waiter?

Moshe ordered some Mogen David wine. But Murray said, "Water, no ice for now, thanks."

Murray perused the tafrit (menu) and ordered borsht, kasha and chicken for his aruchat erev (dinner). Moshe ordered some borsht, kasha and brisket of beef for aruchat erev (dinner). Murray kind of settled down, since all the talk they engaged in so far was small talk and not one word about religion, much to his surprise. Moshe wasted no time in telling him that he had just left Hong Kong and Shenzhen, China where he used to do business at the Lo Wu Commercial City, a giant shopping mall that sells imitation designer, luxury items. It was well known as the "world's capital of counterfeit goods." Here Moshe told him that he used to obtain bogus Gucci shoes, Fendi clothing, and Chanel wallets for a fraction of the prices charged for the real thing.

This last trip though, he said he just went back to visit with friends, hoping to share with them the wonderful life he had since knowing Yeshua HaMashiach. Murray knew Moshe, born and raised in Philadelphia, Pennsylvania and that he had lived near them in the Jewish community in South Philly. He and Murray's parents were friends when he was just a boy of eight. Now that area has been completely run by Vietnamese shop owners. While they ate their meal, Moshe reminisced about the old days. Days after the second world-war had ended.

He asked him, "Murray, do you recall some of the friends and neighbors that owned stores on seventh street?"

"Yes," Murray said, "I remember Bell's Shoe Store, Yetta's handbags and the furrier, Birinbalm. I went to Francis Scott Key elementary school with some of their children."

"Do you remember the Jewish Deli on the corner of Seventh and Winton Streets," he asked?

Murray said, "I will never forget how my mother used to go there to buy candled double-yoked eggs and fresh lox. And how the deli would cut out a pound of butter from a large fifty pound tub in their refrigerator."

"Do you remember Izzie's Soda Shop," Moshe asked him?

"Yes, Moshe," he replied. "I used to love to go there and eat a banana split or buy a hot dog and a soda pop. In those days it was the only place to kind of hang out with other kids, since there were no McDonald's or Burger Kings around at the time." When they completed their meal, Moshe took care of the tab and the tip. Another surprise, Murray thought. After dinner Moshe invited him up to his room for some after dinner Mogen David wine. Murray hesitated, but being polite he accepted his invitation. Upon entering the room, he looked around. The room was adequate, he thought.

"Sit down, Murray. Make yourself comfortable." Moshe motioned to the small dining area near the balcony. It faced a beautiful view of the Mediterranean Sea.

"Here, I'll take your coat," Moshe said. Moshe hurriedly put his coat on a hanger, then pulled out two port glasses from off the shelf. Pouring the wine, he raised his glass, toasting it to their renewed acquaintanceship. As their two glasses clinked, both of them said, "Mazel Tov (Good Luck)."

Moshe sat down across from Murray and said, "Have you heard about the Prime Minister's recent discovery of the Temple Treasures mentioned in the Copper Scroll?"

Not answering Moshe, instead he raised a question, "What have you heard, Moshe?"

Moshe answered and said, "Well, the discovery is considered top secret. But one of the archeologist who works with Felix on the project is a friend of mine. He told me that Felix, after entering the sealed Warren's Gate on the Western Wall, that the Prime Minister had discovered an underground hidden passageway. It began from the Temple Mount, extended for about twelve miles right up to the Valley of Achor, on the borders of the Dead Sea." Moshe heralded the site, stating, "That once the discovery of gold, silver and lost temple treasures were found, not only could the state budget be settled, but it would give Israel the financial freedom it had longed for."

Murray sat there and wondered to himself, how could this little old man know so much about such a taboo subject? So, he asked him, "Moshe, how in heaven's name did you come by what is supposed to be top secret?"

"One of the diggers saw the Prime Minister visiting the site quite often. He saw the Prime Minister remove something valuable. God knows who else he may have told."

Curious, Murray waited to hear the rest of what he had to say. So for now he continued to listen. He, for the life of him, could not fathom Moshe as a Christian caring about politics or the state or the Jews. He felt Moshe's conversion to Christianity would have caused him to leave the Synagogue and relinquish his loyalty to the state. Moshe was so affable. And the more he talked, the more Murray became confused.

"Murray, what do you think all of this means?"

He was pensive for a moment. Lifting his glass and taking a sip of wine, he said, "I believe once this underground city and its treasures are found that it would be an indication that HaMashiach is soon to come."

Moshe, not wasting a moment, put aside talk about the discoveries mentioned in the Copper Scroll and got right down to starting a conversation about HaMashiach. Moshe said, "That reminds me, I need to answer your earlier question, inquiring about the peace you see in me. The joy I have, Murray, which you see on my face and in my eyes has nothing to do with tradition or traditional religion, but a personal encounter I have experienced with the God of our fathers."

What, Murray wondered, would his conversion to Christianity have anything to do with a real Jew, let alone the God of their fathers, Abraham, Isaac and Jacob?

Any fool, his parents had warned him, would know Christianity was a monstrous religious hoax, dressed in the thievery of Biblical terminology. He remembered being taught that Yeshua was an imposter and that is why He died.

"Murray," Moshe said interrupting his train of thought, "Let me ask you a question. Would you be willing to view a greater reality of GOD?"

He put his head down and placed his forefinger to his mouth, as if to silence his own lips. Then hesitatingly he said, "I am not quite sure how to answer you Moshe. But, I am always wondering, when I pray to the GOD of our fathers if I will ever experience a catharsis."

"If you would like to know how to get there, Murray, there is one thing you will need to do and that is to let go of all thoughts about your traditions. You will need to let go of the old paradigms."

"Also, Murray, the experience you have when you pray and the experience I have had are both subjective. But, have you ever wondered how you can tell if your experience is biased or not? Or how can you know or recognize if your subjective experience is a counterfeit or the real thing?"

With a strange confused look on his face, Murray's heart began to pound, his head started to throb and in a frightened tone of voice, he wavered and said, "I'll have to think about that Moshe."

Moshe immediately assessed his confused look and the fearful sound in his voice. He sensed Murray was growing apprehensive about pursuing any deep talk about his Yeshua.

"Perhaps I can use an illustration, Murray," Moshe said. "See if this analogy can help you to figure this out for yourself. Have you ever seen counterfeit money?"

"Why no, I have not, Moshe," Murray replied.

"Then let me share this with you. The government trains the secret service, our Mossad, how to recognize counterfeit money. They do this by having agents study thousands and thousands of genuine bills, then by the time they present them with a counterfeit, they're so familiar with the real thing, they can immediately spot a phony. This is true also concerning outward signs as proof of a genuine experience with GOD. One is that if your experience is genuine, it will become obvious and it will be noticeable because it will lead you to be more holy, as well as to improve your character and help you grow more mature, mentally, emotionally and spiritually. It would alter your philosophy about life, causing psychological changes that would also increase your love of GOD. It would also increase your love and tolerance of others more liberally than you would have prior to a genuine experience."

But, Murray felt more confused. He felt like bolting for the door, however, no matter how eccentric and bizarre Moshe was, he felt he was also good-natured and in a strange way he could not let go of the magnanimous feelings he had toward Moshe. Besides, the questions that Moshe presented to him had never even crossed his mind before and now they peaked his curiosity even more. "Moshe, what you are saying is beginning to sound very intriguing, but how can a Jew convert to Christianity and still be a Jew?"

"Murray, my answer is this. I am now a completed Jew. There is more to add to our Jewish heritage. I am sharing this experience with you because I want to offer you God's gift, a gift that transcends the human consciousness and crosses the boundaries of time. That gift is the promise of everlasting life, starting right now. I want to tell you what I have personally experienced and witnessed myself and to ask you to put aside your fears and any prejudices you may have towards Jewish converts to Christianity. If you can put aside the so called allegations that Yeshua HaMashiach was an imposter and only human, then hear me out and His true identity as the Son of God, the HaMashiach will become absolutely, categorically clear."

"But Moshe, if Yeshua HaMashiach was the prophesied Mashiach, then why are we not living in the messianic age of peace and justice?"

In a gentle, resilient, humble response, Moshe said, "Because ever since His resurrection He has given His peace to those who believe His claims in a revelation that can only occur on a one to one basis. But, when He comes back a second time there will be a mark that will identify that the Messianic age is about to begin. Then the same revelation He has given us on a one to one basis over the past two-thousand years will be the same revelation He will make to all mankind. At that time, instead of a one to one basis, He will reveal Himself to the whole world, all at one time, during one single event. Then, everyone living at that time will know who He really is. That will begin the Messianic Age."

Murray, in a state of excitement, could not come up with a comment. Quietly, he remained pensive.

Moshe continued, "Let me ask you this Murray, have you ever scrutinized the claims of Yeshua HaMashiach? Have you ever read the documentation by the first century Jews who left their eye witness accounts written in the New Testament?"

He said, "No, I have not."

Then Moshe said, "Then let me make this comment. Much about what Yeshua and His early Jewish followers said and did may seem obscure, unclear and hard to understand. I am sure you must have many objections. Perhaps you may be thinking, how our people have suffered, along with many others, of course, knowing they have felt the sharp blade of the crusader's lance, the onslaught of the Spanish Inquisition, as well as going through the horrors of the Russian pogroms and in the 20th century, the abominable Holocaust. But, in spite of all these detestable events giving Christianity a black eye, I want to ask you Murray, personally, would you be willing to put all of that on the back burner, so to speak and listen to me, objectively?"

"I am willing to listen, Moshe." He felt strange hearing himself say those words. In his conscious mind Murray really wanted to leave, but something, some unseen force was holding him back. It was as if he was physically paralyzed, riveted to the spot, unable to move. He had mixed emotions. He was both frightened and excited at the same time.

"Let me start from the beginning," Moshe said as he poured himself some more Mogen David and nudged Murray, as if to ask him if he wanted some. Muray nodded a "no" and Moshe continued. "It all started while I was a practicing Orthodox Jew. I, at that time, believed as you do, that if I followed the Law I would be saved. However, I realized that I could never say I followed it perfectly every moment of every day. The reality of this fact dawned on me one day while I was reading the Pentateuch, Deuteronomy 27:26. Let me read it for you Murray," Moshe said. Then Moshe turned to that location of scripture and started to read out loud, "Accursed is one who will not uphold all the words of this Torah, to perform them."

"Then Murray," Moshe continued, "After much hiboneut (contemplation) I asked myself the question I am now going to ask you. Can you or I or anyone say they have kept all the law? And what about our forefather Abraham? He lived at a time when the law did not even exist."

Feeling tongue-tied, Murray replied, "But Moshe, that is why we have our day of Atonement every year. You as an Orthodox Jew know that."

"Ah, Murray, now we come across another obstacle. Yes, we do observe such a day, but we offer no animal sacrifice and no blood is poured out, no laying on of the priests' hands on the head of the animals and no Levitical priests to perform those things required by the Law, which actually classifies this as a violation of the Law itself. Here, let me turn to Leviticus 17:11. Read this for me, Murray."

Reluctantly, he began to read, "For the soul of the flesh is in the blood: and I have assigned it to you upon the altar to provide atonement for your souls; for it is the blood that atones for the soul."

"What does that mean, Murray," Moshe asked? "Does it or does it not mean that the Jews of today are legally left without a substitute for our sins? No, GOD has never left man without a way to approach Him in their sinful state. And did not Abraham receive GOD's approval simply by faith alone?" Moshe continued, "Let me read to you from Genesis 15:6." Moshe began to read ardently, "... And he (Abraham) trusted Hashem and He reckoned to him as righteousness. So, Murray, what today is left for the Jew? We have no temple, no altar, no sacrificial animals, no Levitical priesthood."

Murray said, "But Moshe, we have been told by tradition that this is a myth."

"Well then Murray, does that mean that large portions of the Torah written by Moses are false?"

"Why, I don't know how to answer that statement. I never looked at it in that way. But, what about all the Jews for the past two thousand years, Moshe, are they out in the cold?"

"Murray, there is only one way I can answer that. GOD knows the heart and mind of all men, women and children. He is a merciful GOD. He would accept anyone that exercises belief in Him. However, He is also a GOD of justice. He will judge each person individually. For this point in time, Murray, you must answer for yourself. Murray, GOD honors faith, but you can also read for yourself how GOD feels about anyone who is not ignorant of Yeshua HaMashiach, His Son, yet still rejects Him. Turn to Proverbs 30:42 and read for yourself that God has a Son."

He said, "You read it."

Moshe, sensing Murray's growing fear, calmly turned to the verse and read it out loud. "Who established all the ends of the earth? What is his name and what is his son's name, if you know?"

Moshe calmly closed the Bible. "Murray, if you doubt all that I have told you so far, then let me make a suggestion. Go sincerely to the GOD of our forefathers, and ask Him yourself, if it is really true that Yeshua HaMashiach is His Son, and ask Him if Yeshua is really alive, and if so, would He reveal the truth to you. Would you like me to lead you into this type of prayer," asked Moshe?

He responded, "Moshe, suppose I do hear from God myself, won't people call me psychotic?"

"Murray, if that were true, then we would have to give that label to Moses and all of Israel. They heard His voice when they were at the foot of Mt. Sinai. They were so frightened that they told Moses not to let Him speak, but for Him to speak to Moses only."

Moshe got down on his knees, beckoning Murray to do the same. At first he hesitated, but very touched by Moshe's display of goodness and sincerity, he found himself kneeling down beside him. With closed eyes, Moshe uttered this prayer, "Oh GOD, our Father, GOD of Abraham, Isaac and Jacob, I come to you humbly asking you to forgive our sins, enlarge our hearts, making them more like Yours. Reveal the truth by Your grace, mercy and love, to Murray concerning Yeshua, Your Son, in His life, death and resurrection power. Send him Your promise of peace that You give to all who open their hearts to You, seeking a sincere, unprejudiced answer. Guide us; illuminate us. Open the door as to where he should go and close the door where he should not go. Help Murray to empty himself, ceasing all doubts, opinions, suppositions and preconceptions he has as to the reality of Yeshua's true nature, who is equal to You and the Holy Spirit." Having completed this prayer, Moshe then asked Murray, "Would you like me to lead you in the sinner's prayer?"

He unexpectedly found himself willing, but questioned Moshe. "What does the sinner's prayer mean?"

Moshe answered saying, "This prayer will go to the Father requesting your sins be forgiven by the shed blood of His Son, Yeshua HaMashiach, as an atonement for your sins. This will make the way clear for you, Murray, to establish a personal relationship with the Father, the Son and the Holy Spirit. Once you complete this prayer in humility and sincerely mean it, then Murray your name will be written down in the Lamb's 'Book of Life,' granting you to start the promise of eternal life to be with GOD, now and forever, and at the time of HaMashiach's reappearing, being granted a new body, like His. Here, let me read this to you." Moshe opened his Bible and began to read out loud from John 1:11-12, "He (Yeshua) came unto his own and his own received him not. But as many as received him to them gave he the power to become the sons of GOD, even to them that believe on his name."

"And now I will turn to some other words recorded by this Jewish fisherman, known as the Apostle John. Here, Murray, read these verses," Moshe said handing me his Bible.

Murray, still on his knees, took the Bible from Moshe. His hands were trembling and his body perspiring. He still could not understand what force was keeping his knees bolted to the floor, listening to words he never dreamed he would listen to, let alone read the New Testament out loud. However, he felt moved, as if a gentle breeze was blowing, leading him to follow Moshe's genuine love and guidance. Somewhat reluctantly, he then began to read the verse of scripture that Moshe had turned to out loud, the Gospel of John 3:16–18.

Reading once again out loud, he began, "And as Moses lifted up the serpent in the wilderness, even so must the Son of man be lifted up: That whosoever believeth in him should not perish, but have eternal life. For God so loved the world, that he gave his only begotten Son, that whosoever believeth in him should not perish, but have everlasting life."

Murray placed the Bible onto the bed, leaving it open to the verses he had just finished reading.

"Now, Murray," Moshe said, "Put your name in the place of the word 'whosoever' and read this verse again."

He focused on the sentence and read, "That Murray who believeth in him should not perish, but have everlasting life."

"Now, does it say, you may receive it, or can you have it right now," Moshe said?

"Have it."

Moshe continued to tell him God would then, once he committed himself, come to dwell within him, making him new. Individually, He would guide and direct him, and work on improving his character, helping him to become more holy.

Turning the pages of the Bible to another section of scripture, Moshe read out loud from I Corinthians 15:51–57, "Behold, I shew you a mystery: We shall not all sleep, but we shall all be changed, In a moment, in the twinkling of an eye, at the last trump: for the trumpet shall sound, and the dead shall be raised incorruptible, and we shall be changed. For this corruptible must put on incorruption, and this mortal must put on immortality. So when this corruptible shall have put on incorruption, and this mortal shall have put on immortality, then shall be brought to pass the saying that is written, Death is swallowed up in victory. He has destroyed death forever (Isaiah 25:8). O death where is thy sting, O grave, where is thy victory?"

Moshe turned the page and once again handed Murray his Bible.

He asked, "Now Murray, would you read from Romans 10:8–11?"

He read, "That if thou shalt confess with thy mouth the Lord Jesus and shall believe in thy heart that GOD hath raised him from the dead, thou shall be saved. For with the heart man believeth unto righteousness; and with the mouth confession is made unto salvation. For the scripture saith, Whosoever believeth on him shall not be ashamed."

"Would you stop there for a moment, Murray," said Moshe? Murray placed his hand on the top of the Bible, and gave Moshe a stunned look.

"Now Murray, this is the hard part. Are you willing to make a sacrifice to GOD?"

"Do you mean an animal sacrifice," he asked?

"No," replied Moshe.

"Here, let me clear up any confusion you may have about the need for animal sacrifices for today. I'll read from Mark 12:28–34. It happened that during Yeshua's time on earth that the Jewish scribes came to Him. This is what transpired. And one of the scribes came, and having heard them reasoning together, and perceiving that he had answered them well, asked Him, Which is the first commandment of all? And Yeshua answered him, The first of all the commandments is Here, O Israel; The Lord our God is one Lord: And thou shalt love the Lord thy God with all thy heart, and with all thy soul, and with all thy mind, and with all thy strength: this is the first commandment. And the second is like it, namely this, Thou shalt love thy neighbor as thyself, There is none other commandment greater than these. And the scribe said unto Him, Well, Master, thou hast said the truth: for there is one God; and there is none other but he; And to love him with all thy heart, and with all the understanding, and with all the soul, and with all the strength, and to love his neighbor as himself, is more than all burnt offerings and sacrifices."

"So, you see Murray, in this scripture what God really wants from you is your love. To love His word and to love His Son."

"You made your point, Moshe. I understand," he said.

"Well then," asked Moshe, "Would you be willing to receive Yeshua HaMashiach as your HaMashiach? And would you be willing to make the sacrifice to confess to others that you have decided and received Yeshua as your personal Lord and Savior?"

"Is that the only sacrifice I would have to make," he asked?

"Well, let me put it like this, it would mean that you would start a new life, one completely different from the one you now lead.

Your life will improve. You will be with others like myself, who meet weekly, giving each other support. At first you may loose your family and friends, but you can expect GOD to help you and them through this transition. You can expect joy in sorrows and peace in the midst of turmoil."

"Moshe, to tell you the truth, I cannot understand what is keeping me glued here to the floor on my knees. I know it has to be something stronger than myself, but I will promise you that I will read the New Testament and ask the GOD of our fathers to reveal the truth concerning Yeshua's nature and His position, but I need some time to think about this. I am not sure what I should do right now."

"Murray, let me lead you in the sinner's prayer now. You never know what will happen to you once you walk out this door and then it well could be too late." Moshe said, "I know the doubts and fears you are going through Murray. I know because I have undergone these same doubts and fears."

Suddenly, for no explained reason, Murray got very quiet. Silently to himself, he thought, "I am not sure if I can do this. I have always demoted Yeshua, following others who dismissed Yeshua's claims about His true nature, being GOD who became a man and then went back to His place as the Son of God." However, Murray, in a small voice, said, "Moshe, I am not really sure, but I'll try." Moshe turned towards him with tears in his eyes, liquid beads rolling down into the creases of his aged face, wiping the tears away from his face with his hands.

Moshe said, "Murray, repeat after me these words: Father God of Abraham, Isaac and Jacob, please forgive my sins, especially that I believed what others had to say in rejecting Yeshua. I now ask You to forgive me for this. I ask You to reveal Your Son to me. Help me to accept the only acceptable sacrifice for my sins through His shed blood."

Murray, not use to this mode of intimate praying, started out in a halting voice, so low, Moshe could barely hear him. He then repeated this simple prayer with Moshe and the instant he finished praying, an overwhelming peace came over him. Feeling somehow deeply happy inside himself, a happiness that made him feel like he was smiling from his head right down to his toes. He felt light, as if someone had lifted a heavy weight from off of his shoulders. He felt as if the mundane external world was slipping away, transporting him into a world beyond boundless time and the limitations of space. He felt like he had entered eternity, a place that did not have emotion, as we know it. And if anyone were to ask him what it was like, he could say, it was a feeling of being constant, unlike any other experience he had ever had in his whole life.

He could hardly believe what he had just prayed, but the peace and joy he felt at that moment was so exquisite, he could hardly contain himself and he found himself giving Moshe a bear hug.

Moshe hugged him back, then stood up. Murray followed. Moshe handed him, whose hands were still shaking, a copy of the New Testament.

"Murray," Moshe said, "All I ask is that you read this with an open mind and heart. Here is my business card with the address on the back of it. This is the location where Jews who believe in Yeshua too, meet together on a weekly and sometimes bi-weekly basis. I would like to invite you now to go there with me tomorrow at eleven o'clock and bring your questions with you. We can go over them after the service."

Murray, kind of staring as if he was in a trance, smiled and said, "Yes, tomorrow is good. I usually spend the day in my apartment, but early tomorrow I'll be at work in parliament, finishing up some uncompleted paper work, while the Jerusalem day celebration is on, and since Jaffa Road is just a few minutes from there, I should have no difficulty getting there on time."

Moshe walked him to the door, excited and happy, and handed him his hat and coat.

"Shalom, Murray, see you tomorrow," Moshe said.

He said a quick, "Shalom," left the room, taking the stairs to the garage level of the hotel. He needed a few minutes to get a grip on himself. He paced slowly through the garage, found his car and got in. Driving home he felt as if he was riding on air. Even the heavy traffic which usually frustrated him, this time it didn't even phase him.

****

Besides the President's Residence, Felix maintained a condominium in the King David Hotel as his home. On the evening of June 4th, immediately after the conclusion of the Jerusalem Day celebration, a day celebrated each year, commemorating the end of the six day war and its subsequent 1967 reunification of the City of Jerusalem, Felix, now Prime Minister, held a post celebration at his condominium.

Having concluded the celebration on Ammunition Hill, several members of the Parliament, bodyguards and other well-wishers attended who had received a special invitation. Murray Andrews was among one of those invited. Much to his surprise he wondered why he had been invited.

Murray entered the King David Hotel. He always enjoyed his visits here. The surroundings and the decor were always so enthralling.

However, as many times as he had visited this hotel, he had never been up to visit Felix's condo. A large crowd surrounded the elevator, so Murray decided to take the stairs, leaving the crowded elevator to others. He climbed the two flights of stairs and entered the hallway. He didn't have to knock on the condo's door; it was left open, with bodyguards flanked on each side of the door. Murray presented his invitation to one of them, then stepped inside the hall. Handing his coat to the maid, he glanced up and down the entrance hall, all the while glancing at the walls and floors, richly decorated with Chinese plaques, a foyer table and chairs and an exquisite Chinese rug on the floor.

As he stepped into the large living room, what he saw cast Felix into a different light. He thought his decor would be more Victorian in taste, never imagining he would see ultra modern sofas and mirrors. Mirrors, it seemed to be, were everywhere. Even the vertical blinds were mirrored mylar, casting reflections, as if one was looking at himself in an arcade's maze of mirrors.

Stepping onto the rug, Murray felt the plush cushion under his feet as he walked onto an enormous Persian rug that covered the floor. Murray mused, this was the rug he had heard everyone talking about. The one that Felix was said to have purchased for $25,000 while on his trip to Madras, India. On the walls Murray saw exquisite paintings that looked like they were original paintings by Monet, Picasso and Rousseau. Several Chinese sitting chairs surrounded the room as well as three ultra modern sectionals, all in glorious white, leaving enough sitting room for all the guests.

Looking at all this, Murray couldn't help feel overwhelmed by it all. This setting was elaborate, quite ostentatious, swank and palatial to say the least. Three servants scattered throughout the condo offered guests a supply of unending hors d'oeuvres. One room held a bar, which was open for drinks. Making his way toward the bar to get a glass of wine, he caught a glimpse of the large dining room, enough to seat about twenty-five people. As he continued his entrance he shook hands with several other high-ranking Parliament figures.

Reaching the bar, he saw Benny, Felix and Fillmore standing together engaged in conversation. He caught their attention. They each acknowledged his presence in a glance of eye to eye contact. He decided to wait for a better moment to speak to them. Perhaps he could find out about the secret discoveries of wealth Moshe had told, regarding the Copper Scroll.

Then a bell rang and the maid declared, "Dinner is ready." Murray searched the table for the place set with his name card and sat down. He noticed that the name cards for everyone were tucked onto silver rings decorated with a large silver rose bud with a cloth napkin rolled up in the ring. Luxurious, but very practical, thought Murray, noting how everyone found seats with ease. How very personal and warm, he thought as he looked at each place setting adorned by a 3 x 5 picture frame listing the menu and individual silver topped salt and pepper shakers were set at each place setting. Fine china, nestled on brass servers atop a lace "Star of David" tablecloth and a miniature vase which held a fresh rose for each person. This was elegance indeed. Perhaps, he had underestimated Felix after all.

Wine poured freely, which Murray indulged in, never caring for hard liquor, his favorite being Mogen David. The meal was sumptuous, with choices of chicken, brisket of beef or salmon and of course, borscht with sour cream for soup and plenty of a variety of vegetables. Desert was a specialty cake made with liquor and a liquor icing. Murray had never been to such a feast. He was very impressed. As dinner concluded, some guests left. But Murray milling around became engaged in a conversation with the Israel Antiquities Director, Sol Cohen, formerly of the Israel Geology and Geophysics Institute in Holon, Israel and former President of the Israel Institute for Talmudic publications. Sol had successfully implemented the vast Med-Dead Sea Project. It was a project that would create a pipeline going directly from the Mediterranean Sea and stretch across the dessert up to the Dead Sea in the vicinity of the Valley of Achor, some fifteen miles from Jerusalem. It would bring the waters of the Mediterranean Sea to the Dead Sea using a hydroelectric plate that would produce enough electricity to supply the whole area.

"Sol," Murray inquired, "What is the current status of the Med-Dead Sea Project?"

Sol replied, "We are ready to implement construction. Hopefully our engineers who are working on the Mediterranean side will catch up with those who are working on the Valley of Achor side."

Kind of surprised Murray's ears perked up at the mention of the Valley of Achor. He knew that information about this area was a taboo subject and not one for casual conversation, however he pursued it.

Sol, feeling good from all of the best liquor he ever had, went into brief details, revealing secrets of how Felix had managed to dig under and around the Temple Mount, and how Felix had discovered hidden chambers breaking through section after section of a large tunnel. Sol, speaking in an eager but hushed voice said to Murray, "Felix has discovered some of the regional, palace and hidden temple treasures listed in the Copper Scroll."

Murray caught off guard, startled by Sol's gossip mongering asked, "How was Felix able to go undetected?"

"Genius, sheer genius, such a rare bird that Felix," Sol went on. "The work," Sol said, "Was done at night by specially assigned diggers dressed as Arabs, so as to attract the least attention. They in turn bribed the guards. These diggers were under orders of strict secrecy, however, several other unorthodox archeological groups were digging on the Dead Sea end, beginning on the floor of the Valley of Achor, just below the caves at Qumran and that's how word leaked out. There were," he continued to ramble on, "Some arm-chair archeologists who had discovered a gold vein, but notice of this was kept under government confidentiality, until such a date when this work would be completed."

"Murray," Sol continuing to speak in a whisper said, "If word leaked out about Felix's discovery of the treasures, it could lead to war. Although," he paused for a moment, looking Murray right in the eye and saying, "I feel war is inevitable. These treasures really belong to us even though they are in territory now under Arab control."

Sol's whispered braggadocio ended quite abruptly when Fillmore stepped in ending their conversation. Murray, not one to be fooled, interrupted Fillmore before he even got the chance to say a word.

"Fillmore," he said, "How good to see you. Listen, Sol and I have been discussing the Copper Scroll. Since it has been more than a year since any information has been released by Felix, I am going to request a report on the status of the operation involving the Copper Scroll."

Stunned, Fillmore, not one to discuss "top secret" matters in public under any conditions, abruptly ended the conversation, saying that, "His limo had arrived." Then with eyes cold as steel he looked at Murray and Sol and in a voice full of consternation he said, "I want to see both of you in Felix's office, Monday morning, 8:00am sharp. Goodnight gentlemen," he huffed.

Shaken by Fillmore's grasp of the gravity for discussing top secret operations, Murray couldn't get away from Sol quick enough. He said, "Sol, talk to you later. I see someone I need to talk to."

Sol in a sharp staccato voice said, "Fine, see you later too!" The celebration went on into the evening, with most guests departing by nightfall. It was then that Felix found himself alone with Murray Andrews.

As I eyed Murray, Felix noticed that there was something very different about him. Somehow he looked vibrant and alive, instead of morose and downcast, especially considering the long day of celebration and the approaching lateness of the hour.

"Murray," I said, "You look extraordinarily vibrant and alert for this late hour. What is your secret tonight?"

"Do you really want to hear the truth," he asked, in a strange hesitating voice?

I looked deep into Murray's eyes. I noticed Murray's usually intense cold stare had somehow turned softer.

I said, "Go on."

"Felix, just yesterday I discovered the most profound truth concerning 'that man.' It has been one of the most fascinating experiences of my life. I found out who Yeshua HaMashiach is."

"You what," I replied in astonishment?

"Felix, what I am about to say is not a subject for debate or opinion and definitely not just a subjective experience for me, but it is for anyone who will open their heart and mind. It all happened like this. I was on my way, leaving the Parliament building, headed for home. It was raining out so I bought a cup of coffee to warm me up. As I got up to walk to the train, I was unexpectedly approached by a friend of my father's whom I had not seen in a long time. In fact, the last time I had seen him he was in his early fifties, when my family and I lived in Philadelphia. I was only about ten at the time, but I never forget a face. His name is Moshe Rosen. He too, though in his eighties I assume, looked as if he hadn't aged at all. He was as vibrant and alive as I look to you right now. I questioned him then, as you have questioned me now. And what happened to him has now happened to me. It all started on the same day we attended the Great Synagogue together. After services we had dinner at the Hilton Hotel, where he was staying. After dinner we went up to Moshe's room for a nightcap. It was there that I had quite a personal experience. I found myself, against all odds, getting onto my knees and asking the God of our fathers to reveal the truth as to whether Yeshua was His Son, the HaMashiach. I also asked Him was Yeshua still alive today and was He interested in a personal relationship with me?"

I was shocked and feeling like I would burst, but kept calm and said, "Go on, I am listening Murray."

"I can't explain exactly how I felt, but I must admit at first I felt confused over the fact of relating to a personal God. I was not sure I could accept that. I had a lot of mixed feelings. When Moshe first confronted me, I wanted to leave. Instead I found myself glued to the spot, as if some invisible force was leading me to stay and go through this act of prayer that resulted in my own personal conversion and commitment to accept Yeshua HaMashiach, along with all of its ramifications. Once I made this decision, Felix, it was awesome. I was astounded."

"For the first time, I was able to see a reality of God that I had never known before. Moshe then invited me to a meeting the next day, a Saturday. He said I would find other Jews who had gone through this same experience and to come and see for myself how they, like him, were full of joy and peace too, now that they knew who Yeshua was. I was going to reject his invitation because it was our Sabbath, but my feelings were so free and happy, I decided to go."

"And so, we decided to meet the next day at the Central Bus Station on Jaffa Road. We walked all the way from there, past Independence Park, where today's celebration had begun, headed just south of Aaron Road, entering a small building next to the YMCA. The room was rather plain, but the people were happy and excited. As the main speaker began, I knew I was sitting in a room filled with what I would in the past have called 'traitors,' Messianic Jews, whom I at the time also believed to be not Jews at all, but Christians who were born Jewish, later converted to Christianity and used the term Messianic Jews to hide from being called Christians. However, the speaker cleared up this misconception by telling those who attended why they do not use the identifying word of Christian."

"He explained that Christian means one who accepts the common doctrines of Christianity and follows HaMashiach, whereas the identity they do adhere to as Messianic Jews is because it means that they have not only embraced the claims of Yeshua HaMashiach as revealed in both the Talmud and their fulfillment as witnessed by many Jews and recorded as such in the New Testament, but that they are still practicing intently the summation of all the Law: To love GOD, our neighbor and ourselves, including the observance of all of our Jewish feasts. I fought my feelings to leave. Instead I decided to stick it out and see for myself what these people were up to."

Murray could tell Felix was ready to explode, but he held back, he was sure out of common courtesy.

So, he went on. "One thing I did notice was that the speaker, all during his speech, never referred to Jesus, but instead he would say, 'HaMashiach' or 'Yeshua.' He had a way of making the abstract real and his philosophy practical. He was a skilled wordsmith and a creative communicator. I felt here was a spiritual giant whose words left me with the feeling of being a spiritual pygmy. He made the scriptures sound exciting and not merely a collection of religious teachings or out of date ancient narratives."

"When he concluded, he introduced a group of men and women who got up and danced to what sounded like Jewish music, but the words were like none I have ever heard before. I found myself attracted to their expressions of joy and happiness."

86

Felix though listening intently to him, Murray noticed was now visibly very uncomfortable. He was unable to sit quiet any longer and listen to Murray. Felix lit up a Camel, took a long, slow drag, and said, "So, you've read the New Testament have you?"

"Well, yes," Murray said, "But what really startled me is that I found myself actually praying first and asking our God, the God of Abraham, Isaac and Jacob to reveal Himself to me. And He did!"

I got up from my chair, almost tripping over my feet. I said, "I cannot believe what I just heard you say!"

Quickly, Murray retorted, "Felix, I had a theophany. It was the most awesome, spellbinding moment in my life. When I began to pray, internally, I heard a voice say, 'This is it! Murray, I am it! I am Yeshua! I am God!' The voice I heard had no inflection in a non-acoustic medium. Unlike human transmission, it was spoken telepathically, transmitted via radioactive neurological propagation."

My expression was dumbfounded. My eyes rolled back up into my sockets. I got up from my chair with a look of total disgust. Raising my voice, I said sharply, "Murray, that's it! I must insist that you stop this conversation. Put these thoughts out of your mind where they belong."

"Felix," Murray said in an excited tone of voice, "Don't look at me like I am meshumadim (crazy person). This really happened. I know all of this may be frightening to listen to. However, what I am telling you, that most people are frightened when they are unable to understand or comprehend subjective, mystical experiences."

Glaring at him angrily I said, "That's it! Murray, you've crossed the line. You're on the wrong road. You and your crazy psychotic ideas can leave." Then grabbing him by the arm I steered him toward the door.

I said, "Murray, what you have told me, you may as well have slapped me in the face or hit me over the head with a hammer. I want to see you Monday morning in my office at eight o'clock sharp!" Quicker than a blink of an eye, Murray grabbed his coat from off its hanger in the hall closet. I quickly walked past him and alerted the guards, instructing them to escort him out the door.

Flanked one on each side by Felix's bodyguards, they escorted Murray down the hall, down the steps and out the back door of the hotel. However, in some strange and unexplained way he stayed calm, maintaining a peace he could not explain. All the while feeling as if he was in some other dimension, and not here on earth.

Meanwhile, he decided to put in a call to his father. He needed to vent himself. Picking up the receiver, he dialed his father's telephone number.

Felix said, "Fillmore." (He never called him dad or father.) "Fillmore, this is Felix."

Fillmore replied, "What is going on Felix? Why do you sound dreadful?"

"It's Murray, that beast! That absolute zero, a bete noire."

"And to what does he owe these honors," Fillmore asked?

"He's gone off his rocker!" In a huff, I crushed my cigarette out in the ashtray. My hands were shaking. I said, "I always knew Murray was eccentric, bizarre, unconventional and a true blue, sui generis, if there ever was one! But this takes the cake!"

"Hold on Felix," Fillmore said, interrupting me. He said, "Felix, stop going on a long string. What is this diatribe about? What has he done to warrant such caustic remarks?"

"Fillmore, I have had it with him! We had an intimate discussion about GOD and he went haywire on me. He says he has converted!"

"Converted to what," asked Fillmore?

"He said that he believes that Yeshua HaMashiach is GOD. And that he has become a part of the Messianic Jewish movement. He said he is still a Jew, even though he is now a Christian."

"Felix," Fillmore asked, "And for that you're going to fire him?"

"What else can I do?"

Fillmore suggested, "Let's continue this subject when I stop in to see you in the morning. And by the way, you will need to call Sol on the carpet."

"Why," I asked?

"I overheard Sol tell Murray details about your discovery of the Copper Scroll."

"Did Sol tell him everything," I asked?

"It looks that way," said Fillmore.

"Then who else knows," I asked exasperated?

"See you in the morning, Felix. We will talk about it then," Fillmore said and hung up.

I was fit to be tied. I hung up. Then I quickly put in a call to schedule a session of Parliament to proceed with criminal action against Murray and Sol.

Fuming to myself, I thought, in the interest of national security, Murray and Sol would have to pay for this incredible breach. I felt quite strange, angry at Murray and Sol, yet inquisitive and exhausted emotionally. I sat down in my recliner, pushing it back into its reclining position. In spite of my frustration and anger against Murray, talking about GOD always made me think back to the time when the entire family had left New York and returned to Israel. It was on the eve of the colossal birth of our nation. Soon after that event, Sarah, my mother, passed away, a victim of a terrorist bombing.

Holding a lifelong sense of wonder toward the beauty of being, I was always what I would call "an atheist at heart." Yet, the one thing I could never accept was a belief in the GOD of my fathers. However, I always kept occupied with physics and its relation to philosophical issues. It was the event of my mother's death that triggered my search for the meaning of life. Why, I wondered, had my mother been taken from me in such a horrible way? Why do the best of the best die young? Looking back now I remembered how during my teen years I would spend hours pouring over Fillmore's enormous collection of the great Rabbi, known as Moses Maimonides, and his monumental contributions to the world. His genius was in the fields of medicine, astronomy, physics, metaphysics and other profound branches of science and philosophy.

Reading page after page, expounding the difficult topics of life and death and all that comes in between was astounding. So, was his light into our mortal years here on earth and our hope for a heavenly state of immortality. Yet, as much as I wanted to know God and even after exploring Maimonides through and through, examining the great Rabbi's subjective and objective views, I was never able to make a paradigm shift. I was unable to cross the bridge that could lead to a real and active faith.

Undaunted however, I wanted a spiritual life, one I wished I could have shared with my mother. I tried. Oh how I tried. Once, soon after my mother's death, I continued this quest.

I remembered how excited I was about the Hasidism Pietistic movement, by studying their fascinating current literary masterpieces, hoping it would help me unlock its mysteries.

Even when I was up into my early forties I remembered how excited I was when a three-day symposium was held in Jerusalem, entitled "Maimonidies as Physician, Scientist and Philosopher." Maimonides was also known as the "Great Rambam." Why, I asked myself, even after attending that symposium, why am I still in doubt about the reality of GOD? Whenever there is talk about GOD, what makes me become like a storm raging across the sea? Why were my emotions tossed to and fro? Saddened by my mother's death, I had hoped that one day I would transcend my unbelief. As I reflected on these questions I knew that if I would ever be able to believe, it would only be because of my mother's great love of God and what I had learned from the "Great Rambam." Deep inside I felt that if I could have shared in my mother's life with GOD, it would somehow have drawn me closer to her before her death. Missing her presence filled me with great emptiness. How I missed her was beyond words. But, at least I had fond memories of her. I embraced those memories now.

I will always cherish the early days of my youth spent with her and Fillmore when we lived in Brooklyn. As if it were yesterday, I recalled how in those "good times," how she would always speak "out loud" to GOD and even "louder" in "bad times." Yet, even up until the time of her death I was never able to enter into her experience of faith and her life with GOD.

****

Headed down the hall, towards his office, Benny would embark upon the preliminary preparations for this incredible journey into the unknown. He was ready to meet his destiny and the fate of the state and no doubt the entire world.

Benny knew Felix would shortly present the "Chondriana Operation" to the Parliament. His steps increased their pace as he hurried to get started. As Benny swiftly rushed by the large marble columned hall, he brushed past Murray Andrews, Minister of the Interior and head of the National Religious Party or NRP in the government.

"Good morning, Murray," he greeted him.

Murray, a young, tall, rugged, muscular man with high cheekbones and dark brown eyes, eyes that almost looked black, eyed Benny up and down. Murray managed a quick, "Hello." Not giving Murray another thought, Benny continued to quickly descend the stairs, headed towards Felix's office, as Murray followed close behind him, ready for his encounter with Felix. Murray had no idea what would transpire once he entered Felix's office. He knew that he was not high on Felix's "good boy" list and he was not looking forward to this meeting. He sensed complete disaster up ahead. Murray, intellectually honest and steadfast, was also known for being egocentric and because of his openly displayed stubborn streak some referred to him as having the mind of a rock.

Murray approached Felix's office, knocking on the door, then throwing it ajar, he entered the somewhat usually quiet enclave, and slapped his original report onto Felix's desk.

In a gruff voice, he squeaked out a bare, "Good morning, Felix, Fillmore."

"Good morning," I uttered in a hasty manner.

Fillmore nodded his head acknowledging Murray's presence, giving him the cold shoulder in a surly look.

"Sit down, Murray," I said as I motioned for Murray to sit in the chair next to my desk.

Murray ignored Felix's request to sit down. Instead in a feverous tension filled voice, he said, "Felix, what the hell is going on? Not only is Iraq and its allies against us but also word has it that factions from every country have raised up their armies against Israel. Ciphers are coming in from counter-intelligence all over the world. Hell, even the ROM, the head of the Israeli Secret Service, the Mossad can't keep up with the Stringers."

I broke out into a cold sweat. Beads of salt ran down my forehead, along my cheeks and on into the corners of my mouth. Quickly, with one swoop of my handkerchief, I wiped my face clean. My deep set icy blue eyes penetrated Murray as if I was boring a hole through him. I composed myself. I had a sense of peace once I had made my decision to go ahead with the Chondriana Operation.

"Murray, you're fired," I said!

Murray said, "Are you out of your mind, Felix? For what reason?"

Handing Murray my write-up, I said, "As of today Murray, you and the NRP are outlawed!"

I meanwhile pressed the silent button, summoning security. Security arrived in seconds and placed Murray under arrest, cuffed him and escorted him out of the building.

Fillmore said, "I wondered when you were going to do that Felix."

Then I retorted, "Yes, it's about time we are rid of that rock head!" Relieved that the task of firing Murray was over, I issued a directive for selective elimination of the other traitors, the Messianic Jews and the NRP. Then, I summoned Benny on the telephone intercom.

"Benny," I said, "Are you finished with your preliminaries?"

In an excited tone of voice, Benny replied, "Yes!"

I said, "Then it's time to come back to my office. I need you and Fillmore's signatures on the directive."

Benny arrived at Felix's office.

"Felix," he asked, "What happed to Murray?"

"I fired him and outlawed him, his party, and the Messianic Jews."

"Why," asked Benny?

"For security infractions against Murray and religious extortion, which the Messianic Jews are guilty of in their conversion strategies."

Meanwhile, Sol entered Felix's office after a slight knock on the door.

I said, "Come in."

Sol, sober now, knew he was in trouble. Before Sol could even say hello, I said, "Sol, I am giving you immediate notice that you will vacate your position in the Parliament due to the security breach and malafide interpretation you shared with Murray in conversations that were overheard by Fillmore."

"Felix, I can assure you it will never happen again," said Sol.

"You can answer in this write-up," I said as I handed him his walking papers. Sol left Felix's office, surprised he had not been arrested. He knew it was too late to mend the breach.

Speaking to Felix, Fillmore said, "That motor mouth should have followed the Greek god, Harpocrates, the god of silence."

I let out a belly laugh and exclaimed, "Fillmore, you always outdo yourself!"

Benny, sitting quietly breathed a sigh of relief and said, "Good riddance!"

****

Meanwhile, out on bail, walking the distance to the railway station, headed for home, Murray put his hand in his jacket pocket, and pulled out the business card Moshe had given him. He needed someone to talk to. He felt like he was going to burst from the strange feelings that filled his emotions of joy mingled at the same time with an indescribable sadness. Murray telephoned Moshe from the station.

"Moshe," Murray blurted out.

"Murray, what is it? What has happened? Where are you calling from?"

"Moshe, I attended a post Jerusalem Day celebration held by Felix at his condo. Somewhere around nine o'clock, when all the guests had left, I engaged in a conversation with Felix about my experience with you and how Yeshua was now influencing my life."

"Do you want to talk about it now," asked Moshe?

"Yes," he answered and then went on to relate all the details which had transpired when he was with Felix.

Moshe said, "Murray, I am sorry to hear that you were escorted out of Felix's condominium. I am concerned for your safety. I suggest you put in a call to the other members of the Knesset informing them of the situation. Murray, call me as soon as you hear from them. If you feel up to it, I want you to know I am available to come and see you at a moment's notice."

"Yes, meet me in an hour at Hebrew University, on the second floor. The room that has its lights on will be the room we will be in. I'll put in a call to the other members of the Knesset in the NRP, Barry and Marvin Cohen and David. And thanks Moshe for being there for us."

He hung up and then followed Moshe's suggestion and phoned all three members of his party and scheduled a meeting to take place within the hour at a special private conference room at the Hadassah, Hebrew University Center.

Emotionally still ragged, he was anxious to speak with Barry. Barry fortunately was at home when the telephone rang.

"Hello," Barry answered as he cradled the phone to his ear.

"Barry, this is Murray. Some urgent events have occurred and I need to meet with you, Marvin and David Blum within the hour. Meet me at the Hadassah, Hebrew University Center."

"What seems to be the problem," asked Barry?

"Barry, right now I cannot tell you over the telephone. Will you meet me in an hour or not?"

"Alright, Marvin is here. I'll give David a call and tell him you have scheduled an emergency meeting. See you then." With that he hung up and notified David.

Murray was on his way, happy with the fact that their meeting was after dark. Meeting while it is dark had its advantages. With empty parking lots and empty rooms and only security guards in place, most of whom he personally knew, would guarantee them absolute privacy.

Still emotionally shaken, yet somehow filled with an unusual sense of great peace, he headed for the center. He arrived at the University, as the others were parking their cars. He tipped his hat in welcome and headed up the stairs to the second floor conference room. He informed the security guard on duty that a meeting was to take place. Unlocking the conference room doors, he turned the lights on and waited for the others.

One by one, the other three Knesset members entered the room and sat down.

Murray stood up and thanked them for their quick response to attend an emergency meeting.

Without wasting any time, he started relating all of the events that had happened over the past few days that had eventually led up to his conversion to Yeshua HaMashiach and his encounter, and being fired and subsequently evicted from Felix's condo an hour ago. He hesitantly relayed the facts too about their party, the NRP and the Messianic Jews now being outlawed by the Prime Minister's Directive. A long silence followed his revelation. At the same time, a knock was heard on the door.

At first the men were apprehensive, but relaxed once they saw Murray calmly walk over to the door and open it with a smile. It was Moshe. He introduced Moshe to the men, reassuring them that no one else knew about their meeting.

Two out of the three members, Barry and Marvin Cohen, were brothers. Both stood up and gave Murray and Moshe a handshake and an unexpected smile. At first Murray could not figure out what was going on, until Barry spoke up and in a clear, happy tone of voice admitted he and Marvin too, several months ago had secretly become Messianic Jews or Completed Jews, as some referred to themselves. Barry related how he and Marvin had successfully kept this quiet, and maintained their new beliefs secretly.

However, the only other remaining member, David Blum, upon hearing this news was left in a state of temporary shock. When he first heard Murray, then Barry and Marvin publicly admit that all three had secretly associated with and believed in the teachings of the Messianic Jews, he felt like he was covered in a thick blanket of fog. His face turned white and his eyes looked like they were going to bulge out of their sockets. He started to cough. His shoulders drooped. His body went limp.

When Murray saw what a profound effect all of this had on David, he asked him to speak his mind.

David, cleared his throat and said, "All of you know that I am a devout Orthodox Jew, but you two, I knew were once with me. What is going on here? Isn't it enough we had to deal with the illegitimate faith of the atheists in our government who surrounded us, and now this? If I can say this without being irreverent, what in heaven's name could be so powerful as to cause this insanity? How can you believe in three Gods?"

Feeling encouraged that he now had the two brothers on his side, Murray said, "David, we have not lost our minds. We have not ceased being Jews. What has happened to us and caused us to experience such a profound paradigm shift has been completely under the control of the Living God. David, are you willing to hear what we have to say? Do you think you can remain open and objective and I might add fearless? Are you willing to listen to the complete and thorough revelation we have been given about the greatest Jew of all time, Yeshua HaMashiach?"

David sat dumbfounded. He was so shocked he could not answer a word, but nodded with his head up and down as if to say, "Yes."

"David," Murray said, "In regards to believing in three Gods, this is not true and I know Moshe here, a more seasoned believer, can prove it. Moshe, if you would?"

Moshe, stood up, facing the four men, he looked into their eyes. There were tears brimming in his and he noticed that they too were almost at that point.

Overwhelmed, Moshe picked up his Bible, opened it and prayed, "GOD of Abraham, Isaac and Jacob, I come to you at this moment in gratitude that I can face these men and call them brothers. Because of our belief in Your Son, Yeshua HaMashiach, we have all gone through tremendous mental, emotional and spiritual changes. Changes that are sometimes frightening and sometimes exciting. Be with us now, leading us and guiding us in the way we should go. Give peace and blessings to David, who may feel strange and confused as to what has happened to us all. I ask it in the name of Your Son, Yeshua."

"David," Moshe said, "If you feel uncomfortable and feel you must leave, we will understand. But if you want to stay, you are most welcome. Perhaps I can help clear up any confusion or misunderstandings about all that has transpired over the past two days."

David, still stunned said, "Yes, I am astonished, however I want to stay and hear what you have to say."

Moshe then began, "I am sure you will all agree that the GOD of our fathers nature is omnipotent, omniscient, and omnipresent. Well, this same nature I have come to believe is shared also by His Son, Yeshua HaMashiach and the Holy Spirit."

"I will start with the word Elohim. What does that name mean?"

Barry replied, "We were taught that it means GOD, and that Elohim, in Hebrew, is known as a plural number."

Moshe said, "I used to believe that GOD was only one person, however, after careful investigation and study I have come to believe that GOD, as three persons, is not a mathematical one, but a unity, united like one. This is seen when the scriptures refer to a man and a woman united in marriage being referred to as one."

Moshe asked, "How do I know? Well, I will ask you, David, this question. What does the Tenach mean when speaking of Baal?"

"GOD," answered David.

"And Baalim?"

"Many of them."

"And Seraph?"

"An angel with six wings."

"And Seraphim?"

"Many of them."

"Then if Baalim and Seraphim are plural, is not Elohim the same?"

David remained silent, still dumbfounded by what was being said all around him. His head pounding and his heart confused, he remained temporarily silent.

Moshe continued, "Now what about the Shema?" (The Rabbinical name of the great confession of Deuteronomy 6:4, "Hear, O Israel; HASHEM is our God is the One and Only.")

Moshe asked, "What is the meaning of the fourth word Elohenu?

David boldly speaking up said, "One Lord."

"Then," Moshe asked, reading from Isaiah the 53rd chapter, "What is the meaning of the following words found in the following verses?"

"Abbothenu," Moshe said?

"Our fathers," David replied.

"Of cholayenu," said Moshe?

"Our sicknesses," David replied.

"And peshaenu," Moshe said?

David continued to answer, "Our transgressions."

"And avonathenu," Moshe said?

"Our sins," David stopped there.

"Then David," Moshe said, "If abbothenu means our fathers; cholayenu, our sicknesses; peshaneu, our transgressions; and avonathenu, our sins; surely elohenu means our gods."

"The words gentlemen, 'The Lord Our God is One Lord,' is true. But one in the same respects as once again I repeat Genesis 2:24, which speaks of a man and a woman when they become husband and wife, become one. It does not mean they become one person or one physical body, no, but it means that they now act as one. Meaning they do everything together. They now live together, they eat together, they plan together, and they create children together. They are united in planning and action. They both have a human nature, but working so close together that they can now be referred to as one. And so it is," Moshe continued, "With the Father, the Son and the Holy Spirit. They all have the same nature, a divine nature. And they too, work so close together and are so united that they never do anything alone. They act as one and speak of themselves as one."

"A rather simple analogy and one I hope will not be taken as my being irreverent," said Moshe, "And that is the egg. We have the egg yolk, the egg white and the egg shell. So although they are plural in nature, we call it an egg, singular. Each part joined together, making up one egg."

Joyfully, he presented a clear picture of the true nature and being of God. Speaking softly, he said, "My hope is that we can all live in peace." Then looking at David, Moshe said, "Think about these things David. Search out the remaining truth for yourself. For we all must answer to GOD individually. David, can I ask you to stay as I pray a concluding prayer before we depart?"

David, not wanting to be the odd man out said, "Of course."

Moshe bowed his head, closed his eyes and proceeded to pray once again. Moshe prayed out loud, "Father GOD of Abraham, Isaac and Jacob, reveal the absolute reasonableness of surrendering to Yeshua HaMashiach as GOD and no longer demoting Him and dishonoring Him. Help us to obey Your Word. Reveal the facets of Your character for some who may need to correct any distortions. Reveal Yourself in personal ways that cannot be refuted. Frustrate our enemy, Satan, and his plans to destroy and deceive. I believe almighty GOD in the power of Your divine intervention and providence, leading all of us present here to this point and place in time. I ask this in the name of Yeshua, my Savior. Amen."

Upon opening his eyes, Moshe saw that David had quietly slipped out during his closing prayer. Putting his arms around Barry and Marvin, he gave them both a brotherly hug. Giving Murray a firm handshake and a hug, he then asked them all to meet him the following day, saying he would call them with the time and location. They agreed. Exchanging business cards, they handed Moshe a card with the telephone number where they could be reached. Each man exited the building, happy, yet sad for David.

Meanwhile, Felix had called the seven members of his Likud Party, informing them that he had fired Murray, stating that Murray had committed a faux pas, making sure they understood that this was not going to be a laissez-faire. He also made sure that they understood clearly that they needed to form a consensus to formally outlaw and remove Murray and all the other members of the NRP from office, outlawing the NRP and all Messianic Jews. He then commenced to establish Marshall Law and to resurrect the use of the guillotine as the form of execution for his party and all those who now followed Yeshua HaMashiach!

Chapter 3

Chondriana

"The danger of the past was that men became slaves. The danger of the future is men may become robots."

~Erick Fromm

Relieved that Murray, the NRP, Sol and the Messianic Jews are now history, I let out a deep sigh, cleared my throat and in an explosive tone of voice I burst out, "Today, Benny and Fillmore, we are going to take the world on a journey never experienced before in all the known history of man at war! Soon, we will introduce the Chondriana Operation to the world. The political and military application of the science of genetics will reach the heights of all technical imagination. This change brings with it a new direction. The impact and immensity of the Chondriana on the twenty-first century will reach the zenith of change and it will set the world stage for a permanent world peace!"

I continued, "And the Chondriana will surpass all and any weapons used in all of man's history!"

Then turning toward Benny, I stared intently into his eyes, telling him, "Benny, in a few moments I will be presenting the Directive, Operation Chondriana, to the Parliament. Once this has been done, there will be a changing of the guard. You will receive the operational code to begin mass production of Chondriana. Gentlemen, I believe we have even outstripped DaVinci himself!"

Benny sat quite pensive while I sat and gloated. Benny would say my ego was rising to its pinnacle, like a mountain climber who has reached the top, but then must go back down. Benny hated my boasting. He branded me as conceited. And he accused me of self-idolization.

He said I was like a balloon, full of hot air. And he was not going to be around when it burst. Benny was skeptical, even accusing me of developing a God complex!

Unexpected fear must have suddenly gripped Benny. His body looked as if he was full of lead, completely paralyzed. For a few seconds, he remained mute. The reality of my command that they were about to create life on an expansive scale never before embarked upon by either men of science and technology, must have finally sunk in.

I said, "Benny, Fillmore, the time for a miracle to save our country has arrived. We have it made. This army is prolific. They can replicate themselves quicker than a nanosecond, yielding two-hundred million in one day!"

Benny started to tremble, like a tree blowing in hurricane winds.

I said, "Having dark thoughts again Benny?"

He replied, "Felix, how will we control an army that cannot be killed? One that could, if killed, resurrect themselves back to life within three days!"

"Benny, I have already created a code for that."

"And when, Felix, were you going to let Fillmore and I in on it?"

"Well, as a matter of fact, right now."

I said, "Benny, snap out of it! Instead of fear and doubt, think about the priceless wealth of the second Temple treasures, and the massive sixty-five tons of silver and thirty-five tons of gold we now have procured."

Out of the vortex of his fears and back into the realities of the moment, Benny snapped back, "Don't bark at me Felix, I am not a dog!"

Exasperated, I changed the subject. I said, "Benny, notify the Bodes,* the Malots,* the Diamonds* and our security forces in other countries and brief them on all that has transpired. I'll be giving Parliament this Directive within the hour."

I signed and then placed the Directive for Operation Chondriana and the Declaration of War in front of Benny and Fillmore and said, "Sign here."

Both signed the Directives. Now Benny could begin immediate mass production. Immediately, I put in a quick call to the seven members of my Party, the Likud. I informed them that I had fired Murray and had outlawed Murray and all but one of the MKs in the NRP or the National Religious Party of the Knesset.

Joel Kline answered my call. I said, "Joel, Murray has committed a faux pas. He made a security breach and my action was not going to be a laissez-faire."

Joel asked, "What do you want the Party to do, Mr. Prime Minister?"

I replied, "I need the Likud to form a consensus to formally remove Murray, and all but one of the MKs in the NRP, except David Blum. In addition, I am putting into effect previous legislation to outlaw all Messianic Jews."

Joel said, "Considerate it done, Mr. Prime Minister." And he hung up.

Completing my call to the Likud, I said, "Benny, Fillmore, this is it, let's go!"

Fillmore hesitated, and said, "Felix, I am fearful that your decision to mass produce the Chondriana as a war machine not only defies any rational analysis, but I fear it would cause a veritable genetic disaster. What prevents them from being created like that monster army of Hitler's?"

I was flabbergasted. I yelled back and said, "Fillmore, how dare you even put me in the same category of that insipid monster?"

"Well, Felix, I apologize. But, what guarantee do you have that they will not turn out to be ruthless, remorseless, unstoppable? Not only would the production of Chondriana defy rational analysis, but I fear some may even end up calling you a crackpot, while others would be skeptical that it could be done at all. And what about capturing a backlash of condemnation from the global community?"

I replied tersely, "Fillmore, from the beginning you were aware of these questions. I know you are afraid now that it is clear we are moving ahead, but calm down. I have all the codes to control them."

Fillmore said, "Yes Felix, I guess I have stepped over into my human reactions, but let's hope we will not become the laughing stock of the scientific and intellectual global community."

I replied, "Fillmore, have confidence in me. I will not let you or the country down."

With that we left the office headed for the emergency session of the Knesset. None of us uttered another word as we descended the stairs, entered the auditorium and sat down in our respective seats.

I stood up before a grim Parliament. Facing them, I approached the microphone.

Feelings were running high. The air in the Parliament was filled with apprehension and mistrust, so thick I could cut it with a knife.

I motioned towards Rabbi Jack Wood, a Sephardic Jew and one of my advisers, to approach the microphone. He approached the microphone. I stepped aside.

Rabbi Wood was a little rolie-polie fellow, but sharp as a tack. He bowed his head, his long pe'ot or curled side locks fell across his face as he made the blessing Noten Teshu'a, then he sat down in the row with the rest of his Orthodox political group, The United Torah Party.

As Rabbi Wood took his seat, I approached the podium. Hovering over the microphone in a low-pitched voice, slightly quivering, I glanced across the faces of the members of the Parliament and preceded to present what had up until now been covert operations.

I spoke, "Gentlemen and all members of the Knesset, we have, as most of you are aware, having been briefed, a grave situation standing before us. What has transpired in the last few hours seems to be incredulous. However, we are not without hope. I want to brief you in response to the imminent threat of nuclear attack against us by Iraq and their take over of Jordan by its Ten Nation League and their allies."

"Despite our policy of nuclear opacity our military has completed the Sampson Option, Israel's top secret nuclear arms build-up. Pending your approval I have issued a Directive to implement a Declaration of War by implementing our Nuclear Response Plan. I have already put the nation and the military on our highest state of alert according to Operation Daylight."

"I have also put the following on high alert: the State Attorney General, Larry Heim, the Knesset's Law Committee, the Defense Ministries, the Scientific Affairs Liaison Bureau, the Deputy Commander of the Police Investigation Division, the Commander General of Security, along with the Institute Mossad and AL, our special super secret Division of the Mossad, and the National Emergency Policy alerting the Shinbet and the Shaback.* I have also issued a directive to activate the Kidon Assassination Unit, but only as a last minute action. With your vote of approval, I will also implement two new covert operations: Operation Chondriana and Operation Achor. These two operations have been planned and are ready for immediate implementation. They will give us not only the opportunity to become feared by the nations who surround us with malcontent, but will give us a reputation that will surpass even mighty Rome who had built the largest army in the world."

"First on the agenda is Operation Chondriana."

"Gentlemen, we are prepared to face the threat of our extinction. How? By cloning a two-hundred million man army. I will describe this army called Chondriana. They begin as miracle microorganisms. They are organisms that are living and they are super-intelligent. They are pre-cellular, a pre-cursor to the mitochondria. It is a form of life from which all other life forms exist, including Homo sapiens. It is regarded today by the scientific community as the inner-space of microbial life. These clones will not be 'electronic chromosomes placed into robots using creative software.'"

"Neither are they the 'creation of a neural network incorporated with billions of neurons.' Neither are they the creation of a synapse-like program used to store electronic data. They are not 'thinking computers,' nor are they machines with body parts."

"Instead, this operation will use synthetic fusion, chemicals and or physical stimuli such as electric shock in nuclear transplantation, producing an army of cloned human men. This method differs from reproductive cloning that is done by implanting a cloned embryo into a woman's uterus, leading to the birth of a cloned baby. The most startling fact is that we can replicate the Chondriana in such rapid speed that we can, as I previously mentioned, replicate 200 million within one day! Added to this stupendous feat is that once they are cloned they will not require food or medicine and if killed, they will be able to resurrect themselves within three days! They are eternal!"

"This operation in the field of genetic engineering and microbiology was designed by Benny Stein, Minister of Defense, my father, Fillmore and myself. A project of this magnitude will give us two-hundred million soldiers who will be indestructible and more than capable of wiping out all of our enemies!"

103

"Why, you may all wonder, do we need such an enormous army? The answer is that Iraq has made an alliance with China. They are sending two-hundred million men to attack us and right now they are ready to cross the dried up Euphrates river."

Every eye was fixed on me. Some gasped and others, in shock, remained mute.

"To those of you who may have concerns that this colossal amount of human clones could get out of hand, I have this to say. We have in our possession a method of control which I must for now keep under wraps. In order to meet any type of crisis in this respect I have developed a special control code. This will be your insurance should something go wrong, or if any other emergencies were to arise."

"Gentlemen, Israel, small now in comparison to other world governments no longer will be small but larger and with an unlimited indestructible army, made up of males only, who can replicate themselves, are stronger than our top Ayret Matlal, Naval Commandos, top intelligence group, equivalent to the former American Seals. And I might add, superior even to the world renown Spartans."

"Therefore, with an entire race of universal soldiers who will have unlimited facets of thinking, without a conscience, values, opinions and who would never get sick or die, would make Israel invincible!"

Those last words sent a wave of confusion throughout the Parliament. Some members tried to interrupt me, yelling out loudly, "You crackpot! What are there, if any, unwanted consequences?"

Before I could respond to that question I was interrupted again. This time by Jacob Cohen, a liberal in my party, the Likud. In the past he had been in favor of using genetic engineering to clone endangered species, and to clone in order to preserve the Einstein's and the Beethoven's of the future. He spoke up and said, "How do you plan to control them? And without a conscience, would they have the capacity to supplant us?"

I could feel myself growing red. Beads of sweat poured down my face. I cried out, "Gentlemen, gentlemen, please get control of yourselves. May I repeat, we have controls set in place. They are 100% safe."

Joel Cramer yelled out, "And where is the money for this enormous expenditure?"

I replied, "I will get to that shortly. You will all have a chance to discuss this."

"Now let me continue. What I have to say next should put your minds at ease."

A great hush fell on all the members of the Parliament. Some fumed silently.

I continued, "Gentlemen, our second step is to start therapeutic cloning, also called 'stem cell therapy,' used to clean up all of the major diseases of the known world. We will be able to take genes from patients' own cells to repair and/or treat diseases of the body or due to those who have been injured. After years of debate about destroying human embryos to obtain fetal stem cells performed by nuclear transplantation, it has been concluded fetal stem cells are no longer necessary. Today, by use of biotechnology, stem cells can be obtained from fetal umbilical cord blood and or adult tissue. Our third step is to increase the quality of life for all mankind. How? By putting a stop to the aging process, using a technique in microbiology. It will stop telomeres at the end of chromosomes from shrinking."

The Chairman of the Law Committee, Attorney General, Jay Rothenstein, raised strong objections.

I said, "Gentlemen, I see it's time to hold open discussions to your objections." I stepped aside and motioned for Jay to take the podium.

In a sudden unexpected calm tone of voice, I said, "Jay, proceed."

In a sense of triumph, Jay slowly walked up to the podium and taking the microphone in his hand, he began to speak. Addressing the Knesset, he said, "Mr. Prime Minister and all MKs, Louis Pasteur once said, 'In the field of observation, chance favors the mind that is prepared.' Nevertheless, I object to this directive for utilizing a prepared, cloned army of synthetic humans as a war machine. I consider it to be an expensive disaster. In addition, it is a known fact that there is a ban against cloning by all nations of the world. Therefore, this action is illegal. I will put you on notice that I will conduct a full investigation to be led by the State Attorney General, the Commander General of National Security and myself!" Weak cheering spread throughout the room.

In a huff, Jay left the podium and took his seat, swearing under his breath and disgusted by the thought of taking a risk with something that had never been tried before.

Zachary Levine, head of the Hatehiya, the Israel Renascence Party and former head of the Med-Dead Sea Canal Project, felt he had to speak up in his support of me.

Zachary, a cool, calculating, tall distinguished man with a lanky appearance, quickly stood up from his chair and approached the mic. Addressing all present, he said, "As you are aware, gentlemen, our party realizes the importance of mysticism for revolutionary movements."

I trusted that all things would work out well for the nation. He continued, "As you know, we, my party and I, believe in the Kabala's teaching of Golem: How to make a man from dirt and special words. Because of these beliefs I feel that this Directive is justified by our Prime Minister."

Ignoring the babble going on among some of the other parties, I gave Zachary a big grin.

Zachary turned towards me, shook my hand, and said, "Good luck," and left the podium feeling like a million bucks.

Loudly vocal, Joel Wolf of the Histradrut, the Israeli Labor Federation, usually a man of few words, started a squabble, instigated no doubt by his fear about the real outcome of such a Directive. Even though he was a man able to carry out unpleasant and sometimes dangerous affairs of state.

Approaching the podium, he gave me a look of utter horror. He spoke up, going into a rage about "Sending a cloned army to save the day without knowing how sound the outcome would be." He said, "We are not going to fulfill Erwin Chargoff's words and make this operation 'a gigantic slaughterhouse, a molecular Auschwitz.'"*

Echoes from the Shaz Party, an ultra orthodox Ashkenazi Haredim, which controlled the Department of the Interior and the Meretz Parties, presented their objections, followed by the Hadash Party. Even a few in my own Labor Party cried out a resounding no! But, loudest of all was Irving Stein of the Rklah, Israel's Communist Party.

Irving Stein stepped up to the podium and gave me a nasty, "If looks could kill." With smoke practically coming out of his ears, he curled up his lip and said, "This is monstrous! It is and has been plainly indicated by all the nations that this type of cloning is under a global ban."

Addressing me he said, "Mr. Prime Minister, despite political rhetoric, how do you plan to overcome the world's anger?"

I replied, "Mr. Stein, this is my plan of action. By giving all the nations of the world our knowledge to use Chondriana strictly for humanitarian and peaceful purposes only." I said, "To wipe out disease and increase the quality of life for all."

"To date, this has been a covert operation, but from this moment on it will be open to not only national view but also to world view. Besides," somewhat gloating, "Most nations do not believe anyone really has the ability or the technology and even greater the funding to pull off such a prodigious task! Still, some no doubt will call the Chondriana Operation subversive. But, with the threat we now face, it is the only weapon that will seal our safety."

To cool things down and to give the MKs the opportunity to hash out my Directive, I ordered a short recess.

Stepping down from the podium, several parties among themselves began to question me regarding the finances to back up the vast replication of a 200 million man army of cloned men.

MK, Jerry Epstein, excited, walked up to me and said, "Felix, your scheme is brilliant. But when and how in hell do you expect to pay for all of this?"

Addressing the small group of MKs surrounding me, I replied, "Let me assure you as soon as I reconvene Parliament, I will discuss in detail Operation Achor."

After the short recess, everyone took to their seats, anxious to hear about the money pot I alluded to in my statement of Operation Achor.

Reconvening the session, I replied, "Gentlemen, up until this time this has been a covert operation, but from this moment on it will be open not only to national view but to world view." I felt my ego reaching to the heights of narcissism and somewhat gloating.

I said, "Most nations do not believe anyone really has the ability or the technology or the funding to pull off such a prodigious task. Still, others, no doubt, once they hear about it, will call Operation Chondriana subversive and insane. Yet, the threat to our continued existence as a nation makes it the weapon that will secure and seal our safety."

Ishmel Kaziak, MK of the Agudat Party, represented by the religious Jewish Orthodox community, shouted, "We are in imminent danger of being wiped out and you can stand here talking like all we have to do is butter our bread?"

Shouting back, "That's enough out of you! If you have anything more to say you're invited to speak at the podium."

Ishmel said, "Watch it you bulldog! I am ready to write you up!"

Ishmel was someone to reckon with. As publisher and editor of the daily newspaper for the party, the Hamodia, he could paint me black to the public.

Holding my tongue, I ordered a fifteen minute break.

During that brief interlude, various parties held heated discussions. The most boisterous members, after much rhetoric, they quieted down. Anxiously, like teenagers waiting for their Bar Mitzvah they could hardly wait to hear about the money bags I was going to propose that would finance the replication of a cloned army.

Most parties expressed astonishment by the grasp and comprehension of my Directives, resolutions and plans of action in assessing the terrifying events surrounding us. Some still grumbled as they returned to the session.

With great confidence and calm I approached the mic. "Gentlemen," I said, "I know there has been much question by all about financing such an enormous production. Many of you are no doubt asking yourselves how can we afford such a phenomenal operation. Let me explain."

"Over the past year, we, that is Benny Stein, Fillmore and I, have implemented Operation Achor. We, as geologists and primed archeologists, have uncovered a maze of four hundred tunnels never before discovered. These lead from the Temple Mount through to the Negev Desert. Also as you know it is sometimes called the Wilderness of Zin. T.E. Lawrence and his companion Sir Leonard Wooley once surveyed this desert area. It goes as far south to the Aqaba at the lower tip of the Negev, also known in biblical times as The Valley of Achor. At the time, a survey was to commence. It covers the entire country of Palestine. Queen Victoria and the Archbishop of York, who in 1865, in London, formed the Palestine Exploration Fund, sponsored it to accomplish this project. However, this particular area, the Aqaba at the lower tip of the desert did not come under the exploratory warrant issued. Nevertheless, the two men went ahead, curious to know more about this strategic point. The first agent of the Palestine Exploration Fund, also an officer of the Royal Engineers, began serious archeological excavations. His experience in the work of digging mines and tunnels for military purposes gave us a map, long lost but which had been given to me by an old Bedouin. It was through this map that it showed a never seen before, an entirely new location of the Temple Mount. This then led to my discovery of the previously undiscovered and unknown tunnels. Beginning from this new location of the Temple Mount and going through approximately twelve miles of tunnels with many undiscovered chambers and ending at the Valley of Achor some twelve and a half miles and ending below the caves of Qumran, on the edge of the Dead Sea."

I said, "The most intriguing find was in the tunnels leading up to what is known today as Cave Three. It was in this cave that I found several previously undiscovered chambers. It was in these chambers that I found a massive amount of gold and silver veins. Enough money to last us for the next thousand years! And that's not all. Deep inside one of these chambers held the glorious treasures of the Second Temple."

A great hush filled the room. Everyone present sat stunned and no doubt excited about the discovery of such vast amounts of gold and silver. Most were overwhelmed that the Second Temple treasures really existed and now discovered to be real.

Then quite unexpectedly, sharp words and criticism between parties accused me of being, "A modern day Malthus," a demographer who had been an economic imperialist. Others were fearful that my action if carried out would saturate the world, accusing me of being an eliminationist that in turn could cause a high degree of anti-Semitism. Still others felt terror at the thought that once this news was out, "There would be more terror. Terror with no turning back!"

"Gentlemen," I shouted! "Please put your doubts and fears aside! These are Jewish treasures, not Arab or Muslim. As far as rights go, these treasures belong to us!"

Overcome with a sudden rush of excitement and bewilderment, the Parliament went into an uproar, most giving me a standing ovation, drowning out the opposition.

Still some said, "Let's wait and see."

Others said, "This has never been done before, it could fail!"

Acknowledging their fears, I said in a firm staccato voice, "Gentlemen, what we are about to commence to do is not going to fail! Chondriana has been tested and retested. All of our experiments have been 100% successful! And now with the new found treasures to back it up and with plenty left over, our government will know no bounds!"

This fantastic discovery now shortly would cast me in a much better light, causing a complete paradigm shift among almost all of the MKs that were present.

A vote was cast. Seven of the thirty-five parties abstained from the vote. The twenty-six remaining parties were the first to swing into my camp. They were more than willing to comply with my Directive to create a nationally cloned army. The Knesset also approved by a majority vote my Declaration of War against Iraq and its newly formed Ten Arab Nations, including their allies. Also approved by a majority vote to agree to establish Marshall Law. Thus overriding the blocking parties and overshadowing the fears that a cloned man-made army might malfunction and possibly overpower the human race, relegating all real humans to complete extinction!

In a state of excitement over the success of the votes and anxious to implement my Directives, I approached the podium. Standing in front of the microphone with my cigarette hanging out from the corner of my mouth, I inhaled, taking in a long slow drag and blew out the smoke. As the smoke circled the air, I took my last drag and put the stump out in the fancy ceramic Italian ashtray given to me by Alandro Pasqual, the Italian Ambassador to Israel. As I pressed the butt out, flicking its last ash, my body trembled and in a display of seismic emotions, I summoned every ounce of courage and said, "Gentlemen, the results of the vote reveal that twenty-six parties have agreed to begin mass production of Chondriana, giving the issue the majority vote. Our Minister of Defense, Benny Stein, will commence immediately with production. I hereby notify the Chairman of the Parliament that production of cloning a Military Army is on!" To further assure the Knesset, I said, "Now regarding the threat of nuclear attack against us, I have this to say. There is no way in hell that Iraq or any of their alliance of nations is gong to attack us! If they did, they know it would be curtains for all of them as well. We are in too close of a vicinity for them to risk themselves."

Taking my pen to hand I swiftly signed the Declaration of War and issuing a general alert to evacuate all cities in our country. Then I handed Benny the code to start mass production of Chondriana.

To further assure the Knesset, I said, "Now regarding the threat of nuclear attack against us, I have this to say. There is no way in hell that Iraq, their new formed ten nation pack or any of the nations are going to attack us!"

Jacob Levick, editor of the Israeli Newspaper, Yediot Ahronot, rudely interrupted me. He stood up and shouted out at me, "Are you insane, Felix? Have you lost it? What you are saying now has as much value as those ashes you keep flicking off of your cancer stick! Your defense is as fragile as a clay pot!"

Ignoring the insult, I spoke out loud and in a sharp tone of voice. I responded to Jack's remark and said, "Our enemies are full of hot air! Let me put your questions, fears and doubts at rest and brief you. If they plan to nuke us, they being in close geographical proximity would pose a threat not only to us, but also to all the countries surrounding us. It would leave Egypt, Syria, Saudi Arabia and Jordan with a nuclear dust that would make their countries uninhabitable for over forty years! So, I am going to call their bluff. When they see 200 million men that all look alike, marching their way, they will be dumbstruck! It will make their hair stand on end and their eyes pop out of their sockets! When the Chondriana prove themselves to be impregnable it will be so shocking that it will quickly relinquish our enemies' threats and they will abandon their daring plans to wipe us out! They will have to surrender and then we will take over control of Jordan, pushing them back into their own territories!"

Everyone sat astounded by my reasoning, everyone except Jacob Levick. Shattering the silence he screamed out, "Felix, you are so cocksure of yourself and your plans, but what if you have miscalculated?"

I replied in a roar, "Rest assured Jacob, we have covered all bases. We have looked at all possible scenarios and this plan is ninety-nine and nine-tenths percent sure fire perfect! We will Fete D' Accompli!"

"Now getting back to the agenda," I continued, "Now, gentlemen, second on the agenda is legislation implementing an enforced Directive for selective elimination and crimes of missionary activity. Today, I am signing this legislation into law. I will read the brief."

Jerry Epstein leaned over towards me and handed me the brief. Once I held the brief in my hand, sweat formed on my brow as I read it.

"The Parliament has been briefed in a report given to them by security who work at Hebrew University. This report states that all but one member of the NRP has converted to what is called an aberration of Christianity, and that these MKs have made a security breach concerning Operation Achor. The Parliament has reached a consensus to dissolve the NRP. A Directive has been drafted and dictates they can no longer hold their present seats in the Knesset. Warrants for their arrest have been issued."

Breaking out into another cold sweat, I completed reading the brief. I felt like I was going to collapse. Grateful for my handkerchief, I wiped my face, then pulled out a pack of Camel's. I lit up another cigarette and said, "Jerry, take the written arrest warrants and hand them to the Chairman."

Jerry drew up the arrest order from the brief and placed it in front of me. Once I signed, then the rest of my party signed the order, one by one, including Jerry.

Jerry stood up. His hands trembling, nervously handing the arrest warrants over to the Chairman, giving me a copy.

Applause broke out, exalting me for bravery. My mood swiftly changed, lifting me up into a state of euphoria. Flicking off the ashes of my cigarette, I stubbed it out in the ashtray. Tilting the microphone in front of me, I addressed the Parliament. I read the weighty, acerbic arrest warrant, denouncing the NRP. Flushed with anger, my face no doubt red as a beet, I spewed out virulent comments against them. I could never have sounded more acrid than at this moment.

A vote was taken. All the members of Parliament gave me a 100% vote. A first of its kind!

Parliament gave me their full support. In full view, before everyone in the Knesset, I said, "Now that the NRP is officially outlawed

I want to make my intentions clear! I am going to wipe all of them out! I intend to use fear, intimidation and din!"

I received another round of exhilarating applause with shouts of approval by all the MKs present.

Strangely, Fillmore felt my actions against Messianic Jews and their leadership of the NRP was deplorable. He said, "This is political murder, legalized terror, that is what it amounts too!" Fillmore's analysis of my actions hit the nail right on the head, but I remained silent, stunned because I had never even approached this topic with Fillmore.

I felt it was time for another recess, so I called for a lunch time recess.

Jerusalem—It was two o'clock. The Knesset reconvened. Excitement was in the air as members took their seats.

I motioned for Rabbi Wood to open the session with prayer. The Rabbi took his place in front of the microphone and stood there with his head bowed in shame. What could he do? The Knesset had already voted on the anti-missionary conversion bill which had gone through several past years wrapped up in controversy and stymied the MKs who continued in caustic rhetoric for it. Finally passing it through the Law and Justice Committee into Constitutional Law passing its final decision in the Knesset. Rabbi Wood bowed his head and uttered a short blessing on the proceedings. He returned to his seat passing by me as I stood up and approached the microphone. He gave me a puzzled look, turning white as a sheet.

I ignored the outward signs of the Rabbi's shame and began. "Gentlemen, members of the Knesset, today, MK Samuel Kline of the Israeli Labor Party and the United Judaism Party's Rabbi Michael Kahn, have co-authored this legislation. This legislation outlaws anyone who preaches with the goal of causing any person to change their religion, will face the following consequences. For the first offence a liable of three years in jail and a $15,000 fine. For any succeeding violations the jail term will be doubled to six years in jail and a fine of $50,000. A third violation will bring death by the guillotine! Gentlemen we will take a short recess. This concludes our session."

Everyone exited the room in stunned silence. Thoughts of annihilation and self-preservation flooded some while others were in total fear of the threat to their existence and perhaps the complete extinction of man himself. What remained certain was that life as they once knew it would never be the same.

Then I gave Benny the go ahead to begin mass cloning production of the Chondriana.

Headed down the hall towards his office, Benny would begin preparations for this incredible journey into the unknown, ready to meet his destiny and the fate of the state and no doubt the world.

Everyone exited the Parliament room in stunned silence.

Reporters from The Jerusalem Report, The Kol-Bi, a regional weekly news magazine, and the HaAretz's, the Hamodio and the Vediot Ahronot quickly exited the Knesset ready to hit the press with this explosive headline news. Out to reach the man on the street, in time for the imminent evacuation of its civilian population.

Thoughts of annihilation and self-preservation flooded the minds of some MKs who heard the news, while others were wrapped up in total fear of the impending threat to their continued existence and perhaps the complete extinction of man himself. What did remain certain was that life as they once knew it was now totally uncertain.

Meanwhile, MKs Samuel Kline of Israel's Labor Party and Joel Kahn of the United Judaism Party approached me.

"Congratulations Felix," Joel said.

Samuel grasped me by the arm, shook my hand and said, "Felix, it's about time you took action on this legislation. Since you have now spearheaded state sponsorship outlawing the NRP and their affiliation with Messianic Jews, I will see to it that your Directive will be upheld."

I was gratified by such overwhelming support.

I said, "Thank you," giving Joel and Samuel a satisfied grin. Then I gave them both a hearty handshake. Yet, my decision to produce massive cloning of the Chondriana as a war machine defied most rational analysis. However, it would propel Israel into place as a prominent world power and change the entire political history of man.

Once the public, by radio, television and newspapers received the news, panic set in. Civilian evacuation began.

Meanwhile, an angry mob of 1,000 Ultra-Orthodox Jews Haredim, gathered outside the Knesset. They had found a group of Messianic Jews, and they spit on them, cursing them, calling them "dogs," saying, "You deserve the guillotine!"

Murray was in this small group above ground. He was captured and arrested.

Murray walked with security in a daze of disbelief. He felt his body go limp. He felt like a zombie. His thoughts drew a blank. Murray, just out on bail from Felix's earlier arrest warrant on charges of treason and causing a security breach of classified information, was rearrested along with the small group of Messianic Jews from above ground.

The guards cuffed and hustled him into the prison van, alone.

"Get in," one of the guards said, shoving him onto the seat. Then they took his handcuffs and attached them to a large chain hooked into the floor of the van.

He sat in silence as the prison van headed towards the county jail.

Full of apprehension, he asked the driver of the van, "How long will I be in the county jail?"

"You will have to ask the Prime Minister that question," answered the guard.

As the guard closed the glass window between them, he locked it in place, all the while sneering at Murray.

To him it was as if time had grounded to a halt. The sting of being treated with contempt at first freighted him. Yet, a strange peace seemed to calm him emotionally. It was surreal to say the least, but he was getting used to it.

Arriving at the county jail, Murray noticed that two other vans had arrived as well. In them there was eight other Messianic Jews whom he recognized. His heart sank. Where were Moshe, Barry and his brother, Marvin?

The prison van came to a halt. The security guard stepped out of the van and unlocked the van doors.

He spoke directly to him, "Hurry up, Murray Andrews, you rock head!"

Then they took him out of the van and walked him inside of the prison. Since there was a civilian evacuation going on they took all prisoners to the basement. Murray was placed into solitary confinement, alone again.

His fears began to slide. He could hear an inner voice echo the Bible verses taken from the Hebrew Scriptures in Isaiah 43:2, "When you pass through the waters, I am with you; through rivers, they will not wash you away; when you walk through fire, you will not be singed and no flame will burn you." These were verses of the Hebrew writings of the prophet Isaiah in the Tanach of Holy Scripture, which he'd read in the past, but never understood what those words had meant, until now. Faith in those words transported him into the realm of joy! He felt excited, happy and free. How strange it was to be bound by physical chains, but set free in his heart, mind, soul and spirit.

Murray glanced at his watch. It was eleven o'clock. What had seemed like seconds since his arrest had been only an hour.

A strong realism that what he felt now was how he felt when Moshe led him to the Lord and he became a disciple of Yeshua, as most, completed Jews referred to HaMashiach. He was so happy inside, he could almost float, knowing anyone else would think he was insane to think and feel like this when he was in jail and possibly bound for death.

The prison guard unlocked his cell door and said, "Follow me, you rock head!"

Flippantly he asked the guard, "How do you know me by that name?"

"Well, all you rock heads are the same, down right stupid and gullible and I might add stubborn too!" The guard then led him to the admission center where he was given a number and a set of prison garb to wear.

The admission clerk said, "Hand over your watch, your wallet, money or any other items in your pockets."

Murray handed over everything in his pockets, but asked the clerk, "Can I keep this?" As he lifted up his Hebrew New Testament for the clerk to see, the admission clerk looked startled, probably wondering what was an Orthodox Jew doing with a New Testament in his pocket, and written in Hebrew and English no less.

"No," replied the clerk, "But after we inspect it, we will return it to you. That is if you are still alive."

"What does that mean," Murray asked as he felt a lump in his throat and his stomach turn?

"Oh, you have not heard? The guillotine is being used to execute all you crazy converts."

Murray stammered, "You, you must be crazy, telling me something like that!"

The guard replied sharply, "I am not crazy, this office received an order to follow out execution by guillotine on all Jewish converts!"

Returned to his cell, Murray watched as the guard left him alone. He changed into the prison garb, placing it over his street clothes, hoping the guard would not notice when he returned. Murray sat down on the cold steel cot and pondered what all of this could really mean. Was this the end? Would he really be executed in such a horrendous, terrifying way, his head chopped off? Was he destined for extinction? Fear of death came over him like a cloud, but he decided to let it go. As suddenly as fear and doubt had darkened his being, he felt it being replaced with a warm, comforting sense of love and protection. He was now able to recognize that what he felt was the presence of God, the promise of the Holy Spirit to lead, guide and comfort him, giving him joy amidst fear and doubt. He knew his life was now in God's good hands, realizing this was grace.

Suddenly the ground moved and formed a fissure two feet wide, swallowing up the steel bars that held him captive. The earth rocked back and forth for about thirty seconds, followed by aftershocks from what could not be anything other than an earthquake. Murray didn't think it was a bomb.

Still, with the bars removed, but his cell still intact, he stepped over the debris of rock and dust. It felt so eerie that there were no screams. Nor did he see another person. Cautiously he walked out the front door of the prison, unseen. He realized that he was possibly the only survivor.

Once he was outside the building, Murray looked at the ruins of the crumbling jail. Seeing no one that needed help, he quickly escaped. Cautious but somewhat confused, he headed for the YMCA on Hillel Street.

Chapter 4

The Valley of Achor

"Whosoever saves a single life is as one who saves the entire world."
~*The Talmud*

Meanwhile, Murray was able to reach the YMCA. It was a small building on Hillel Street, next to the U.S. Consulate and across the street from the President's Residence and Independence Park. He was relieved to see that these buildings had escaped the ravages of the earthquake. But, where were the people? Undetected, he entered the building. When he opened the door to their usual meeting place, he was elated to find Moshe, Barry and Marvin Cohen gathered together. They greeted him. Overwhelmed he blurted out, "Am I happy to see you all in one piece!"

Moshe gave him a big grin and a big bear hug. He said, "What happened to you?"

He replied, "My party, the NRP and I have been banned from the Knesset. We have been outlawed along with all our brothers and sisters and anyone else who will speak to another and influence them to convert to Yeshua HaMashiach. If anyone is caught doing this there will be immediate imprisonment and steep fines and for a third offense, death by the guillotine!"

Moshe took in a deep breath. Barry and Marvin turned ashen. Moshe said, "They finally did it! The Parliament has been trying to pass that legislation into law for years."

Murray said, "I was arrested on a warrant, personally by the Prime Minister in his office. Out on bail, then arrested again outside the Parliament where a riotous group were gathered. But, subsequently I escaped from jail when the earthquake hit the area. I must say, I'm surprised that these buildings are still standing intact."

With tears welling up in his eyes, Murray said, "When my jail cell walls collapsed at first I thought it was a bomb that went off. I then looked all about me, but there were no other survivors except myself. So I took off, hoping I would find all of you. I can hardly believe all that has happened myself."

Then Murray asked, "What about the women and children and our other brothers. Are they alright?"

Barry cleared his trembling throat, "Moshe, Marvin and I were here in this building when we heard the roar of the earthquake when it hit. Praise God, all are safe and sound. We are just about ready to send everyone down into the underground bunkers we built. Our engineers have cleared them for safety. The earthquake did not cause any damage."

"Others will be arriving in two's to avoid obvious attention," Moshe said, "Let's join hands and give our Father thanks for His profound love in helping us to seek Him and for revealing Himself, and for protecting us from injury and death. Hallelujah and Mozel Tov," he blurted out! Then bowing his head, Moshe asked them to bow their heads. Moshe began to lead the prayer in earnest. He said, "Father God, of our fathers Abraham, Isaac and Jacob, we come to You asking for Your help. We ask for Your protection. Keep us and all those who belong to You safe. Give us wisdom. Guide us in this tense and dangerous situation we find ourselves in at this time. Amen."

Everyone joined Moshe and said, "Amen."

Then Murray spoke up and said, "I am terrified, Moshe, now that we are on the government's death list. Yet, somehow, I have a strange peace concerning our fate."

Marvin said, "Moshe, I can say that I too feel odd. I am frightened, yet I feel happy both at the same time."

Barry then said, "How unusual it is to face the threat of death and not to worry about the outcome for our lives. To trust in the power of God is most awesome and personal indeed."

Marvin said, "Great peace belongs to those who love God." He said, "Let us pray once more. Dear Lord, Yeshua, it is to You we bring our requests. All of us have been outlawed by our respective government. You know our fears. They are real. We ask You, oh Holy and Loving GOD, to give us wisdom and understanding in the way we should go. We need Your direction and guidance. We need Your strength and we need courage, courage to stand for the revelations which You, Yourself has given each one of us gathered here today. I pray, oh God, that You may continue to dwell in our hearts through faith, that we will be able to comprehend Your love and that we may be filled with all the fullness of Your grace, love and power; that we may be sincere and without offense, that we may be filled with the fruits of righteousness and knowledge of Your will. Amen."

Everyone present added their amen. Moshe stood up and said, "I have contacted several of our brothers and sisters in the Lord. They should be arriving any moment. Murray, you were not here when we made these arrangements. I want you to know that the Lord has prepared a place for us to be safe. Below this building, there are vast subterranean underground caverns. They are built on four levels with hidden chambers and secluded caves. The area is about four hundred and twenty-five acres in size, going down to a depth of two hundred to four hundred feet. It can be entered from this building to tunnels that extend all the way up to the Valley of Achor, about twelve miles south of Jericho on the Wadi Qumran, next to the Dead Sea. For months we have been storing food, clothing and arranging sleeping quarters, resting places for as many as one hundred and forty-four thousand. Food supplies should last for more than three years. The government built these tunnels and their chambers for our rulers as a hiding place. It was abandoned several years ago at the end of the Cold War between Russia and the USA. Our engineers tell us that they are so secure even the Buster Bombs cannot penetrate them."

"That is wonderful," Murray said.

A rap could be heard at the door.

Moshe said, "Don't be alarmed Murray. It is our brothers."

Moshe answered the door and two men entered, giving Moshe a hug, and sat down.

Moshe reassured everyone and said, "To avoid being seen and not creating a noticeable crowd, we will be receiving two people at a time to enter below us."

Moshe introduced the two men who would lead everyone safely to the Valley of Achor. "This is Jerry and Stan," he said. "They will lead the way through the maze of tunnels. Then, each one will return here and lead two more at a time. We will start the process now."

"Murray, you and Marvin can go first, then Stan will return and lead the next two that arrive."

After several hours, over 100,000 people found refuge in the Valley of Achor, next to the Dead Sea, which lies 1300 feet below sea level, the lowest place on earth.

Barely two inches of rain falls each year into the Dead Sea that retains seven times the salt found in the oceans of the world.

"Below us," Moshe reassured everyone who entered, "We have worked out a system for meals and sanitation. For services there is also a cave as large as an auditorium. It will seat all of us."

Some of the children were given tasks to keep them busy and groups were divided by age and given the appropriate instructions and reassurances for their first night together.

A Messianic Jewish service was planned for after meal time. Children were assigned to meet with a special instructor to lead them in a time of worship, praise and Bible study.

By six o'clock everyone was below, safe and secure. By eight o'clock the service began.

Someone opened with a prayer. Then Barry led the service in preaching. But special for the night, Moshe would share his testimony. Murray could hardly wait to hear it.

Barry, never hesitant said, "Brother Moshe, let us all hear your experience in meeting Yeshua. May it give everyone here strength and courage."

Moshe began, "Brothers and sisters in Yeshua, first let me say, I am happy we are safe down here. Praise the Lord for providing us with this shelter from the storm raging above us. We want to assure you all that we have enough supplies to last us for three years. Hopefully, we will not have to be here that long. Living in the underground will be very difficult, but we have special airways we can reach without being detected. God has given us the wisdom, grace and the know how to keep us safe. We have several safe houses prepared for women and children so that they can live above ground at different intervals as needed. When I was asked by your leadership to speak, I prepared a birthday celebration, a spiritual birthday celebration." With that Moshe began to share what happened to him on that special day when he was born again.

"It all started one day, when someone handed me a copy of the Delitzsch, a copy of the New Testament written in Hebrew and English. It included highlighting of the many prophecies taken from the Hebrew Scriptures predicting the signs in which we would recognize the promised HaMashiach. I had in the past heard many negative things about Yeshua and the New Testament. I was led to believe that the Messianic Jews were a cult, full of heresy. To the Jews, I believed in the same GOD that they did, only now I also believed in His Son, Yeshua HaMashiach that they are still waiting for. Born and raised as a Jew, I had grown up a block away from the synagogue that my family and I attended. It was there I attended Hebrew school and like many others, received my Bar Mitzvah. Even though I attended all the High Holy Day services and weekly Shabbot, I never felt I had a personal relationship with GOD. I wondered many times, how did our ancestorss speak about GOD so intimately and I could not. Trying to find the living GOD I joined the Ultra-Orthodox Jews, the Haredim. I was also very active in my support of the State of Israel, being active in the 1952 bond program in the United States. I led the campaigns for Brandies University, the B'nai Brith and other Jewish organizations. I must admit, I, like many other Jewish people held a superstitious fear and an unreasonable aversion of the New Testament and to Yeshua HaMashiach Himself. The paradox being that I was highly literate of both, yet I held onto these narrow minded beliefs. Then one day, I remember it well. It's as if I had just read it yesterday. An article by a noted Jewish scholar of the Reform School of Judaism, perhaps some of you may be familiar with Claude Montefiore and his two-volume work called 'The Synoptic Gospels.' These had come across my path by a friend whom had given it to me as a gift for our friendship. I read these words declared in his work and I'll repeat them for you."

"We Jews do not mind saying that the greatest influence upon European and American history and civilization has been the Holy Bible.

121

But, we too often forget that the Bible that has had this influence is not merely the Old Testament. It is the Old Testament and the New Testament combined. And of the two, it is the New Testament that has been of greater importance for us today. If, he said, it be an improper ignorance not to have read some portions of Shakespeare or Milton, it is I am inclined to think, a much more improper ignorance not to have read the Gospels."

"After reading this profound statement, I came to realize I had to find out for myself exactly what the New Testament had to say. I began by obtaining a copy of the Delitzsch written in Hebrew on one side and English on the other side, from the public library. Taking it home, not wanting anyone to see me with it, I put it inside of my jacket pocket. I started by reading the Book of Matthew. After reading the first few chapters, I was shaken. I began to tremble. For instead of an anti-Semitic book and hatred for the Jews, I discovered a book that had been written by Levi, a Jew also known as Matthew writing to other Jews about 'that man' as many of our Jewish faith always referred to Yeshua HaMashiach or the Anointed One. My impression or opinion about Yeshua HaMashiach began to change. Slowly as I continued to read this sometimes forbidden and taboo New Testament, I began to see more clearly that Yeshua was a good man, but His claims about Himself were not accepted by the Jewish leaders of that time and all the Rabbis since then. Then I asked myself whom should I believe, them or Him?"

"For a long time I had a deep yearning for GOD as a person. Was it possible? I began to search further. Completing my reading of the New Testament, I then searched for more facts. I wondered were there any other Jews that felt like I did right now? If so, where could I find them? By what I believe to be divine providence, I came upon an ad in the paper, bluntly saying that there were Jews for Jesus, or Yeshua as they refer to Him. To my surprise I found that there were many Jews who believed in Him. There was one group known as Messianic Jews. I telephoned the number listed in an ad in a major city paper and found myself being invited to their service. It was there that everything clicked. I realized we Jews had not been following the laws of forgiveness as given by Moses, but if I accepted the sacrifice of Yeshua, I could receive forgiveness not just once but every time. Whenever in my human weakness and failure I could ask Him for forgiveness and receive it, therefore always given a chance to make a fresh start. I clung to every word spoken by the Apostle and Jew, John, found in 1 John 1:9, 'If we confess our sins, he is faithful and just to forgive you and cleanse you from all unrighteousness.' And besides forgiveness, I received unconditional love, personal communication with GOD through prayer and meditation, along with the promise of the free gift of eternal life to all who believe in Him. This gift began the very moment I accepted Yeshua HaMashiach as my personal Lord and Savior. Gradually I learned to leave all the layers of hate and the prejudice, which in the past I felt against Christianity, for all the evils committed against us, the Jews. I now realized that sometimes God has some bad children who are disobedient, who do not listen to Him. They give God a black eye. We cannot blame Him for their evil actions. This is what I found free will to be about. Then I began to look at our own history as recorded in the Hebrew Bible. I read it not only as a record of our history, but also as the truly inspired Word of GOD. I began to see that all of the predictions by all of the Hebrew prophets who predicted the coming of HaMashiach matched the identity of Yeshua. One by one, I compared over some forty prophesies predicting Yeshua's first coming. He being the only one who has already fulfilled all HaMashiach's prophesies."

"As I did this my fears and doubts about Him began to disappear. These prophesies created a biographical puzzle that only the true HaMashiach could fit so completely and perfectly. They authenticate Yeshua HaMashiach as that person. The odds of any other person fulfilling them are one in thirteen trillion. No one else can match those odds. And so I became certain that Yeshua HaMashiach is the Messiah, as I refer to Him."

Murray snapped in the present moment hearing Moshe's voice. He continued, "Now, turn in your Bibles to Isaiah the fifty-third chapter. The issue here is the identity of the suffering servant. Now, many of us Jews have been told that this entire chapter refers only to the nation of Israel, and that they are the suffering servants. If that was true it is plain to see that how can you answer the question, I ask you, how can Israel die for Israel? However, many of these verses I do believe apply to the nation of Israel, while others in these verses cannot apply to precisely that one meaning. For instance this was not always the case. As I researched the oldest commentary on the Hebrew Scriptures, the Targum, I found that these Aramaic paraphrases of ancient Hebrew manuscripts were translated in about the first or second century BC. It was upon reading the following words that I found my doubts and fears completely gone. I will ask you to read along with me, the following: 'Behold, My servant the Messiah shall prosper, he shall be exalted and great and very powerful. The righteous one shall grow up before him, lo, like sprouting plants ... all who see him shall become wise through him. All of us were scattered like sheep ... but it is the will of GOD to pardon the sins of all of us on his account. Then I will apportion unto him the spoil of great nations ... because he was ready to suffer martyrdom that the rebellious he might subjugate to the Torah. And he might seek pardon for the sins of many.' In the Talmud, Sanhedrin 93b, 200-500 AD, and in Talmud, Sanhedrin 98b that several discussants, disciples of Rabbi Yehuda Ha' Nasi, suggested various names and cited scriptural references in support of Messiah's name. He said the sick one is his name, for it is written, 'Surely he has borne our sicknesses and carried our sorrows and pains, yet we considered him stricken, smitten and afflicted of God.'"

"Friends, it was not until the 11th century AD that the Rabbinical interpretation of Isaiah fifty-three began to change from meaning one individual to meaning the entire nation of Israel. A well-respected member of the Midrashim did this. However, there were many dissenters and today there are still some who hold onto the original Messianic view of it being interpreted as predicting one person. Even the 14th century Rabbi Moshe Cohen Crispin felt that to apply the suffering Messiah of Isaiah fifty-three to the nation of Israel distorts the verses of their natural meaning. And that this prophesy was delivered by Isaiah as the divine command for the purpose of making known to us some future Messiah, who is to come and to deliver Israel. And I repeat that this makes sense, otherwise how can Israel deliver Israel?"

"There are also other reasons why the Messiah could be identified and proven true and that he is an individual and not a nation or whole body of people. Note verse 9 of Isaiah fifty-three. First of all, the suffering servant is referred to as an 'innocent person, without sin.' Second He is said to have 'made His grave with the wicked but with the rich after his death, because He had done no violence nor was any deceit in his mouth.' Whereas, Israel is referred to by all the prophets to have suffered punishment for its many corporate sins."

"Also, not to be overlooked is the fact that the nation is referred to by GOD in the female gender. Turn with me please to Isaiah 51:3. 'For the LORD has comforted Zion; He has comforted all her waste places, and hath made her wilderness like Eden, and her desert like the garden of the LORD.' But note, in Isaiah 53:12 where it refers to the suffering servant in the male gender, along with the fact that his end was death. Let me read for you, 'Therefore I will divide him a portion with the great and he shall divide the spoil with the strong, because he poured out his soul unto death, and he was numbered with the transgressors, and he bore the sin of many, and made intercession for the transgressors.' It can also be said that the nation of Israel has suffered but never died. Isaiah makes it very clear that a 'righteous servant' would suffer rejection, physical abuse and death in order to pay or atone for the sins of all mankind."

"Now my dear friends, when you compare these verses with those of Yeshua as recorded in the New Testament it becomes without a doubt that what He Himself said was His purpose in coming. Let us turn to John chapter three verse sixteen where we read, 'For GOD so loved the world that He gave His only begotten Son, that whosoever believeth in Him should not perish but have eternal life.'"

"And so, in conclusion my dear brothers and sisters, it was then that GOD became my Father. We can expect the fury of our enemy, many who believe he is a myth or figment of our imagination, but to us we do real battle mentally, emotionally and spiritually with our invisible adversary, Satan the devil. Not the one pictured with red horns and a pitchfork in his hands, but the one we must resist. And who if we resist will find peace and confidence in the Messiah. He will lead us and direct and guide us in the reality of every moment of every day."

"For your own edification, I am handing out an outline of my testimony, listing thirty-eight specific prophesies identifying the fingerprint of the Messiah in the Old Testament as fulfilled in the New Testament by Yeshua HaMashiach."

"I will close now in a word of prayer. Dear Lord, we praise and thank You for the revelation of Yourself, Your Son and the work of the Holy Spirit as a person to each and every one of us gathered here. We thank You for sending Him to develop our character, granting us self-knowledge and above all making those of us gathered here to become a completed Jew. Amen."

And everyone said, "Amen."

Murray got up and said, "Would all the women and children stand on the right side of the wall? We will hand out supplies and blankets. Barry will lead you to the sleeping areas. I would like to ask the men to set up sleeping bags and to set up the signs for sanitation. Our meal will be ready in an hour. Women and children first."

Melvin and several other men volunteered to fold up the chairs and assist the other men in setting up sleeping arrangements with name tags going from last names starting with A on up to Z. Everything was going smooth. Some were still fearful, but they stayed calm as others wrapped their arms around their shoulders and as special women volunteered to help those with children. No one knew what to expect next. Their faith was being tested for sure.

Moshe put worship music CDs on in his CD player. It helped keep the crowd calm.

Chapter 5

The Valley of Achor,
A Door Of Hope

"I will speak to her heart. I will give to her, her vineyards from there and (make) the Valley of Achor (Troubling) into a portal of hope; she will dwell there as in the days of her youth, and as the day of her ascent from the land of Egypt."

~Hosea 2:15–17

"The divine flash illuminates and strengthens the power of the mind on all its levels, logical and imaginative."

~Herbert Weiner

The musty smell of dirt in the underground safe house permeated the air. Muffled sounds, like the rumbling of thunder, startled Murray who was having difficulty adjusting to the dimness of the underground chambers.

Moshe was with him. He gave Murray a wink and with a wry smile he said, "The war has started. What you hear overhead will shock everyone. But, more shocking is this latest report telling us that the Prime Minister has created an army of cloned humans, 200 million to be exact. The report calls these cloned human Chondriana. They are marching directly above us now. They are headed toward Jordan in route to the Euphrates River where 200 million Chinese terrorists, now allies of the newly established ten Arab nations, in a coup, which has taken over Jordan. But, the good news is that they will be fighting a losing battle. Why are they fighting a losing battle? Because today, nature is on our side and a 'Genie,' the name for the ultimate sandstorms, has brought their march to a halt. And the Chondriana reportedly are marching forward against them. We have reports that the Chondriana are invincible. For even when they are killed, they can resurrect themselves within three days."

Murray was flabbergasted. "Moshe," he asked, "What should we do? We have all of these men, women and children to protect. Will we be safe?"

"Murray," Moshe said, "Don't be afraid. God is with us! He will let us know what we should or should not do. Right now there is an emergency civil defense evacuation in place and the Prime Minister has enacted Marshall Law. Marvin and I have decided to close the upstairs safe house. All of us will remain down here below in the Valley of Achor. Most of these walls are reinforced. Several of our men are engineers and they have seen to it that we would survive even in the event of a nuclear blast. Lord willing that won't come to pass. Even the newest weapon, Cave Buster Bombs, cannot penetrate us."

Marvin, who was sitting quietly, spoke up. He said, "Murray, that should be a relief for you to know."

"Yes, thanks," replied Murray.

Marvin continued to speak. He said, "In a few minutes, Barry will be coming down below as soon as he finishes closing the upstairs safe house. We, Barry, Moshe and I have decided to set up a brief meeting to keep everyone informed about what is going on outside and to reassure them of their safety. Considering what is taking place above ground, they will be relieved and resigned to stay here below with us. After the meeting we have plans to continue special sessions with our small group of elders, we will call them School of the Prophets."

Moshe said, "We formed this group about a year ago in anticipation of the coming of the Lord. We felt we needed to encourage and protect our brothers and sisters from the great deception that will soon come upon us. You are invited to join us, Murray." Then he handed Murray a list of topics, along with a glossary listing the terminology that they were going to use in their discussions.

Moshe continued, "This school was created to guard against any self-deception."

"We believe one of the true signs that predict this coming deception will come about immediately before the Lord's second coming. The deception the evil one creates will be a lie and he will try to make all Christians believe it. The lie he will create is that Yeshua is not coming back a second time! 2 Peter 3:3–4 says, 'Knowing this first, that there shall come in the last days scoffers after their own lusts, and saying, Where is the promise of His coming? For since the fathers fell asleep, all things continue as they were from the beginning of creation.' Therefore, we, who are the elders in His service, want to warn everyone here about this coming lie and to keep them strong in every aspect of life and thought, while we are confined in these caves."

Murray took the list of topics and the glossary of terminology along with their real meanings and read it to himself, unaware that the Chondriana continued to march overhead. The list includes several signs of this coming deception, among them, widespread death by war, anarchy, earthquakes, famine, disease and inflation. Inflation will be so severe that a loaf of bread, if you could get it, will cost twenty dollars a loaf! The stock exchanges of the whole world will die in one day! Global immorality, witchcraft, theft, drugs used by whole populations and worldwide violence will abound.

Moshe continued, "Our list will also include the following topics: the Antichrist and his code number 666 along with the significance of our new third Temple rebuilt right next to the Dome of the Rock, discovery of the Ark of the Covenant, the final earthquake, the comet and an asteroid predicted to hit earth, as Yeshua predicted in the Gospel of Matthew 24:29–30 and in the last book of the Bible, the Revelation, its advanced intelligence interpretation."

"Quite an important list of topics," Murray said excitedly. "But, is it not possible to interpret the Bible anyway you wish to? How do we know the truth from a lie?"

Marvin, always one to interject his comments, stood up and walked over to Murray. His dark bushy eyebrows furrowed above his brown eyes in an arch. He put his arm around Murray and said, "Murray, do you have any paper money on you?"

Murray put his hand into his pants pocket and pulled out the few dollars he had on him. Handing them to Marvin, he said, "Will this do?"

Marvin grasped the money, taking one bill out and running his rough-hewn hands over it, and smoothed it out.

"Now, Murray," Marvin said in his low-gravel voice, "Could you tell me if this bill is a real one or is it a counterfeit?"

Murray looked up at Marvin who towered over him. At six foot seven he could never be missed. "Well, I cannot, but I fail to see what that has to do with knowing the truth about God."

"Well Murray, if you were to study a genuine dollar bill over and over, repeatedly, eventually you would be able to spot a phony bill. So too, our study of the Word of God in Holy Scripture, led and guided by the Holy Spirit who teaches us the truth, by way of our conscience, and the ability to discern what is true and what is false."

Then Moshe, filled with the Spirit and with a glowing smile said, "Murray, by saying everyone can interpret the Bible any way they want is true, but without HaMashiach and the Holy Spirit, what they learn will be a lie."

Murray, a little taken aback by Moshe's statement, kept humble and asked, "Why would it be a lie?"

Moshe continued, "Let us see what the Bible has to say to us, whether it contains the absolute truth or can one be a Christian and believe whatever he wants? To answer that we must first and foremost ask this question: Are you in a personal relationship with Yeshua HaMashiach? If a person is not, then he is open to all kinds of error and the Bible can then easily be misinterpreted. Secondly, if a person does not have the right motive and is not sincerely looking for GOD and His truth, then that person will not find the truth, unless he has a change of heart. So true motives, humility and a clear and clean conscience is the prerequisite to learn the truth about GOD and His Word."

"If we want to know the truth," said Moshe, "Then we must look to Yeshua and the instructions He has left us. Now turn in the written record of your Bible to the passage found in the Gospel of John 14:6 and the words of Yeshua spoken to His true disciples."

Murray took his Bible, opened it eagerly, turning to the passage. Clearing his throat he started to read, "Yeshua saith unto him, I am the way, the truth and the life, no man cometh to the Father but by me" (John 14:6).

"Now Murray, read John 14:26 and verses 16 and 17," Moshe requested. Placing his finger on the verse, Murray read, "But the Comforter, which is the Holy Ghost, whom the Father will send in my name, he shall teach you all things, and bring all things to your remembrance, whatsoever I have said to you ... And I will pray the Father, and he shall give you another Comforter, that he may abide with you forever. Even the Spirit of truth whom the world cannot receive because it seeth him not, neither knoweth him: but ye know him for he dwelleth with you, and shall be in you."

"Now," Moshe said, "All the body of HaMashiach must go to the Lord and ask the Lord to give us the meanings of His words. And we are told that understanding His words, which would include prophesy, would require the anointing, and that it is Yeshua who gives this anointing to us, by the Comforter, the Holy Ghost. Now Murray read this in 1st John 2:27–28."

Murray leafed through the pages of his Bible and read, "But the anointing which ye have received of him abideth in you and ye need not that any man teach you: but as the same anointing teacheth you of all things, and is truth, and is no lie, and even as it hath taught you, ye shall abide in him. And now, little children, abide in him that, when he shall appear, we may have confidence, and not be ashamed before him at his coming."

"Now Murray, what do these scriptures say we must do once GOD gives us the Holy Spirit and we receive this anointing?"

Murray answered, "He will teach us individually and that our part is to abide in Him."

"Yes," said Moshe, "But what does it mean to abide in Him? Murray, you have a King James version of the Holy Scriptures with the Scofield footnotes. Will you go to the bottom of page 1136 to footnote three? It is on the same page as chapter fourteen and fifteen of John's Gospel. Will you please read it out loud for us?"

Murray found it quickly and read, "To abide in Christ (HaMashiach) is on the one hand to have no known sin that has not been judged and non-confessed, no interest into which He is not brought, no life which He cannot share. On the other hand, the abiding one takes all burdens to Him, and draws all wisdom, life and strength from Him. It is not ceasing consciousness of these things and of Him, but that nothing is allowed in the life which would separate us from Him."

Moshe said, "That is, I feel, a clear understanding of the part we must play. So let us close our eyes for a few moments and quietly clear our conscience. Then let us pray and ask the Holy Spirit to guide us in this sacred endeavor."

"Barry, would you lead us in prayer," asked Moshe?

"Yes," replied Barry, usually quiet and somber compared to his extroverted brother, Marvin, spoke up. Closing their eyes and bowing

131

their heads, each one of them took a few quiet moments to reflect. Then Barry began his prayer.

"Holy Father, you who sent your Son, Yeshua HaMashiach to enter our dimension and who in turn sent us the precious person of the Holy Spirit, we now ask Him to enlighten us. Keep us from all error and evil. Father, give all of us gathered here in Your holy presence clear understanding and guidance during our stay here. Amen."

Everyone then followed with a concerted, "Amen."

Barry then took the lead and said, "Murray, turn to Hebrews 1:1."

Murray turned the pages until he came to the book of Hebrews. Then Barry asked him to read the verse.

He began to read, "God who at sundry times and in divers manners spake in times past unto the fathers by the prophets."

"Now stop there, Murray," said Barry. "Now what does it say about how GOD spoke to men in times past?"

He said, "It's clear that He said by the prophets."

"Okay," said Barry. "We know these are the prophets of Israel and their writings about GOD can be found in the Hebrew Scriptures, the Tanach, or as some call them, the Old Testament. Now," Barry continued, "What does verse two of this chapter tell us, Murray?"

He read, "Hath in these last days spoken unto us by his Son, whom he hath appointed heir to all things, by whom he also made the worlds."

"Now Murray, who does this verse say is our creator and who speaks to us now?"

He answered and said, "Now it's quite clear to me that Yeshua HaMashiach is the Son, who has the truth and we are to listen to His words."

"Okay, now let us go to John 16:13. It reads," said Barry, "As follows, 'How be it when he, the Spirit of truth is come he will guide you into ALL truth; for he shall not speak of himself; but whatsoever he shall hear, that shall he speak; and he will shew you things to come.'"

Barry asked Murray, "Now can you see how we can arrive at the truth, Murray? Can you see why we need to follow Yeshua and learn of the words He spoke to the Apostles, as recorded in the New Testament for our benefit?"

Barry went on, "Murray, turn to John 17:1 and 8 where Yeshua is praying to the Father on behalf of His followers, and read it."

Always a little nervous when he had to read, Murray cleared his throat and read, "These words spake Yeshua, For I have given unto them the words which thou gavest me; and they have received them and have known surely that I came out from thee, and they have believed that thou didst send me."

Always inquisitive, he asked Barry, "Well what about people who are critical and say that GOD could never be that narrow and only have one way to find Him and follow Him? How do we answer them?"

"It all hinges on what Yeshua prayed to the Father in John 17:14 & 17," said Barry.

Moshe said, "I'll read that Barry." So Moshe read, "I have given them thy word and the world hated them ... Sanctify them by thy truth; thy Word is truth."

"So Murray," Moshe said, "The truth is that Yeshua is the only GOD you can have a personal relationship with. It is a fact that even if you tried you could not have a real relationship with Buddha or any other so called gods. We will consider for discussion now, Romans chapter one. We find it makes it clear that everyone has the knowledge of God built inside of them."

"And with that let's leave the judgement of those who cannot receive these words up to GOD to handle. For whom are we to judge their hearts? Something only God can do."

Marvin stepped into the conversation and said, "Gentlemen, brothers, let's stop here. It's time to set up the meeting, informing everyone about what is going on overhead. It will be our responsibility to keep them informed and encouraged. After giving them a short briefing, we'll all eat dinner. Then Barry, Moshe, Murray and I will meet back here in the Library to resume our study of the topics of The School of the Prophets."

One by one, Marvin, Barry, Moshe and Murray left the room and entered a larger auditorium. It held seating arrangements for upwards of five-hundred people. It was 6:00 p.m. The seats filled up quickly. Not one chair was empty. Everyone was quite hungry, so Moshe approached the mike and said, "Brothers and sisters, please remain seated. Dinner is being made ready and will start in fifteen minutes." Everyone sat down. The room grew quiet as Moshe began to speak.

"Brothers and sisters, let us open with a word of prayer."

Everyone bowed their heads and Moshe opened the meeting with a word of prayer. "Dear heavenly Father, we approach Thee with great praise for all You have done and are doing on our behalf. We thank You for Your protection here below in the Valley of Achor. We thank You for providing the many caves turned into sleeping quarters for Your sons and daughters. We ask You now in the name of Your Son, Yeshua HaMashiach, that You comfort all of us. Let us feel Your invisible presence. Keep our confidence in You to protect us from the threats of death by our very own government. Remove all fears and apprehensions of the parents here, concerned for their safety and the safety of their children. We look to You for guidance, peace and direction. Thank You for this place and thank You for the caves in which we have been able to store food for a very long time. Amen."

Everyone followed with an amen.

There were a few murmurs that could be heard, but for the most part everyone had strong faith and were trusting GOD to take care of them. Most of them felt as secure in GOD as if they were in a wheel barrel being pushed by a tightrope walker crossing over the Niagara Falls.

Moshe said, "Brothers & sisters, we have received a report that the Prime Minister of Israel has cloned an army of two-hundred million men and that they are marching overhead right now to fight against the new Ten Nation Arab and Muslim governments who in a coup have overtaken Jordan. In addition, their Chinese allies have formed an army of 200 million and they are ready to cross the dried up Euphrates River. However, by God's divine providence, a huge sand storm is holding them at bay. We want you to have confidence that no matter what goes on above us, these caves and rooms have been secured by our engineers to withstand even the strain of nuclear weapons." With that Moshe said, "You can approach any of our elders with your questions and comments. Dinner is ready now so you are dismissed for dinner. May God bless it in nourishment to our bodies, amen." Everyone followed with an amen.

Dinner was over and everyone was preparing to settle down for the night, except for the small group of elders.

Murray was the first one to enter the Library where The School of the Prophets was to regather. The walls were filled with books lining the shelves. A small portable fan made a steady hum, circulating the damp, musty smell of earth clinging to the ceiling, walls and floors. A large table sat in the center of the room with several books piled upon it. This room was not as dark as some of the other caverns. The florescent light helped create a brighter atmosphere.

At least Murray felt less claustrophobic. If there was anything he couldn't stand, it was being in a dark or even dimly lit room. He always needed light and lots of it, especially when it came to reading. As he looked around the room he saw several chairs placed in a circular pattern, the unfolded chairs were placed on top of a large tapestry rug. He hoped the rug would help keep the dampness in the room to a minimum. He couldn't stand his feet being cold. Besides these petty dislikes, Murray was grateful he was not above ground facing the horrors of war, the threat of a cloned army or facing the guillotine.

One by one, Marvin, Barry, and Moshe entered the auditorium and greeted Murray. Before they sat down, Moshe opened the meeting in prayer.

"Brothers and sisters," he said, "Let us bow our heads for a word of prayer."

While everyone bowed his or her heads, Moshe began. "Father God, Yeshua our redeemer, and Holy Spirit our teacher, we glorify Your name. We thank You for creating us and caring for us by bringing us into holy union with You. We ask that tonight You will comfort all of the men, women and children who are here below. We are safe but under the stress of having to live underground for what may be a great length of time. Minister to all our needs, Lord. Help us who are elders to remain fully yielded to the Holy Spirit as we search Your Word and Your revelations so that we can set an example of complete surrender to You for them to follow. Grant that we might lead Your people, gathered here in this our underground safe house, into holiness. Enlighten us, help us to show Your people that Your Son and our HaMashiach are the center of all things and of all prophesy. Bless our small group here gathered together to learn Your will, Your meaning to all that we will cover in The School of the Prophets. Thank You, Lord, for all of Your goodness, all of Your mercy and all of Your truth. Amen."

And everyone joined in saying, "Amen."

Moshe addressed everyone present and said, "Marvin, Barry and I have been meeting together over the past year. During that time we formed what we call The School of the Prophets. Recently we have added a new member, Murray Andrews."

"We know that one of these schools existed during the time of our early fathers and we felt led by the Holy Spirit to form one during this most pivotal time in our history. We want you to know that we are happy you have joined us. We will cover all the topics listed on the handout now being distributed to you."

"These topics focus on the events that are now happening. They're also to prepare and to lead God's people through the time of Jacob's trouble, and to protect you by warning every one of you of what we think is the coming great deception. We will share with you what we feel the Holy Spirit has led us to know, what this great deception is spoken by the Apostle Paul who indicates that it is a benchmark that would precede Yeshua HaMashiach's second coming."

Moshe then said, "Barry, why don't you start the meeting."

Barry, smaller and thinner than his brother, Marvin, nodded to Moshe and said, "Let me start by informing you about this place where we are meeting today. It is a historic site. It is the same location where HaMashiach went to be baptized by John the Baptist and where later many came to decide that Yeshua was HaMashiach. We elders have formed The School of the Prophets to clarify what these events mean. We will explain the rules we relied upon for interpreting and understanding the last book of the New Testament, the book of Revelation. We will also relate its prediction and the things we are now going through and what we may face up ahead."

Opening his Bible he turned to Revelation 19:10. He read it out loud, "'For the testimony of Yeshua is the spirit of prophesy.' We are," said Barry, "Therefore going to follow the Lord's method of interpretation for the Revelation as seen and recorded by John the Apostle under the direct command by the Lord Himself when He said to John, 'What thou seest, write in a book, and send it to the seven churches.' Our first topic will cover some basic scriptural rules to follow under the heading, 'Interpretation.'"

"Is there an actual Bible example that makes it plain enough and simple enough to use when interpreting the Bible? And if so, what scripture tells us that it is the same method Yeshua used? It can be found in Luke 24:27. Murray, would you read this verse for us?"

Murray stood up, quickly turning to the verse. He cleared his throat and began to read out loud, "'And beginning at Moses and all the prophets, he (Yeshua) expounded unto them in all the scriptures the things concerning himself.' And so, 'The messenger became the message.'"*

Barry said, "Thank you, Murray. Now here is a list** of thirty out of more than three-hundred*** Hebrew Testament prophesies that Yeshua completely fulfilled at His first advent. Familiarizing yourself with the list will help you with your own private study time."

Barry continued, "Just let me use two scriptures to consider concerning the accuracy of this list of prophesies. This list includes those that Yeshua had no control over. For instance, note Zechariah 1:12-13, 'And I said unto them. If you think good, give me my price; and if not, forbear. So they weighed for my price thirty pieces of silver. And the Lord said unto me, Cast it unto the potter, a goodly price that I was priced at them. And I took the thirty pieces of silver, and cast them to the potter in the house of the Lord.'"

"Immediately after Judas betrayed Yeshua, he realized his sin and tried to rectify it by going to the Jewish leaders to give them back the thirty pieces of silver. The Jewish leaders refused to take it back. In anger, Judas threw the thirty pieces of silver back into the house of the Lord."

Murray interjected a comment and said, "That is really awesome. I can see that Yeshua had no control over what Judas would do. But He knew he would do it!"

Barry went on and said, "Now Murray that was one event that Yeshua had no control over. Murray, now read another one taken from the Psalms in Psalm 22:16-19."

He stood up and read out loud, "... For dogs have surrounded me; A pack of evildoers has enclosed me, Like (the prey of) a lion my hands and my feet. I can count all my bones; they look on and glare over me. They divide my garments among themselves, and cast lots for my clothing."

Once he stopped reading, Barry then asked him, "Murray, what method of punishment was used to execute criminals in Rome before the year 200 B.C.? Was it the popular method of crucifixion?"

"No, stoning was used by the Jews," he replied.

"Right," said Barry. "Crucifixion was unknown among the Jews themselves as a method for capital punishment in the years prior to 200 B.C."

"In addition," said Barry, "Has anyone from the beginning of time until our very present other than Yeshua HaMashiach fulfilled Genesis 49:10? 'The scepter shall not depart from Judah, nor a scholar from among his descendants until Shiloh arrives.'"

"The answer is no. Why is the answer no? Because all the genealogical records from Adam to Yeshua HaMashiach begin and end as recorded in Matthew chapter 1. Today, there are no records to be found anywhere from the time of HaMashiach until now. So, from that time until our time no one remains to fill the bill, so to speak. This reason can be said to apply also to Deuteronomy 18:15 and 18."

Barry read out loud, "A prophet from your midst, for your brethren, like me, shall HASHEM, your God establish for you to him shall you hearken ... I will establish a prophet for them from among their brethren, like you, and I will place My words in his mouth. He will speak to them everything that I will command him."

"Now I ask, has any one person other than Yeshua HaMashiach been able to fit this description? Only Yeshua HaMashiach fits this description. He always made the claim that He was sent from GOD to speak the words of GOD and that these words he spoke were from the Father in Heaven and not His own!"

"Witnesses in Yeshua HaMashiach's day recorded that many saw Him as 'that prophet,' the one Moses said to look for. 'Then those men, when they had seen the miracle that Yeshua did, said, This is of a truth that prophet that should come into the world (John 6:14).'"

Barry, usually somber, began to show more intense enthusiasm and excitement over their discussions. He interjected, "Moshe, will you record our discussions?"

Moshe said, "Sure Barry, I have been doing so all along. First on our agenda, it is necessary to formulate a statement of our purpose and the reasons for forming The School of the Prophets. It should be noted that we are composing a statement with the spirit of openness and accountability to both GOD and the body of our HaMashiach. It will prove to be a statement that will be freed, so far as is possible, from mere theological concepts and presuppositions. Instead we will rely heavily on using prayer and careful research. We will compare significant historical facts and compare them with the outline of the Revelation given to the Apostle John."

"Note, two facts stand out when considering Biblical interpretation. One is that all He has given us in the Revelation is an outline. And second, the fact that the dimension of time is missing, creates for us a daunting task. However, we are going to compare subjective and objective facts, thereby giving everyone here the chance to make an independent judgment. In addition, we will not use any personal political theory of interpretation, but only use what Yeshua spoke of in reference to political things involved in the Revelation's outline."

Marvin interrupted Barry, making a suggestion. He said, "Let's include that we surrender any egotistic desire to control the text as well as to avoid empty speculation or conjecture. Instead we will let the scriptures speak for themselves. Also, we should mention that we intend to avoid the semantic path which can lead to misinterpretation, confusion and error. To avoid misinterpretation, confusion and error, we are including a glossary of terms with their definitions, using them only as a guide. And to repeat, we will follow Yeshua's method of comparing scripture with scripture. First, we will go over the scripture that is predicted, as a future event, then compare it to the scripture showing how it was fulfilled and came true by Yeshua HaMashiach."

Barry replied, "How does that sound to you Moshe, Marvin and Murray?"

Moshe spoke up and said, "Definitely well worded and to the point. I agree we accept this as our first statement."

Murray said, "Well I am not as knowledgeable as all of you are, but I feel that it makes sense to someone who is new in understanding the Words of GOD. So, from that viewpoint I agree with you Barry, Marvin and Moshe."

"Well Marvin, what else do you have to say," asked Barry? Marvin was surprised that Barry had not, as his usual self, spoken up sooner than this.

Marvin said, "I agree. It sounds like it is incisive indeed. I believe it will convey accurately how we intend to approach such complicated prophecies. Our intention is not to be dogmatic."

Barry said, "Good, then we can proceed with our objectives. Here is what I propose to say under that heading."

"Our objective and purpose is to support the body of Yeshua, by preparing them to be ready for Yeshua's coming, with their lamps full of oil. We will do this by offering them courage, consolation and confidence. Especially teaching scripture that will give them a strong faith in discerning GOD's Divine Providence, His lead and instructions so that they will know what actions they must take in order to abide in Yeshua, both now in the present and daily. And to always be ready for the coming of our Lord."

Barry asked Moshe, "Are we going too fast?"

Moshe said, "No, I am able to keep up."

Barry went on, "If anyone has objections or comments, speak up and we will find the answers." Barry continued to speak with continued enthusiasm and excitement. He said, "Let us include that our insights will not be apologetic, expository or orthodox, instead, they will be an unprejudiced exegesis. And this method will be followed in order to help the entire body of Yeshua to grow in holiness and continue in the joy of the Lord. Let me read 1st John 4:1–3, 'Beloved, believe not every spirit, but try the spirits whether they are of God ... Hereby know ye the Spirit of GOD: Every spirit that confesseth that Yeshua HaMashiach is come in the flesh is of GOD.' Now, Murray, what can you glean from this verse? What do you think it means," asked Barry?

He answered, "The fact that stands out clear to me is that Yeshua, in total humility, chose to put aside His own rights, privileges and prerogatives as GOD to become a man. I would call what He did a process called self-emptying."

Murray said, "Emptying Himself, He became flesh, a man."

"Yes," Barry said, "That is correct Murray."

Barry went on and said, "It is important at times to clarify some of the terms. For instance, the flesh means the self, all of your psychological and intellectual faculties, as well as your five senses, what you can see, hear, taste, touch or feel. It includes emptying aspects of the mind. Emptying itself of all preconceptions such as our formulating assumptions, presumptions, suppositions and projecting the future, what you can only imagine will happen. Now I am not promoting that we

139

are to be empty headed. No. What I believe is that we take all of these various levels of thinking and put all of them on the back burner until we clear the mind and see their reality. If we compare what Yeshua said, 'To be like little children.' Now little children have uncluttered minds. So, we can aptly say that we must have clear minds. Self-emptying is clearing the mind of all of our opinions, holding them at bay."

"As an example, ninety-nine percent of all of the worry that the unregenerate mind thinks never happens. In a paraphrase of Luke 12, Yeshua, Himself made it clear that all worry, of believers and non-believers, is a waste, when He asked the disciples who could make themselves with all their thinking to grow a foot. It is common sense that thinking will not change your height. Yeshua's use of this illustration was telling us it's a waste of time and a waste of the mind to worry. Why? Because all the thinking you can do will never cause a change; only prayer to GOD can. The fact that Yeshua gave up everything, including all of His prerogatives as GOD, was a true act of humility. It shows that He put GOD the Father's thoughts, opinions and commands first. So, when GOD says in Philippians 2:5, 'Let this mind be in you that was in HaMashiach Yeshua,' it means we must at all times practice the art and act of humility before GOD by subordinating all of our thoughts and our actions. Keeping our mind free from worry will eliminate a cluttered mind full of waste and leave room to hear from GOD."

"Did not GOD instruct us to 'Be still?' So, we need to stop all unnecessary thinking. I use the illustration of someone trying to find the radio station one wants. If one is to get to the right station he must pass the static or he will never hear the station he wants to listen to. All worry is static. Tune it out. Turn it off. Stop it! This requires discipline and cooperation with the Holy Spirit. With His help and our willingness and humility it is possible."

Murray spoke out and asked Barry, "Then once we clear our mind of wasteful and cluttered thinking, how do we test the spirits, to see if they are true or false?"

Barry spoke up and said, "If anyone is, be it people or organized religious bodies that do not believe that Yeshua is GOD who became a man and not a man who became GOD, they are classified as false or lying spirits. All religious cults and false religions, with false doctrine follow this course and demote Yeshua. Some in error believe He was 'just a man,' 'a prophet,' or 'a God,' and not 'Almighty God.' Along with others who teach, He is 'not the Son of God.' This is the first litmus test. Ignore anything they have to say or teach."

"Now Murray, this scripture proves those who believe the lie that Yeshua is not 'Almighty God' who became a man, is proved by comparing it with this scripture in Hebrews 1:1–2. Would you once again read it to us out loud?"

Quickly he turned the pages of his Bible to those verses and he read, "God who at sundry times and in divers manners spake in time past unto the fathers by the prophets, Hath in these last days spoken unto us by his Son, whom he hath appointed heir of all things, by whom also he made the worlds."

Murray said, "This scripture proves He is also our Creator."

Barry said, "Yes, Murray. And what else does this verse tell us," he asked?

Murray said, "According to these verses of Scripture, there is no one other than Yeshua HaMashiach, our Yeshua, to bring us the truth. The Scripture is clear enough to me. There is no one else, period!"

Barry in joy, raised his voice and exclaimed, "Then blessed are we the so called narrow minded!"

Marvin blurted out, "If it were not sacred and so true, we could almost gloat before others that, yes, there is only one way! I repeat what Yeshua HaMashiach, our Yeshua, said in John 14:6, 'I am the way, the truth and the life.' To repeat the Scripture, I repeat again what Yeshua said, 'I am the way, I am the truth, I am the life!'"

Moshe, chimed in and said, "Okay, brothers, we will keep all the Scripture verses in our statement, but I am leaving out the blurt you gave us, Marvin," he chuckled. "Let's be sure to include the topic, 'How to abide in Yeshua.'"

Barry went on, "Yes, I agree with you Moshe."

Marvin joined in and said, "Yes, absolutely."

"Okay, Murray," said Barry, "Now read 2nd Peter 2:1."

More at ease now, he read, "But there were false prophets also among the people, even as there shall be false teachers among you, who privily shall bring in damnable heresies, even denying the Lord that bought them, bringing upon themselves swift destruction."

"Now," Barry said, "Scripture shows us that GOD will not let the prophesies contradict the Scriptures. For GOD will never permit His true body to speak contrary to His written words. However, our objective is to assist our brothers and sisters in avoiding damnable heresies, lies, doubts and the coming great deception, mentioned in 2nd Thessalonians 2:1–3 and 11, which reads that it will be a strong delusion due to come prior to the Lord's arrival for us. We want to negate the fears, doubts and lies."

Murray said, "Barry, you're right. I need reassurance. I am sure the others with us will need it."

"Yes," said Barry, "But we want to make sure we are not creating unnecessary fear in our brothers. We will need to hold on tightly to GOD's Word, by believing every word and understanding its true meaning. But that is not all we must do. We must not focus wholly on the signs received. Why, you might ask? The answer to that is found in 1st Peter 1:13. Let's include it on our list. It will bring hope to everyone. I will read it. 'For the grace that is to be brought unto you at the revelation of Yeshua HaMashiach. Wherefore gird up the loins of your mind, be sober, and hope.' Therefore we must be sure to include that the Lord will send us the grace to get through this terrible time of persecution and deception."

Murray asked Barry, "Are we in the time of 'Jacob's Trouble' now?"

Barry went on, "Almost every Christian especially those who are suffering persecution, from the first century up until today, believed the Lord would come in their time and in each century they were wrong! Yes, HaMashiach may come at any moment, but no predictions prophesied prevents the Christian from the hour when He comes for us, at the hour of our death. Can you see the difference Murray?"

He replied, "Wow, I'll say. So instead of being overly concerned that we look for these signs to occur, we should always be ready and alert every day, keeping our relationship with Him continually active and alive, because we do not know if our physical death will come first and we would go to be with Him or if it will occur when the signs indicate the time of His second coming has arrived."

Marvin said, "Actually if we are still living and the Lord returns, it will be first to gather us together, His body of believers. So, we can say He is coming again for us as the first part of His second coming."

"He will come, quietly and unexpectedly, like a thief, for us first. It reads in Matthew 24:44, where Yeshua said, 'Therefore be ye ready; for in such an hour as ye think not the Son of man cometh.'"

And, Marvin continued, "Also, Moshe, please record this verse found in Matthew 25:13, 'Watch, therefore,' Yeshua said, 'for you know neither the day nor the hour wherein the Son of Man cometh.' The only thing we will know is the season of His coming that the signs reveal."

"The book of Revelation indicates that at His second appearance He will be coming back to earth and it will be at that time that He will openly, not to individuals or privately as He has over the past two thousand years revealed Himself, but all at once, immediately to the entire world of unbelievers."

"Coming in a spectacular way, Yeshua in His very own words tells us the exact one and only sign or event that all people will see Him all over the globe, all at one time. Let us list this in our statement of purpose." Barry said, "I will read it out loud. Everyone turn to Matthew 24:29 and 30. 'Immediately after the tribulation of those days shall the sun be darkened, and the moon shall not give its light, and the stars shall fall from heaven, and the powers of the heavens shall be shaken. And then shall appear the sign of the Son of man in heaven: and then shall all the tribes of the earth mourn, and they shall see the Son of man coming in the clouds of heaven with power and great glory."

Barry stopped reading there. He asked Marvin, "Would you like to continue, Marvin?"

Marvin with a smile of confidence on his face said, "Yes, I would like to continue." Marvin said, "Topics we covered in our School of the Prophets will read as follows: The Temple, The Ark of the Covenant,* The Anti-Christ, The Code of the Anti-Christ—666, The End of the World, The Time of Jacob's Trouble, The 7th Trumpet, The End of the Thousand Year Rule, The Supernatural Experience of the Baptism in the Holy Spirit."

"We also acknowledge that the Lord has given us only an outline of the events to take place as depicted in the last book of the Bible, The Revelation of Yeshua HaMashiach."

"Since we only have an outline," Barry said, "It is evident that the details will come when the fulfillment comes. Therefore, we will use the following rule to govern their interpretation and the possibilities that seem clear. We also have concluded that we have no way of judging the future, other than looking at what the prophesies which have occurred in past events, i.e., if a literal interpretation was given in the past then a literal interpretation must be given for the future. This same rule will apply to the spiritual interpretation of a verse or verses, of course within their context."

Marvin then called on Barry to speak. He said, "Barry has done research concerning questions on our first topic, The Temple being rebuilt as one of the signs signaling the return of HaMashiach and of the end of the world."

Barry, always serious and studious began, "There have been in the past two temples, first the Temple of David, second the Temple rebuilt by Nehemiah and later refurbished by Herod the Great. We know that the second temple was completely demolished and never rebuilt until our present time. Oddly enough it stands out that both the first and the second temple were destroyed in different years but on the same exact day, April ninth."

"Well, where does that leave us," asked Marvin? "Since Paul wrote that the Antichrist would be sitting in the temple, being worshiped as God (2nd Thessalonians 2:4)."

143

Murray interjected and asked Marvin, "How then do we rectify this with the prophesy written by Zechariah in Zechariah 6:12 and 13?"

Marvin said, "Go ahead and read it to us, Murray. We will include all of these verses with our statements and the interpretations of prophesy put together by us."

Quickly he leafed through his copy of the Holy Scriptures and read, "Say to him, said HASHEM, Master of Legions; Behold, there is a man, his name is Zemah, and he will flourish in his place; he will build the sanctuary of HASHEM."

Marvin said, "That is a very well thought out question, Murray. Moshe, what is your response to Murray's question?"

Moshe looked up from his writing, ran his hand over his beard, looked at Murray, smiled and said, "This is only my opinion, but there is a very strong possibility that the Temple of today's Jewish Orthodoxy has put to use in their present Great Synagogue. The third temple is the one that has been taken over by Iraq's newly formed Ten Nation Arab's and their allies is being used by their leader, the Antichrist, to 'exalt himself as God, in the temple of God.'"

"However, I will note in our statement that the present Great Synagogue is being used as the third temple for the following reasons: first, it is the first central house of worship for Jews in more than nineteen hundred years. And that sacrificial worship services in the temple are sacrificing animals and doing so as we speak."

"This would mean therefore that the Antichrist has appeared at this time according to 2nd Thessalonians 2:3–4. Now if this is to be true then what does Zechariah 6:12–13 refer to? Here we come across another temple, this time to be built by a man of God's choice. That would mean then that there is a strong possibility that this Temple will be the fourth temple to be built. This will be the temple built for the millennium rule of HaMashiach, by HaMashiach."

Barry continued, "Now back to the third temple. The Apostle Paul now reveals the fact that it now exists, and is important to us. In 2nd Thessalonians 2:1–4, we read, 'Now we beseech you, brethern, by the coming of the Lord Yeshua HaMashiach, and by our gathering together unto him, That ye be soon not shaken in mind, or be troubled, neither by spirit, nor by word, nor by letter as from us, as that day of Yeshua is at hand. Let no man deceive you by any means: For that day shall not come except there come a falling away first, and that man of sin be revealed, the son of perdition; Who opposeth and exalteth himself above all that is worshiped; so that he as God sitteth in the temple of God, shewing himself that he is God.'"

144

Murray spoke up again and asked the question, "I am perplexed. If the Jews today are using the Great Synagogue as the third temple, how can its location be authentic? Especially since the Great Synagogue is over a mile west of the Dome of the Rock, where once stood the first and second Temple."

Moshe replied, "Murray, Barry has a possible answer to that."

Barry spoke up and said, "There remains an intricate and compelling argument that the first and second temples did not sit where the Dome of the Rock (the Haram esh-Sharif) is today. Dr. Asher S. Kaufman has written an article giving them a new location."

"Since an archeological excavation of the temple site is barred by the Muslims, Dr. Kaufman used other means, i.e., using ancient Jewish literary sources and modern aerial maps with detailed measurements of numerous ancient hewn rock cuttings, cisterns and wall remains on the Temple Mount to guide him. He locates the first and second temple sites being thirty-three feet north of the Dome of the Rock."

Murray said, "This should solve not agitating the Arabs. And since the third Temple is as we know now being used today for animal sacrifices then that would leave the fourth temple to be built by Yeshua in the Millennium."

Moshe, Marvin and Barry gave an energetic amen to that!

Marvin asked Moshe, "How is the documentation coming along?"

Moshe replied, "Great! That concludes this topic. Let's continue with the next one."

Marvin and Murray said, "Yes, let's go ahead."

"Our next topic," Barry said, "Is The Ark of the Covenant."

Marvin asked, "Shall we include the description of the Ark in our statement?"

Moshe replied, "Perhaps if we list where the description can be found in scripture verses that should be sufficient."

Marvin, Barry and Murray agreed that should be sufficient. "I'll list Exodus 25:1–40 and Exodus 37:1–9."

"Sounds reasonable to me," said Marvin.

Barry said, "Okay," and Murray said, "Yes" too.

Excitedly Murray jumped in and asked, "Does the Ark still exist? Will it be found? I've heard rumors that whoever finds it will rule the world. Is this true?"

"Hold it, Murray," Barry said, "One question at a time. Moshe, what do you have to say in answer to Murray's questions?"

Moshe stroking his beard and with a twinkle in his eye, looked at him and said, "Well Murray, Moses was told to make the original

145

Ark, after the pattern shown to him by GOD. In our Mission Statement we refer to this as recorded in Exodus 25:40. Perhaps we should also mention that there is only one place in all of Holy Scripture where the Ark of the Covenant is called the Holy Ark, or the Aron-Ha-Qodesh. It is found in 2nd Chronicles 35:3. Let's include this fact and this scripture in our statement. We are also told that the Ark rested on a platform or Bema, a raised prayer platform."*

"Since the destruction of the first temple in 586 B.C. the Ark has disappeared from Jewish history. So, where is the Ark today? Some think it is hidden in a deep secret cave, built by Solomon.* Warren's Gate came within thirty to forty yards of a hidden chamber wall, in the late seventies and eighties, think that the original gate, known as Warren's Gate, came within thirty to forty yards from the hidden chamber located beneath the present Temple Mount, since first temple times.** The Ark of the Covenant was claimed to have been seen by one of the Rabbis but Muslims sealed this entrance," Moshe continued. "But, today there is also a group in Israel calling themselves Ne'emanel, 'Ha Habayil,' the 'Faithful of the Temple Mount.' They are braced that they can reach this tunnel by another entrance called The Cave of Zedekiah. They claim, 'This entrance is located in the underground caverns of the Quarries of Solomon. It descends from this entrance near the temple mount all the way down to the Valley of Achor.'* The very spot we are now standing below ground with our safe house above it."

Moshe said, "Rumors have it that the original Ark is in Ethiopia."

Murray asked, "Can that be true?"

Moshe replied, "Let Barry fill you in on that Murray."

Barry answered, "There are many replicas of the Ark of the Covenant. We believe that the Ark residing in the church of Axum, Ethiopia is one of those rumors. There are also other replicas of them in Elephantine, Germany, Turkey, here in Israel at the Great Synagogue and for that matter, as we all are aware that every synagogue has one for memorial purposes."

Murray said, "Yes, and I have seen the one in the Great Synagogue. Reports have it that it cost two-hundred and fifty-thousand dollars."

Barry went on, "Some Muslims and some Jews feel that whoever finds the Ark will rule the world. That is one of the reasons why Hitler, in 1935, sent out a contingent to find the Ark."

Barry chimed in and said, "Seventh Day Adventists feel they will be the ones to discover the lost Ark. They base this on the fact that only a saved or godly person, meaning a Christian, will discover the Ark. I have even heard of a writer whose cousin is somewhat of a psychic. She asked her cousin if she would help her locate the Ark, but her cousin, said, 'No, its taboo.' In other words, it is sacred. Hands off."

"Even more peculiar and bizarre still is a report that someone in America actually believes the Ark is hidden somewhere in Arizona and that it was brought there by the Vikings and that is one of the reasons they believe that the United States has had such phenomenal growth and power."

Moshe interjected and said, "Let us read and record what God's Word says about the Ark."

"Go on," said Barry.

Moshe turned to Psalm 132:8 and read, "'Arise oh Lord and enter your Temple with the Ark, the symbol of your power.' It's plain enough I would say that the Ark is a symbol of God's presence."

Barry said, "Amen." Barry then handed me a very large Bible and asked me, "Now what about the verses found in 2nd Maccabees 2:1-7, Murray? Will you read these verses for us?"

He replied, "Sure will," as I flipped through the books of the Bible known as the Apocrypha.

Marvin interjected and said, "Before you read, Murray, I would like to make a comment about the Apocrypha. There are several other books included in the Apocrypha. Most Christian fundamentalists and many protestant religions do not accept these. However, the Catholics do include them in their Douay Version of their Bible."

With that said, he began to read. "It was also contained in the same writing, how the prophet, being warned by God, commanded that the Tabernacle and the Ark should accompany him, till he came forth to the mountain where Moses went up and saw the inheritance of God: and the Ark, and the altar of incense, and so stopped the door. Then some of them that followed him came up to mark the place but could not find it. And when Jeremiah perceived it, he blamed them saying: The place shall be unknown till God gather together the congregation of the people and receive them to mercy."

Now Moshe asked him, "What does that tell you about the possibility of finding the Ark, Murray?"

Murray replied, "According to what I have just read, it will not be found until the Lord gathers His people."

Barry asked Murray to read Jeremiah 3:16–17.

Anxiously he turned to the verses and read, "Then when your land is once more filled with people says the Lord, you will no longer wish for 'the good old days of long ago' when you possessed the Ark of God's Covenant. Those days will not be missed or even thought about, and the Ark will not be reconstructed, for the Lord himself will be among you and the whole city of Jerusalem will be known as the Throne of the Lord, and all nations will come to him there and no longer stubbornly follow their evil desires."

Murray was stunned. "Why, I have read these scriptures several times and never once noticed such a clear comment. We will not need the Ark of the Covenant!"

Barry said, "This is proof conclusive that we today who already have God's presence within us will not need the Ark anymore because we have Him personally dwelling in us!"

Barry spoke up and said, "This definitely is one scripture we must include in our statement. It should put to rest any questions or curiosity about finding the Ark."

Barry, Marvin, Moshe and Murray, though awestruck, all agreed.

"Now," Barry continued, "There are other scriptures that we should include that make it even more clear why we will not need the Ark of the Covenant. Let's turn to 1st John 3:23–24. 'And this is his commandment that we should believe on the name of his Son Jesus Christ, and love one another, as he gave us commandments. And he that keepeth his commandments dwelleth in him and he in him. And hereby we know that he abideth in us, by the Spirit which he hath given us.'"

"Also," Marvin said, "Let's include 1st John 4:11–16, where it tells us once again why we do not need to find the Ark of the Covenant. 'Beloved, if God so loved us, we ought also to love one another ... Hereby know we that we dwell in him and he in us, because he hath given us of his Spirit. And we have seen and do testify that the Father sent the Son to be the Savior of the world. Whosoever shall confess that Jesus is the Son of God, God dwelleth in him, and he in God. And we have known and believed the love that God hath to us, God is love: and he that dwelleth in love dwelleth in God, and God in him.'"

"Murray," Marvin asked, "What can we conclude according to these scriptures?"

He replied, "Today, we do not need to find the Ark of the Covenant."

"But, why do we not need it, Murray?"

He felt so awe struck he could hardly speak up. Practically stuttering he said, "Because God's presence resides in us. His Shekinah Glory is already in us. We have communion with Him and He communes with us by His Holy Spirit."

Barry said, "Yes, and it is clear from Exodus 25:22 that Almighty God would meet with Moses at the Ark and that is where He communicated with Moses. But now He speaks to us individually, directly, by means of His Holy Spirit. Sometimes in our intuition or our conscience, other times by way of Divine Providence and if we are quiet enough, we may hear Him speak to us, telepathically in our mind, literally our thoughts."

Marvin went on and said, "The Apostle Paul sites the details concerning the Ark in Moses' day and under Jewish Law up until Yeshua HaMashiach came with God's new and better way. And what better way than to have Him dwell in each of us?"

"Let's list Hebrews 9:1–28 and Hebrews 10:1–20, quoting them in their entirety in our statement. Moshe, would you make a note of that," he asked?

Moshe replied, "Yes, I am doing that right now."

Murray interjected, "But how do we explain Revelation 11:19 where the Apostle John saw the Ark in Heaven?"

Marvin said, "In Exodus 25:9, the Lord made it clear that Moses was to make the Ark according to the pattern shown him which was the heavenly Ark."

Sheeplessly, Murray said, "Well I guess that resolves that question."

A knock was heard at the door. Joel, a giant burly man, walked into the room. However, his huge appearance was deceiving, for he spoke very calmly and slowly.

Joel said, "Brothers, sorry I am late, but I had to put on a change of clothes after I sealed the rooms of our above ground safe house."

Barry, Marvin, Moshe and Murray each gave Joel a bear hug and they said, "Welcome."

Then Moshe took Joel's hand and said, "Why you are just in time, Joel. We were beginning to go over our third topic, the Antichrist and the strong delusion he will bring to try and turn us away from loving Yeshua HaMashiach."

"I know that is your specialty, Joel, so I'll turn the discussion over to you."

Joel started to speak, his square jaw jutted out and his bushy eyebrows arched. Holding his Bible, he said, "Moshe, I see you are still taking down notes. Good." Then handing Moshe a stack of papers he said, "These are my notes on the topic of the Antichrist, which I will now be sharing with you. I have condensed them as much as possible so that our statement will not be too lengthy. I thought this might make it easier for you to take them down for the records."

Moshe said, "Thanks, Joel."

Joel said, "I'll read the pertinence of the Antichrist as it is relevant to our current situation."

149

Joel went on, "Our statement for formulating and concluding the facts about the Antichrist is that he is extremely dangerous. He is capable of misleading thousands of the faithful astray. Note, he is capable, but we do not say he will succeed. Praise the Lord, for His grace will be sufficient to keep us, if we stay alert as He instructs us to."

"Our purpose," Joel said, "Is to expose him. Then to protect our brothers and sisters, we will build a wall of protection, consisting of the Word of God in the Holy Scriptures."

Moshe interjected with a question. "It's been said in scripture that Yeshua HaMashiach, after His resurrection, appeared unrecognized. Could His counterfeit, the Antichrist, also catch us napping?"

"Not if we can help it," said Joel. Addressing the others present Joel said, "I have my notes, but where do you want to start?"

Moshe replied, "Let us go to the very first chapter of Revelation, verse three."

Joel opened his Bible and read it out loud, "'Blessed is he that readeth, and they that hear the words of this prophesy, and keep those things which are written therein: for the time is at hand.' So our first step is to be sure everyone reads and hears the entire book of Revelation."

Joel said, "Good, we can also include that we, as The School of the Prophets, today bear the responsibility to biblically inform and educate the minds, hearts and souls of all the believers in our care. Further, that we are now to continue in undertaking responsible study of the 'signs of the times' we are now living in. Not merely religious knowledge, but knowledge of GOD. One of our goals is to build up the body of our HaMashiach. Our purpose is to help them learn what deception is. Deception consists of false beliefs, lies, delusions and doubts, which do not agree with what our Lord has taught us, as recorded for us in Holy Scripture."

"The first big question we ask ourselves is who is the Antichrist? How can we identify him accurately?"

Murray spoke up and replied, "The Antichrist is a counterfeit HaMashiach."

Joel in turn replied, "That is correct, Murray. Now where do we find the scriptural support for that statement?"

Rifling through the pages of scripture in his Bible, he replied, "The one scripture I know about Antichrist is found in first John 2:22–23. It reads, 'Who is a liar but he that denieth that Yeshua is HaMashiach? He is the Antichrist that denieth the Father and the Son. Whosoever denieth the Son the same hath not the Father, but he that acknowledges the Son hath the Father also.'"

"Okay, Murray. What does this scripture tell us about the character of the Antichrist?"

He replied, "He is a liar. And the lie he will teach is that Yeshua is not the HaMashiach. In other words he demotes Yeshua. How? By denying His deity. He will cause many people to convert to his belief that Yeshua was just a man, or a smaller God, but not Almighty God. Over the past two-thousand years there have and still are present today, many who can be called Antichrist, who promote this same lie. In fact first John 2:18 tells us that. I'll read it."

Smiling, Joel leafed through the pages of his Bible and read aloud, "Little children it is the last time and as ye have heard that Antichrist shall come, even now there are many Antichrists; whereby we know that it is the last time." Joel asked, "Now what will make the last Antichrist stand out from among all the other Antichrists?"

Joel asked me, "See if you can find out what will make the last Antichrist stand out as distinct from all the other Antichrists? Murray, please read 2nd Thessalonians 2:3 and 4 for us."

Elated to be among those who made up the School of the Prophets, Murray eagerly read, "Let no man deceive you by any means: for that day shall not come, except there come a falling away first, and that man of sin be revealed, the son of perdition. Who opposeth and exalteth himself above all that is called God, or that is worshiped, so that he as God sitteth in the temple of God, shewing himself that he is God."

When he stopped reading, Joel asked, "Murray, what is it that makes him stand out from all the other Antichrists?"

He replied, "He will sit in the temple of God and make others think he is God. This shows he can be labeled mentally as being one who is psychotic. He will make the claim that Yeshua is a myth, made up by the Jews. And it is he that is GOD incarnate. This would make him the most impious and irreverent of men."

"Now," Joel asked, "What temple could this verse be talking about?"

"Marvin interjected and said, "The third Temple. The one that our Jewish Rabbis have built and are now using," he replied.

Joel said, "Continue with 2nd Thessalonians 2, read verse 9, Murray."

Running his finger down to verse nine, he read, "Even him, whose coming is after the working of Satan with all power and signs and lying wonders."

"So, Murray," asked Joel, "Who is said to be influencing this man?"

I replied, "Satan."

Joel exclaimed, "Yes, and for that reason this man will be the most wicked man of the human race. He will exercise the maximum of malice! He shall never do a good act! He will be nihilistic, destroying morals and all laws, including the Ten Commandments! In other words, he will have no moral character, he will be an outlaw. But he will be so slick that he will be able to cover that up. How? By presenting his own ten codes to replace the Ten Commandments! He will be the sharpest con artist ever."

Joel continued and asked him, "Murray, why is it so important that when this man comes we must be able to identify him?"

He replied, "I am not sure. But, in the past there have been others who fit the identification marks of the Antichrist."

Joel replied, "Yes, in the past we could say other world leaders have risen that were identified as the Antichrist. To mention a few, there was Nero, Attila the Hun, Alaris the Goth, Napoleon, Stalin, Lenin, Mussolini and Hitler. If ever anyone came close, it was Hitler. For he slaughtered six million Jews, he was also a great orator, conceited, took drugs and dealt in the occult. He and all of these men were military geniuses, tyrants, violent men, murdering millions of people, many their own people. And what about the Communists of our present day and of China's Chairman Mao? He even has an Antichrist bible called, 'The Thoughts of Chairman Mao.' All who follow his doctrine believe that, 'Belief in God is a superstition.' You could therefore conclude that any of these geniuses with cruel instincts at being evil could be the Antichrist. For he will destroy all faith in the Bible, saying it is all a lie."

Murray asked Joel, "What then identifies the final Antichrist as different from these men?"

Barry, who had been quiet for quite some time now, spoke up, "A fact that was missing when those men were alive is the development of the Information Age, mentioned in Daniel 12:4, 'And knowledge shall be increased.' Instant, international knowledge at the tip of the computer did not exist up until today, in our generation!"

Murray was in deep thought for a moment, eyes glazed over, "That is simply incredible! This is a fact that no one today could deny! This is simply awesome! How I thank the Messiah for letting Moshe come across my path when he did. I am really grateful to be able to understand God and the Holy Scriptures. I want to thank all of you too for patiently disciplining me."

Moshe patted Murray on the back and said, "You're a blessing to us too, Murray."

Marvin then went on, "Let's continue to cover the remaining facts about how we can identify the Antichrist. Holy Scripture indicates that this man will be a brainstorming commercial genius, an international banker. He will take economic control of the world, as Daniel 11:43 indicates, 'He shall have power over the treasures of gold and of silver."

"Now notice Murray that in all of previous history, there is not one person able to accomplish this since the global community and the opportunity to take over the one world government, one world economy never existed until now. The policy of 'brainstorming' also never existed until Alex Osborn developed it in the early 1950s. A genius, Osborn introduced masterpieces with a single brush stroke, inventing revolutionary theorems overnight. Initially he designed the technique of 'brainstorming' to increase the creativity of American scientists and engineers. The technique allows any idea on the table. Criticism is not allowed. Bizarre ideas are welcome; and no critiquing takes place until the ideas are generated."

"Now, Murray," Marvin went on, "Also, one missing factor in prophecy is the time element. However, a verse in Daniel identifies a characteristic about what type of time it will be that will differentiate it from any other time in prophetic history. Daniel 12:1 distinguishes it as, 'A time of ... trouble such as never was since there was a nation.' It is apparent that he will appear at a time of international chaos. And it is apparent that this has happened right now."

Murray asked Moshe, "What can we expect to happen next?"

Moshe spoke up, pushing his spectacles up off his nose and said, "I can answer that. The urgency is that we are able to discern what is going on in the real world up above us and what is going on this very moment shows that he has appeared. Now we all know that this latest report reveals that Iraq has set up a new ten Arab Nations Coup forming an international political alliance that has taken over Jordan with intent to claim the treasures, gold and silver veins. We still hold the Title Deed to the land where these are located. It will mean that we have a wicked fight to hold our claim of that property, notably the area surrounding the George Alenby Bridge. To secure our land, they, along with their allies and their armies, are marching against Jerusalem, but are temporarily being kept at bay at the southern tip of the Euphrates River. In our favor, a severe sand storm, a Genie, has immobilized them. This action taken by Ahmet has broken the seven year peace treaty in only three and a half years."

Murray blurted out, "This indicates that the Antichrist's coming is here and that Yeshua HaMashiach will be coming soon for us!"

153

Marvin interjected, "Well, let's briefly go over the fact about the Antichrist. Moshe, jot down the scriptures on the description of the Antichrist and his identifying marks. You can do it in the form of an outline."

Moshe, never lifting up his eyes nodded his head up and down, indicating a "yes" to Marvin, as he continued to record.

Marvin went on, "We will discuss this identification mark which is mentioned in Daniel 11:37."

"Murray, would you read this verse and tell us how does this verse identify him?"

Flipping through the pages of his Bible, he read, "Neither shall he regard the God of his fathers, nor the desire of women, nor regard any God: for he shall magnify himself above all."

Moshe asked me, "Murray, what does this verse tell us about the identity of the Antichrist?"

He said, "He shall not regard the God of his fathers. It seems to me that when the expression, 'God of his fathers' appears in the Hebrew Scriptures, it was used to refer to Abraham, Isaac and Jacob as the fathers of Israel. Would that identify him as an unbelieving Jew? Or perhaps he could be identified as a secular Jew? Might his identity be a Jew who was a believer and ends up returning to God and winds up becoming an atheist?"

Moshe replied, "That sounds like a strong probability, or he could be an ex-Kabbalist or an ex-Hasidic Jew. Or he could be a half-breed, half Jewish and half Arab. There is a strong possibility that he will be an accomplished mystic who becomes an unbeliever. It would be someone who is delusional; who at one time had a relationship with God, then turns around, abandons that relationship and becomes an unbeliever that thinks he is God! This would mean he is psychotic and very dangerous. Worse yet, Daniel 7:25 says that he will actually turn against God and against God's people. 'And he shall speak great words against the most High and shall wear out the saints of the most high.'"

Murray spoke up, "I know that in today's world, when someone claims to believe that he is God, he is looked upon by the psychiatric profession as being psychotic, or as you just mentioned, Moshe, that this makes them delusional. So, I guess that means that the Antichrist will have a major mental illness. It could also mean that he will be a closet drug user."

Marvin chimed in and said, "Murray, the Lord is blessing you with great insight into Holy Scripture. Praise Him!"

"Now," Marvin went on, "What other identifying mark of the Antichrist is mentioned in this verse, Murray?"

Looking through the verse, then looking up at Moshe, Marvin, Barry and then Joel, his face turned red and somewhat startled, he inquired, "Will he be a homosexual? I mean if he has no lust for women, why would the scripture make that point stand out?"

Marvin replied, "Murray, that is also a very strong possibility. Revelation 18:23 and 16:13–14 does mention unclean spirits and that the Antichrist will not be attracted to women, use of drugs, satanic worship and other types of sorceries, including communication with the dead. He will also be someone capable of advanced thinking, perhaps educated by magicians, thereby gaining perfect knowledge of the arts and magic. Indications are that he will hold Ph.D.'s in all of the sciences. He will use technology to promote the occult with magic."

"And all of our intelligence reports identify that Ahmet fits the above descriptions."

Marvin said, "Yes, it looks that way. It is a fact that he will also use religion to draw worship after himself. By doing this he will abolish true worship, rationalizing and distorting the truth. He will be a liar."

"That," Marvin went on, "Leads us to very briefly cover our next topic, the code of the Antichrist, 666."

Murray said, "I have heard so many ways you can interpret 666. Can you cover it briefly?"

"Well," Marvin continued, "We are going to eliminate the usual past interpretations for that number and just say one thing stands out, there are 6,666 sentences in the Koran. Mohammed, one of the many past Antichrists wrote the Koran. My only conclusion is that it could mean that the last and final Antichrist is someone whose mother was Jewish and father was a Muslim and following his mother he becomes a devout Jew. When his mother dies, he converts to the Muslim religion and leaves '... the God of his Fathers.' When his father dies, he turns his back on the Muslim religion and becomes an avowed atheist."

Marvin said, "This leads us into our next topic, what are the signs of Yeshua's coming?"

"Barry will cover this topic, but how about if you continue to read the verses, Murray?"

He said, "I am ready and willing."

Barry, always an astute reader, also had a knack for details. He spoke up and asked him to turn to Matthew 24:1–3 and read.

Flipping through the pages of his Bible, he came to the passages and began to read. "And Yeshua went out, and departed from the temple: and his disciples came to him for to shew him the buildings of the temple. And Yeshua said unto them, See ye not all these things? Verily I say unto you, there shall not be left here one stone upon another,

155

that shall not be thrown down. And as he sat upon the Mount of Olives, the disciples came unto him privately, saying, Tell us, when shall these things be and what shall be the sign of thy coming, and of the end of the world?"

Barry said, "Note, Yeshua places both His coming again, tying it in with the same event as the end of the world."

Then Murray asked Barry, "Wasn't Yeshua telling them when the second Temple would be destroyed? And that did come true when the Roman General Titus destroyed it in A.D. 70?"

"Yes," replied Barry. "He told them the temple would be destroyed. But He did not answer them with a date. He only gave the events that would surround it."

Inquisitive, Murray asked, "Well, then Barry, why didn't Yeshua come back right after that happened? Especially when most of the New Testament writers believed and claimed that His second coming was 'coming soon.'"

Barry said, "That's a good question, Murray, and one that could lead to the very serious deception of doubt. I believe also that this is a question that could lie in the back of some Christians' minds. Now, in order to answer that question, we need to examine it a little further."

"Notice Murray, that Matthew 24:3 states there is a threefold question. One is, 'When shall these things be?'"

Barry replied, "One reason is that scripture tells us that one thousand years is with God as one day."

Barry then asked Moshe to record 2nd Peter 3:8 in their notes. Moshe quickly jotted it down.

Barry went on, "Some will succumb to this deception called doubt. Doubts about the very questions you have and are asking. Is He coming soon? And when is He coming?"

"Murray, please continue reading. Read what Peter had to say about this in 2nd Peter 2:1, Murray."

He read out loud, "But there were false prophets among the people, even as there shall be false teachers among you, who privily shall bring in damnable heresies, even denying the Lord that bought them … "

"Now what did Peter have to say about what these false teachers will say that is deceptive about Yeshua coming again?"

Murray read 2nd Peter 3:3–4, "Knowing this first, that there shall come in the last days scoffers … And saying where is the promise of his coming? For all things continue as they were from the beginning of creation."

"Murray, can you see how people can be deceived? Can you see how creating doubt leads to deception? Can you see how they, like the serpent in the Garden of Eden deceived Eve, will create doubt about Yeshua's words? So, we must watch out for any thoughts that would cause us to stop believing what Yeshua taught us about His second coming."

Murray was astounded by how simple doubt can rear its ugly head. He spoke up and replied, "Yes, I can see people looking back on the past two thousand years and still Yeshua has yet to return."

Barry said, "That fox, Satan, will be hard at work to try and make Christians doubt that Yeshua is ever coming back. We believe that this is the 'strong delusion' mentioned in Second Thessalonians 2:1–4. It will cause many to let the doubt discourage them, and thus, prone to give up their faith."

"After all, He is real to us and it will not matter when He comes back in the flesh because every believer has Him present within himself. He may therefore come for some of us to be with Him at the time of our death. Or we may be one who is alive when He returns to earth. So, either way, we will be with Him."

"However, we need not worry or be anxious about these coming deceptions. Why? Because we are going to prepare information that will help our brothers and sisters here with us to do as Peter commanded in 2nd Peter 3:18, 'Grow in grace and the knowledge of our Lord and Savior Yeshua HaMashiach. Then as now, we can trust the Holy Spirit to help us keep vigilant and watchful and to maintain our relationship with the Lord, daily.' Making sure we go to Him confiding in Him that we are being tempted to doubt."

"This then," Barry said, "Takes us to the second and third part of the threefold question in Matthew 24:3. 'And what will be the sign of thy coming and of the end of the world?' Notice both the signs of His coming are tied into the end of the world. Just in passing let us include what the word 'world' means. It means, system of things or the way the world is run. It does not mean the end of the earth."

Barry continued, "In Matthew 24:4–8 Yeshua gives four general signs: 1) false HaMashiach, 2) famine and pestilence (disease), 3) wars, and 4) increases in earthquakes. After these four general signs, follows one special sign that definitely marks the beginning of the end (not the final end). For Yeshua said in verse 8, 'All these (four general signs) things must come to pass, but the end is not yet.'"

Barry asked, "Murray will you read what sign it is that will mark the beginning of the end?"

He did not hesitate. Running his finger down the page he read Matthew 24:7, "For nation shall rise against nation and kingdom against kingdom."

Barry asked him, "When did this event happen?"

He did not have to ponder over that answer. He just blurted out, "World War I in 1914. It was the very first time in all of man's recorded history that the entire world was involved in one war. Therefore the name given it marks it standing out from all and any other wars by mankind."

Barry said, "Correct Murray. So, the sign, WWI, the year that global war began in 1914 marks that time as the 'beginning of the end.' Matthew 24:9–12," Barry went on, "Tells us other things that will occur during the time of the end. One is that all nations will hate us for believing in Yeshua. Many Christians will be unable to take the persecution and turn their backs on the Lord. And they will go against their own brothers and sisters in the Lord, their fellow Christians. A lot of false prophets will be around. A lot of sin and the pleasures of sin will increase and their love for God will grow cold." He found the scripture and reverently read it out loud, "But beloved, be not ignorant of this one thing, that one day is with the Lord as a thousand years, and a thousand years as one day." Barry said, "So, God's timing and man's times are not the same."

"What is most important for all Christians to understand is that these are going to be. What sign then does Yeshua tell us will stand out that will show that His coming is near and that the final end of this world has arrived?"

Barry noticed that Marvin was getting somewhat restless and needed to have some input into this review of topics, so appropriate to the current events unraveling before them.

So, Barry called on Marvin and asked him, "Marvin, would you please read Matthew 24:14 for us?"

Marvin obliged and read out loud, "And this gospel of the kingdom shall be preached in all the world for a witness unto all nations and then shall the end come."

When Marvin finished reading the text he asked the question, "How will we know when the witness to all nations is complete, and the time for His coming has arrived?"

Barry said, "Good question, Marvin. Read Matthew 24:21, 29–30 and let's see how Yeshua Himself answers that question."

Marvin cleared his throat and started to read out loud. "For there shall be great tribulation such as was not since the beginning of the world to this time, no, nor ever shall be … Immediately after the tribulation of those days shall the sun be darkened and the moon shall not give her light, and the stars shall fall from heaven, and the powers of the heaven shall be shaken: and then shall appear the sign of the Son of man in heaven: and then shall all the tribes of the earth mourn, and they shall see the Son of man coming in the clouds of heaven with power and great glory."

"So then, how can we recognize what will be 'the sign of His coming?'" Answering the question, Marvin went on, "There will be visible extreme geographical and cosmic changes affecting the entire globe. Changes so severe that they will block out the sun and the moon. The only events that could possibly do this is for a direct impact by an asteroid or a comet upon the earth, leaving its scar of a cloud of dust so thick, it would block out the sun and the moon. Or it could occur by a super volcanic eruption. Or a MCGA thrust earthquake. Revelation 6:12–14 reveals this will all happen when the sixth seal is opened. 'And I beheld when he had opened the sixth seal, and lo, there was a great earthquake: and the sun darkened the earth ... and the heavens departed as a scroll when it is rolled together, and every mountain and every iles were moved out of their places.'"

"So, one of these three outstanding signs will signal Yeshua is coming back. But, what does He do before He sets His feet upon the earth? Specifically He mentions the location as the Mount of Olives." Marvin still ready to keep involved said, "Let's turn to Mark 13:27." And he read out loud, "'And he shall send his angels with a great sound of a trumpet,' the one the Apostle Paul talked about in 1st Corinthians 15:53 as the last trumpet. Revelation calls the last trumpet, the seventh trumpet."

"'And they shall gather together his elect, from the four winds, from one end of heaven to the other.' And Mark 13:27 says, 'And then shall he send his angels and shall gather together his elect from the four winds, from the uttermost part of the earth to the uttermost part of heaven.'" Marvin continued, "There is one more important sign which signals Yeshua's return to our terra firma. That is the conversion of our nation, Israel, the political, religious and nonreligious Israel. We find this in Matthew 23:37–39 when Yeshua was speaking to the Jewish leaders." Marvin went on to read it out loud as Moshe continued to record. "... For I say unto you, ye shall not see me henceforth, till ye shall say, Blessed is he that cometh in the name of the Lord." Marvin said, "For them to see Him, He would have to be visible on earth. They would include those written in Revelation that every eye shall see Him."

"Amen," Barry, Joel, Moshe, Marvin and Murray said in unison.

Marvin said, "This topic is over. Now let's talk about the Great Tribulation and, as the Holy Scripture calls it, the Time of Jacob's Trouble.

Right now we are in tribulation, not unlike many of our brethren in many parts of the world today along with those throughout the ages. But, the great tribulation is the worse. Let's list all the verses and let them speak for themselves."

Marvin continued, "Now we come to what follows the catastrophic geographical and cosmic changes that will take place on the earth. It will be our next topic, the Exchange of Government Power."

"It will take place," he said, "At the sounding of the seventh trumpet, which is also the last trumpet." And he read on in Revelation 12:15–18, "'And the seventh angel sounded; and there were great voices in heaven saying, The kingdoms of this world, are become the kingdoms of our Lord and of his HaMashiach; and he shall reign forever and ever.' This ties in with 1st Corinthians 15:23–24, speaking of the resurrection. 'But every man in his own order, HaMashiach the first fruits; afterward, they are HaMashiach at his coming.'"

Marvin said, "In 1 Corinthians 15:51–52, the Apostle Paul says, 'Behold, I shew you a mystery; we shall not all sleep, but we shall all be changed, In a moment, in the twinkling of an eye, at the last trump (7th Trumpet of Revelation 11:15). For the trumpet shall sound, and the dead shall be raised.' So brothers, we have a lot to look forward to."

"Amen," said Moshe, Barry, Joel and Murray, once again in unison.

Murray asked Marvin, "What are we to make of those who predict exact dates for His coming and the end of the world? Such as the Myna's date of December 21, 2012. Or the asteroid Impasse that is supposed to impact earth on April 13, 2021."

"Well, Murray, the two dates answer that question. It can't come in 2012 and then again in 2021 can it? And we have Yeshua's word, 'No man knows the day or the hour.' We only know the season and we only have an outline with no date. This completes this topic."

"Now for our next topic," said Marvin, "Joel will cover it." Joel, stood up, towering over Marvin, giving him a big bear hug.

Moshe, Barry and Murray let out a big laugh. The sight of Marvin standing next to Joel made them look like those American comics in the past known as Mutt and Jeff.

Joel composed himself, letting out a little chuckle and said, "Our next topic is the Millennial Rule of Christ."

"The word millennium, or one-thousand years, comes from two Latin words: mille for 1000 and annum for year."

"So, there are some who believe there will be no millennial rule of Christ."

"They believe and interpret Daniel the second and seventh chapters to be totally spiritual. Thus, they reject a literal 1000-year fulfillment. They believe man will achieve perfection through scientific discoveries. And I might add my own comment on that interpretation. This is one of the most deadly doubts. Why? Science is already doing just that. With promises of the possibility of being able to live for a thousand years and still stay young at the same age of thirty throughout that time. If these promises continue to come true and Yeshua still has not returned, doubt will rear its ugly head and many will believe what the Apostle Peter said would come true. Many will say, Where is the promise of His coming? All things remain the same from the beginning? This is what the Great Deception is!"

"We will not be here for the seven bowls. These believe that Yeshua rules from heaven only and when He does come a second time it will be for the general resurrection of all the dead."

"Now onto Pre-Millennialism. It starts with the prefix 'pre,' which means before."

"Those of us who believe," said Marvin, "That HaMashiach will return a second time, before the start of the 1000 year rule of a literal, political kingdom, as King, together with His saints. It will be worldwide in scope. Today, we and most Christian Fundamentalists hold this belief." Marvin cleared his throat several times. He was nervous talking about Post-Millennialism because of its great tendency for being extremely deceptive.

"Post-Millennialism," Marvin stated, "Starts with the prefix 'post,' meaning 'after.' Those who hold this belief believe that Christ will come after the 1000 years."

"They believe that the Kingdom of God will be literal, but that it will not be set up by Christ. They believe the same as I stated earlier about Pre-Millennialism, that it will be established by human efforts, such as today's expanding knowledge, new discoveries and inventions. They believe that the Church has the responsibility to help bring in the Kingdom. HaMashiach's second coming will occur at the close of the Millennium, as the crowning event of that golden age. This is where we must make sure that our brothers and sisters understand that this is a deception. It will be easy to fall into this belief trap, due to the fact that if we look around us, we do see great developments that appear to be headed in that direction. That would indicate the natural man's view, but Christians must beware of being fooled into this deception."

"What makes me so upset about Post-Millennialism is that it will be so easy to fall into this deception and believe that Yeshua will not be coming back after all. Why? Because people will look back and see how the realities of man's efforts have been expanding and it looks like they will not need Yeshua to come back. They believe they can do it all themselves, that they can bring in the golden age without His divine intervention. We must really watch because many signs Yeshua left us have today been fulfilled. So, it becomes easy for a Christian to be deceived into believing the lie. Peter warned us of this in 2nd Peter 3:3–4, 'Knowing this first, that there shall come in the last days scoffers, walking after their own lusts. And saying, where is the promise of his coming? For all things continue as they were from the beginning of creation.'"

Joel said, "This concludes this topic."

Moshe was to preside over the next topic. So, he asked Barry, "Will you take down the recording of our next topic?"

Barry replied, "Sure Moshe. I am ready. Proceed."

Moshe began, "This will be our final topic. We are including this sacred topic, the Spiritual Experience of the Baptism in the Holy Spirit, because any error or misunderstanding brings with Yeshua's edict of the unpardonable sin to those who ascribe the works of the Holy Spirit to Satan." (See Matthew 12:24, 31 & 32.)

Moshe began, "Let me say from the outset, we, the School of the Prophets have decided to keep this sacred topic as simple as possible and just as easy to comprehend. Our approach will focus on the actual practical side of this supernatural experience. It is a gift that is received as a subjective experience, since each person who receives it, receives it differently. So we will not conduct an in-depth psychological or theological study. However, we will list the benefits when receiving the gift of the Baptism in the Holy Spirit. We will warn of the extreme danger which Christian denominations face who oppose, censure, object and reject belief in the works of the Holy Spirit for today and the gifts of the Holy Spirit when one has received the Baptism in the Holy Spirit. We will include one true actual experience so that it makes clear why we all need to enter into this sacred life giving, life changing experience with the Holy Spirit."

Moshe said, "Before we go any further, I want to make it clear that the Holy Spirit is not a force, not the wind, but He is a real person. He has the divine nature of GOD the Father and GOD the Son. So He is included in the Godhead of the Holy Trinity. He speaks, He guides us and directs our paths on the straight and narrow. And we will refer to Him as 'He.' He is a gift from GOD the Father and HaMashiach, GOD the Son, to His body, His church" (1st Corinthians 12:4–11).

"Who is the person who has sent this gift to us? I'll read whom John the Baptist says He is, found written in Luke 3:16 '... John answered, saying unto them all, I indeed baptize thee with water; but one mightier than I cometh, the latchet of whose shoe I am not worthy to unloose, He shall baptize you with the Holy Ghost and with fire.'"

Moshe then asked, "Murray, will you please read out loud 1st Corinthians 12:7 for us?"

Without any hesitation, he turned to the page and read, "'But the manifestation of the Spirit is given to every man to profit.' One of the benefits it will produce in us is a desire to lead a more holy life. This is what the Holy Spirit will work in us. His work is to conform our character to the character of Yeshua HaMashiach. This can occur in some instantaneously, but always continuously. He will help us advance and grow in virtues and increase in grace. Also we can expect to have a closer union and increased love with and for Yeshua HaMashiach because of the work of the Holy Spirit's power in transforming us. He will help us practice scriptural behavior and living. He will help us follow the advice in Ephesians 5:8, 'Keep on being filled with the Spirit.' He will help us learn generosity and unselfish giving. He will create higher morals and thoughts, keeping our conscience clean and clear. He will teach us humility. He will help us to change the behavior of our attitudes and our desires."

"Our part," Moshe went on, "Will be to cooperate with His work in His leading us into closer union with the Father, the Son and the Holy Spirit, and in practicing the Word of GOD that will help us to accomplish spiritual growth. This is brought out in Romans 12:2, 'And be not conformed to this world: but be ye transformed by the renewing of your mind.'"

"This indicates that we must take action to discipline and to change our old way of thinking and living. We are not to be passive if our supernatural transformation is to take place."

"This is indicated in 1st John 3:2, 'Behold now are we the sons of God … we know that when He shall appear, we shall be like Him …'"

"The Baptism in the Holy Spirit then, awakens our spiritual life."

Moshe continued, "Now we will cover censure against His manifestations, scandalous practices, and counterfeits; and censure and objections by some denominations due to what they call excesses leveled at some people, thereby creating a hindering spirit to His manifestations and His works."

"These Christian denominations know the manifestations and workings of the Holy Spirit yet they object to the workings manifested by His supernatural effects that happen to some people when they receive it, i.e., tears, trembling, groans, loud outcries, fainting, or agonies of the body, ecstasy, and sometimes visions. These manifestations and workings of the Holy Spirit being censured by them brings with it sin. Sin against the sacredness of the Holy Spirit's works therefore unless corrected, they stand on dangerous ground and they face serious consequences. Some which have already started to occur and will increase in severity."

"Now this subjective supernatural experience is controversial and is considered by some Christian denominations to be a deception and they say it is not for today. Or it is from the devil. These are only the opinions of men. There is not one scripture that agrees with their assumptions and these false accusations."

Moshe went on, "The irony is that it is a deception not to believe this holy experience is for today."

"We must recognize that even though speaking in tongues and other spiritual gifts may be abused by some who get carried away while they are under intense thought and strong emotions, it does not mean that they should be prohibited or censured. For those who do prohibit, censure, hinder or attribute the works of the Holy Spirit to the works of the devil, there are serious consequences, i.e., Mark 3:28–30, 'Verily I say unto you, all things shall be forgiven unto the sons of men, and blasphemers wherewith so ever they shall blaspheme. But, he that shall blaspheme against the Holy Spirit hath never forgiveness, but is in danger of eternal damnation. Because they said, He hath an unclean spirit.'"

Moshe continued, "We will list the following scriptures for study. We will encourage all of our brothers and sisters who have not yet entered into this experience to study these passages and then in prayer ask Yeshua our Lord to baptize them according to the patterns shown here in the Word. They are, Acts 2, Acts 8:14–17, and Acts 10:44–47."

"Other warnings can be found in 1st Thessalonians 5:19, 'Do not quench Him,' and in Ephesians 4:30, 'Don't grieve Him.' So, we can conclude that these warnings would include any censure against the manifestations and workings to be included as to quench and or grieve Him."

"The final warning can be found in Matthew 25:1–10. Yeshua Himself said, 'When the Bridegroom cometh' five out of the ten virgins will not have oil (symbol of the Holy Spirit) in their lamps and while they are gone to purchase some, Yeshua arrives and the door is shut. Those without their oil will not make it!"

"Now," Moshe said, "To receive this experience it is required that we, in our minds, relinquish our total selves, mentally and emotionally, realizing the superiority of God in all of our thoughts, words and actions. This is called yielding to the Holy Spirit, completely and voluntarily complying (by being obedient) to all that He reveals to you individually for your sanctification and transformation into the image of HaMashiach. Note, this does not mean being thoughtless or emotionless, but putting our thoughts secondary to His, making His thoughts take first place."

Moshe went on, "This means we must be willing and obedient (Isaiah 1:19) and flexible and not stubborn and proud, not wanting to give up some of our thoughts that may not be in line with God's leading, guiding or directing."

Anxious, Murray interrupted Moshe, "I've never received this extraordinary supernatural baptism in the Holy Spirit. I would like to now."

Moshe said, "Okay. Let everyone here lay hands on Murray and pray for Yeshua HaMashiach, our Yeshua, to baptize Murray in the Holy Spirit."

"Now, just to interject," Moshe said, "Murray, there are some who believe you do not have to lay on hands to receive this experience because of the incident in Acts when the Apostle Peter witnessed to Cornelius and his family and friends and they were all baptized in the Holy Spirit while he was preaching and teaching. But we have other verses showing that they 'laid hands on them.' So we, not wanting to presume upon the Holy Spirit and Yeshua Himself, the Baptizer, we choose to lay our hands and pray for you to receive this sacred baptism." Everyone gathered around him. They laid hands upon him and prayed.

"Dear Yeshua, we are believing here together and asking You the Baptizer to baptize Murray in the Holy Spirit. Murray, receive ye the Holy Spirit. Amen."

Everyone followed with an "amen."

Then he asked them all, "What will happen now?"

Moshe replied, "You will feel the power of the Holy Spirit. He will give you the gift of speaking in tongues, which will validate that you have been baptized in the Holy Spirit."

He said, "But I have not received the speaking in tongues yet."

"Don't worry, Murray, you will. And when you do, tell us about it."

He replied, "I sure will."

Moshe closed his Bible and said, "It's growing late now. How about if we call it a night and get some much needed sleep?"

Everyone agreed and Moshe closed the School in prayer.

Murray tried to get to sleep but a strange tingling went through his body, not hurting him, but it kept him awake. Then he heard a voice say to him, "Get up and go pray.'"

He responded, "I am too tired." He still could not get to sleep because the tingling in his body remained.

For a second time Murray heard a voice say, "Get up and go pray.

He responded once again and said, "I am too tired." Then he heard the voice for the third time, only this time it sounded more firm and added an instruction.

The voice said, "Get up and go pray, and don't look at the clock!"

Murray was very calm. Hearing a voice and not seeing a body did not frighten him. And he knew he was not having a psychotic experience. And he knew he was not mentally ill.

So, Murray finally got up out of bed and fell to his knees. This was the very first time he had ever assumed this position to pray of his own accord.

Murray started to pray. Astounded, he found himself confessing sins he did not even know he had, self-hatred of others.

When he finished praying and confessing his sins, he returned to his bed.

While lying on his back, Murray closed his eyes and across the screen of his mind's eye he saw what looked like a ticker tape going across the screen on the inside of his mind. He also saw a pen. He saw that the pen was really a finger, an index finger to be exact. The finger began writing in what looked like the shape of a needle on a seismograph or a telegraph would record data. It was writing out words, but not in English. He found himself repeating the words as they continued to move, like a ticker tape. These were words that he'd never seen before. Yet, he began to repeat them in his mind as they passed by his inner vision.

Needless to say, he felt so excited he could hardly go back to sleep, but when he did, he felt like he was wrapped in a warm loving peace. It had to be Yeshua God, for who else could transmit a voice and a ticker tape message in another language, one he had no knowledge of and which he could understand. It certainly was not another human calling him via the cell phone!

When he woke up, he dressed hurriedly and walked swiftly over to Moshe's room.

Rushing into the room, he shouted, "Moshe, Moshe, it happened. I received the baptism in the Holy Spirit!" And before Moshe could respond, he excitedly related to Moshe exactly what had happened to him before he fell asleep last night and how he had received his prayer language speaking in tongues.

"Moshe," Murray said, "Even though I have never seen these words that were written out for me, I understood their message. Most of it consisted of high praises to God."

Moshe replied, "We told you that you would experience this wonderful supernatural gift from Yeshua, our HaMashiach. But, yours is only the second one that I heard of that was given this experience in such a rare way."

"Moshe," Murray exclaimed, "I feel such joy and peace. I feel so clean inside. It's wonderful, Moshe!"

Moshe said, "Praise the Lord, Murray. Let's go right on over to the Library. We can join the others and you can tell them how Yeshua has baptized you in the Holy Spirit."

Moshe and Murray walked down the corridor to the Library. However, Murray felt like skipping instead of walking. One could say he was almost deliriously happy. They greeted Joel, Barry and Marvin, saying, "Good morning, brothers."

"Good morning to you both," they all responded.

Suddenly, out of nowhere, a great sound, like the roar of a passing freight train filled the room. The earth rumbled under their feet. All of the books and bookcases fell to the floor.

Joel, large as he was, had been standing and fell to the ground with a large thud. One wall of the room collapsed, sending dirt, rocks, books, chairs and wood flying in all different directions, missing Joel by inches.

Moshe, Marvin, Barry and Murray quickly took hold of Joel's feet and head and carried him out of the room and into the hall, shutting the door behind them.

Murray said, "What hit us?"

Marvin coughing from the stirred up dirt said, "I don't know!"

Barry said, "I doubt that it was a nuclear blast."

Moshe, still holding onto Joel's head said, "It could have been an earthquake, but strangely there are no aftershocks." Then turning Joel's head to the side he saw it was bleeding. "Look," Moshe exclaimed, "The back of Joel's head is bleeding. He's knocked out cold from the blow, but praise the Lord he's breathing okay. Quick, Murray, give me your shirt. I'll wrap it around his head. That should stop the bleeding."

Not wasting a second he quickly took his shirt off, ripping it in half and tied it around Joel's head to stop the bleeding.

It had only been a minute or two since the blast had occurred, when suddenly it grew very quiet.

Moshe took control, "Barry, you, Marvin and Murray take Joel to one of the caves that has an empty bed. Call on one of the

167

paramedics in first aid. See if any of the brothers and sisters have been injured. If they have, reassure them while we check out the cause of the blast, then come back here and we will check out what has happened." Moshe said, "I hope it's not the military looking for us. Perhaps they have blasted the safe house overhead."

Murray said, "Barry, I'll go back into the room and see if the dust has settled and see what I can find out."

Barry said, "Okay, we'll be back as soon as we get Joel tended to and after we have checked on the others."

Meanwhile, Marvin and Moshe had found some blue tarp. Folding the tarp in half they created a makeshift gurney and placed Joel on top of it. With that they left the hall, carrying Joel to first aid.

Murray stepped back into the room. Looking at the rubble he saw a lifeless human hand protruding from the debris. Stunned by the sight, he walked over to the pile of rocks, breathing in the dust still clinging to the air in the room. He stepped over the pile of rocks and cleared away the debris wondering whom it was that lie buried there. Hurriedly, but cautiously, fearful that the rest of the room would collapse, he reached the body. The first thing he did was to check for a pulse. There was none. Then he checked his airway but there was none. The man was dead, too late for CPR.

Hoping to find some identification, he rifled through the man's pockets. The dead man was wearing a military combat suit appearing oddly out of place. All he could find was the name Chondriana 83 written on a tag on his vest. Murray didn't see a weapon.

Murray grew sick at heart that the soldier was no longer alive. He took his jacket off and gently covered the soldier who lay dead beneath his feet. He left the room and entered the corridor.

Just then, Barry, Marvin and Moshe returned to the scene.

"How is Joel," Murray asked excitedly?

Marvin, still coughing from the dust that was still clinging to the air, spoke up and replied, "Well Murray, praise the Lord, he has regained consciousness. He did sustain a large gash on the right side of the back of his head, but the medics felt a few stitches and some rest will be all he will need."

In a sense of relief, Murray wiped his forehead with the other half of his shirt.

"Look," Murray said, "I don't know what has happened yet or what caused the collapse of the wall inside our library, but you should be prepared. There is a dead soldier inside."

Trembling he said, "What if someone has discovered our safe house and had come to arrest us?"

168

"Don't worry, Murray. We are safe. Did you find out his identity," Moshe inquired?

Murray said, "All I found was the name Chondriana 83 written on a tag on his vest."

Moshe said, "However, my big question is, was anyone else with him?"

"No, but it is most logical to believe he was not alone. Although he may have become lost in the labyrinth of tunnels and became separated from others in his battalion."

Barry, nervous but outwardly calm asked, "What do we do now? Shall we bury him first, then shore up the wall so no one else can come through it?"

Moshe asked Marvin, "How do you want to handle this matter?"

Marvin, a quick thinker spoke up and said, "Yes. We can bury him in some extra tarp we have and take him to the tunnel that we used to exit whenever we need to dispose of our refuse. We have plywood there. I'll make a box to bury him with outside."

When Murray heard they were going to go outside he started to get more frantic. Sweating profusely in fear he raised his voice. His words hit the others like a pen dipped in poison. He cried out, "We'll be seen. I tell you! Don't risk it! Why don't you just bury him here, out of sight?"

Somewhat taken aback by his sharp outburst, Moshe responded in a soft, calming voice and said, "Murray, slow down. We will be safe. Don't be frightened. No one will see us. Now, while Marvin and Barry dispose of this poor soldier's body, you and I will enlist the help of two others and we will as fast as possible shore up the wall that collapsed. If anyone does follow the soldier's path into the cave next to our library, they will only see the restructured wall. We will make sure we clean up every splinter, rock or book so that there will be no evidence left to create suspicion of any kind."

Moshe asked both Marvin and Barry, "Did you both check if anyone else heard the partial collapse of the wall in the library? Was anyone alarmed?"

Marvin replied, "Thank and praise the Lord, no. Everyone was still asleep. I am glad," he continued, "That this tunnel is quite a good distance from the people and out of their hearing range."

Moshe said, "Let's get moving. Marvin, you and Barry take the body to first aid." Quickly, Barry helped Marvin make a gurney from a tarp and placed the dead soldier on it.

Barry said to Marvin, "What a relief. I thought we were having an earthquake."

"So did I," said Marvin.

Trying to stifle his cough Murray said, "I thought it was the start of nuclear war!"

Barry dripping wet from the humidity wiped his brow with his sleeve and said, "Murray, let's hope that never happens."

Barry said, "I am going upstairs to see what's going on outside. If everything looks kosher I'll come back and we can carry the body upstairs and bury it outside."

Upon reaching the upstairs room of the safe house, Barry took a pair of binoculars that were hanging on a nail in the wall. Pushing aside the small drape, he peered outside. Hoping, he thought that the soldiers had passed and were gone for now. However, he still had to check all the perimeters outside the house. It was quiet, but that didn't mean they were in the clear.

Barry opened the door. He was sure no one could see him. Slowly he turned the corner of the house. As he checked the south side of the house, all was quiet with no one around. Facing the west corner of the house he noticed a huge unmanned caterpillar crane. Then turning to the north side of the house he saw an unmanned wrecking ball crane. As he crossed the east side of the house, all was still and quiet there too. After carefully checking all the perimeters of the house on the outside, he went back into the house, hoping the front door wouldn't creek.

Calmly, Barry safely descended the stairs unnoticed.

Returning to the library, he saw Moshe and said to him, "Moshe, am I glad to see you! I checked all the perimeters outside of the safe house. I saw no signs of life, but I did see unmanned heavy equipment parked outside. You don't think they are considering leveling the safe house do you?"

Moshe's bushy eyebrows shot up, the creases in his brows furrowed, "What kind of equipment did you see," he asked Barry?

Barry replied, "I saw a caterpillar and a wrecking ball crane. And even though everything was quiet and no one was around to guard or man them, I questioned their abandonment. What I wondered were two large cranes doing outside our safe house?"

Moshe said, "Sounds suspicious to me. But, since no one is around, we can try to safely bury the body without incident. Let's get Marvin and Murray and get this over with as quickly as we can. We will bury him once it gets dark outside. Perhaps after midnight."

And so after midnight they joined together.

Murray asked Moshe, "Moshe, is three feet deep enough to bury the body? I am getting shaky, hoping no one will discover us."

Moshe said, "Yes, three feet should be enough. Let's get out of here as quickly as possible."

About fifteen minutes later they were finished digging and placed the body in the freshly dug grave.

They returned to the caves underground. Then they washed up, had group prayer and bid each other goodnight.

The night passed by silently.

It was five o'clock in the morning. Moshe was always able to wake himself up without an alarm clock. When he was just a small boy, he trained himself every night by repeating right before he would go to sleep, "I am getting up at five o'clock in the morning."

It worked and because of this discipline he was never late for school and had a perfect record of attendance.

Everyone else was on a schedule for taking showers. It had been quite a job supplying clean water and getting rid of waste in the underground. Taking a quick shower, he changed clothes and quietly left the cave and entered a room that was set up to serve as a small chapel.

Fortunately the engineers had carved out this cave to serve as a chapel, so when someone wanted quiet time they had a place to retreat to.

Still, Moshe missed the sunlight that used to stream through his windows at his home.

He missed the chirps and caws of the singing robins and blue jays, along with the other birds that filled the sky with their peaceful and cheerful larks.

After spending half an hour communing with the Lord, he prayed, "Lord, help us do Your will and to prepare scripture that will build up and encourage the body, Your Church. It is imperative and we will need Your strength and comfort so that You can nourish us all at this crucial time. Grant us Your words in scripture that we can use to admonish, encourage and bring hope to all of us gathered here in this underground."

As he continued to meditate on the scriptures, it became clearer than ever that this would be an enormous task. He prayed again, "Oh Lord only You who are all powerful and all loving can help us to reach the others. Only the Holy Spirit can teach us the truth that You know we need to hear right now. Grant us Your continued divine guidance and direction. Help us to recognize the signs of Your divine providence as we set out to lead this large crowd of Your people gathered here, in the Valley of Achor. Amen."

Moshe then walked through a maze of tunnels until he reached the Library where they always held the School of the Prophets' sessions.

171

Moshe pondered over the explosion yesterday in the Library. He was grateful that it was not one of their persecutors. Still he wondered would others, once they found their soldier missing, follow his trail and break through their wall too?

Marvin, rather chipper, saw Moshe approaching the room and said, "Good morning, Moshe. Barry and Murray have been here but have gone to see if Joel is still okay. They will be back in a few minutes."

Moshe returned the greeting and said, "Good morning to you, Marvin. How did you sleep last night?"

"Well, in spite of the fright of falling walls, a dead body, building a coffin then hauling it upstairs, then burying it in stark darkness in fear and trembling, I slept like a rock!"

Meanwhile Barry and Murray checked on Joel.

Joel was sitting up and finishing breakfast when he glanced up and saw Barry and Murray approaching.

Joel said, "No broken bones, brothers."

Barry asked, "What about that lump the size of a golf ball on your head?"

"Six stitches patched me up," replied Joel. "I am ready to start another day. Grateful too that the one wall was all that collapsed."

Murray said, "Yes, only one wall collapsed but after you passed out I found a dead body. He was alone. He's dead. Marvin, Barry and I put together a makeshift coffin out of some plywood we had back in the storage room. Then we buried him upstairs, outside the safe house."

Joel asked the group, "Weren't you all afraid to go outside?"

"Well," Murray said, "Before we went outside, Barry surveyed the perimeters around the outside of the house. He saw no one. Later we all dug a shallow grave. Then we left as quickly as we could."

I said, "The only thing that was odd was that there was some unmanned heavy demolition equipment outside the house. We hope that they were not meant to tear down the upstairs safe house. Marvin will keep checking that out for us."

Joel asked, "What about the wall? Is it still in a collapsed state?"

"No," Murray replied. "Moshe got hold of a few of the brothers and they secured it, cleaned it up and hoped that no one else will come upon it with the same idea of creating a small cave demolition."

Joel got up from his chair and said, "I am going to wash up. I'll be a few minutes. Wait for me and we'll head back to the library together."

Moshe saw Joel, Murray and Barry approaching the library. Running up to Joel, he gave him one of his famous bear hugs and said, "Joel, I am so relieved to see you up and about. Nasty bump on your head though."

"I'll survive," said Joel. "Praise the Lord, I have no broken bones and I only needed six stitches to the back of my head, so I am in fairly good shape."

"Great, that's what I like to hear," said Moshe.

Moshe asked, "Are we ready to bring a living hope to our brothers and sisters?"

Marvin replied, "Yes. Each of us has already completed our assigned topics. We have made them as concise and to the point in an outline form. Some of it is quite deep, but we feel that ninety-five percent of our group should be able to comprehend it. Three of our sisters typed the outlines and made five hundred copies. So we should have enough to pass out. Here's your copy, Moshe."

Moshe reached out, took the outline listing the topics and said, "I'll review the material and we can present it tonight to the brethren. Meanwhile, Marvin is going to find out what he can about the presence of the bulldozers still hanging around outside the safe house."

It was daylight now. The sun's brilliant rays warmed the rooms in the safe house.

Peering through the window, Marvin, while making one of his frequent checks on outside activity, saw clearly that no one was visible on the outside of the house.

Checking as he had the night before, both the back and sides of the house, he felt it was safe to go outside and check all perimeters of the safe house. Upon opening the front door, he was about to step outside when a powerful blast like the roar of thunder pierced both of his ears. The floor rumbled beneath his feet, reverberating with the intensity and swiftness of an earthquake. Quicker than a flash of lightening, Marvin stepped back and quickly bolted the front door and the trap door leading to the underground caves. Zipping down the stairs he headed toward the library.

"Moshe, Barry, Murray," Marvin yelled as he approached the library, almost falling over some debris that had previously fallen from the wall!

Alarmed themselves from the blast heard overhead, but happy to see Marvin was okay, Moshe asked Marvin, "What's wrong? We heard the blast."

Practically stuttering from fright, Marvin let the words tumble out. "Brothers," he said, "Someone is demolishing our safe house. When we buried that soldier and saw all the heavy equipment outside our safe house that is what it must have been there for."

Murray started to shake. "Oh Lord, how will we ever get out? Moshe, will they bury us alive," he asked, his whole body shaking now?

Moshe spoke up, putting his arm around him. He said, "Murray, that will not happen."

"How can you be sure," he asked rather sheepishly?

Moshe sensing the tension in the air, calmly replied, "Murray, we have back up plans. If and when the time comes to evacuate the caves, we have seven other tunnels which lead to the outside."

"What has happened will only affect the safe house. It will mean that we will not be able to bring in any more of our people. But, all of us are safe for now. Perhaps too, those that demolished the safe house may just be part of the war effort to clear away buildings that interfere with the war and the state of emergency that our country is now in."

Not being a seasoned believer yet, Murray blurted out, "How do you know it's not the government looking for us, hunting us down? Maybe they found out where we are hiding?"

Moshe replied, "If that were true they would have come down here and apprehended us before they tore our safe house down."

A look of relief crossed Murray's face.

Marvin, calmer now tried to relieve Murray's anxieties and said, "Murray, we are all down here because we were led by the Holy Spirit to do so. He has chosen this shelter to protect the many men, women and children from the religious persecution by our own government."

Addressing himself to Murray, Moshe interjected and said, "Murray, now is not the time for us to worry. Instead, we are to regard what Yeshua, our Lord, Himself had to say about worry." Turning in his Bible to Luke 12:25, he read, "... which of you by taking thought can add to his stature one cubit? How much is a cubit," Moshe asked Barry?

Barry said, "About fifteen inches."

"Now Murray," Moshe went on, "You no doubt know how much I desire to be much taller than I am. But, is all my thinking about it or are all my thoughts ever going to make me grow a foot taller?"

Letting out a muffled laugh, Murray said, "I guess I will have to get rid of my vain thoughts spent on worrying about things that I cannot change. I can see that worry, as Yeshua said, is a waste of mental energy. It creates negative feelings and promotes negative actions. So, I am going to replace my worry-wart thoughts with good thoughts, faith and trust in Him."

Moshe said, "Murray, that is one terrific insight the Lord has just given you through His word!" Then turning the pages of his Bible Moshe said, "Now turn to Philippians 4:4, Murray."

"Listed here are the thoughts we must use to replace the thoughts of discarded worry."

Moshe began to read and comment as he went along, saying, "Be careful for nothing, but in everything by prayer and supplication with thanksgiving let your requests be made known to God." And Moshe asked, "What does verse seven and eight of this same chapter tell us will happen if we do adjust or change our old, bad habit of worry and turn it into words of praise, joy, gratitude and prayer?"

Handing his Bible over to Murray, Moshe said, "Murray, how about if you read verses seven and eight?"

Murray took the Bible from Moshe's hand. He quickly marshaled his thoughts and read, "And, the peace of God, which passeth all understanding, shall keep your hearts and minds through HaMashiach Yeshua. Finally, brethren, whatsoever things are true, whatsoever things are lovely, whatsoever things be of good report; if there be any virtue, and if there be any praise, think on these things."

Moshe then asked me, "Murray, according to these verses, what then are the good, pure and virtuous thoughts we can think, instead of the vain thoughts of worry and fear?"

He looked at Barry, Marvin and Joel who had been unusually quiet all this time.

Addressing Moshe, he said, "Moshe, show me."

Moshe replied, "Murray, what book of the Bible is on the same page as the verse in the book of Philippians?"

Glancing down at the page, he said, "The book of Colossians."

"Okay," said Moshe. "Now go down to Colossians 1:10–22 and read it."

Moshe, instead of reading the verses, quoted them in the form of a concise outline.

He said, "One, think of ways that you can please God. Two, ask yourself what good deed can I do today. Three, who is giving me a hard time that I can be longsuffering and patient with? Four, obey the command of GOD to increase in the knowledge of GOD."

Murray asked, "But what kind of knowledge?"

"That is a good question, Murray," Moshe said, "We can ask ourselves, is it abstract knowledge or live, active and experiential knowledge of GOD?"

Murray replied and asked Moshe, "What is the difference between the two kinds of knowledge?"

Moshe in turn answered and said, "Abstract knowledge is a mechanical interaction which relies on formulated thoughts or opinions. We call that just head knowledge, without feelings or emotional interaction with the real person of GOD. What I call, all talk, but no action or real experience. Whereas experiential knowledge is real, for instance when we spend time communing with GOD we receive many things that create in us thoughts of gratitude and love for the myriads of things GOD has and is still actively doing for us. With this kind of knowledge, worship and praise toward or in response to Him pours out from our hearts and not just our minds. That is not mechanical or abstract. That kind of knowledge finds out what GOD is like, His character, His actions and the motives for His actions on our behalf. It is the kind of knowledge that fosters our relationship with Him while learning about His personality."

Moshe then instructed Murray and said, "There are six signs or things that you will experience with GOD that will prove that your experience with Him is real, genuine, authentic and not abstract, not just a head knowledge about Him."

"With real experiential knowledge of God, this transpires. First, you will receive sudden illumination in your intuition. It will be illumination independent from your own human reasoning."

"Second, this will be accompanied by an unspeakable delight." (See 1 Peter 1:8 & 1 Corinthians 2:9.)

"Third, your ego will be negated and you will be delivered from self-centeredness."

"Fourth, you will experience a growth in your personality, accompanied with a change in bad habits and behavior, reaching spiritual, emotional and psychological maturity. Now Murray, read Matthew chapters five, six and seven. These verses are the apex toward a Christian's mental, emotional and spiritual maturity. Do not believe the lies of some, even in some so called Christian denominations who (usually those who reject the Baptism in the Holy Spirit) teach that those three chapters in Matthew are for when the Kingdom Age is established on earth. What these do not realize is that when Yeshua sends you the Holy Spirit, He is the one to help in your sanctification and the transformation of your thinking. So, many here today with us can testify that it is their experience. In effect their belief is false and their belief in it has created, on their part, a hindering spirit. So you, Murray, do not have to wait until the Kingdom Age. Your transformation starts in the here and now. In real time."

"Fifth, closely tied to the fourth, your character will improve. This is when GOD's character is experienced in your character. You will become more honest, more giving, more loving and a deeper prayer life will form in you."

"Sixth, the illumination you receive will be indelible. It cannot be forgotten. You will not forget the real thing."

Moshe kept quiet for a few moments, letting what he said sink into Murray's heart and mind.

Letting out a sigh it appeared that I was overwhelmed by the deep and significant answer to my question. Looking intently into Moshe's eyes, Murray said, "Moshe, this is all kind of deep for me to grasp right now."

Marvin interjected and said, "Murray perhaps we can simplify it for you. Let's pray now and ask the Holy Spirit to guide us." Everyone bowed their heads as Marvin prayed.

"Precious Holy Spirit, whom Yeshua has sent to teach us, lead and guide us as we seek You, asking You to help us make Your words easy for Murray to understand. Amen."

And everyone joined in an amen too.

"Now Murray turn to Philippians 2:5–6. When you get to it would you please read it out loud for us?"

Leafing through the pages of the Bible, he found the verses. Reading out loud, he read, "Let this mind be in you, which was also in HaMashiach Yeshua, who being in the form of God, thought it not robbery to be equal with God. But made himself of no reputation, and took upon him the form of a servant, and was made in the likeness of men: and being found in fashion as a man, he humbled himself, and became obedient unto death, even the death of the cross."

He closed his Bible and asked Marvin, "How can I have the mind of Christ?"

Marvin answered Murray and said, "The action by our Lord in these verses indicate the spirit of total humility. God willingly giving up His prerogatives as God and becoming a man, a humble man. These verses show that first and foremost our priority as Christians is to always have an attitude of humility toward GOD and toward our fellow man. Our mind set should be humble. That means putting everyone before us first. That means men and their attitudes to their wives is to be humble and not bullying. That means wives in their attitudes to their husbands is to be humble, in submission, not to confuse it with subjection. And likewise the man must be humble. Approaching each other in humble love, especially when there are differences. It means being good and kind to each other. Wives and husbands must take the admonition of the Apostle Paul when he tells us in Hebrews, 'Don't be like the Jews in the wilderness.'"

"Stop nagging. Stop complaining. Pay attention to the first word, stop! And replace that complaint, that disgruntled spirit with better thoughts," said Moshe.

Murray asked, "Is that what Romans 12:1 means when Paul tells us to 'transform our minds?'"

"Yes," replied Marvin.

177

"In fact, Murray," said Marvin, "Paul admonishes us in 2 Corinthians 10:5 to bring into captivity every thought to the obedience of Christ. Now, is the time I believe," said Marvin, "That I would like to make what it means clear and what it does not mean to bring 'every thought' captive to HaMashiach."

"There has been a misconception that it means we are to have no thoughts of our own. This teaching is a serious deception. It does not mean we are to have no thoughts, but that we are not to have any vain thoughts. What, you might ask, are some examples of vain thoughts? I have the following: worry is a real waste of our thoughts. A critical mind is another waste, as well as a sin against God and others. We are commanded in Matthew 7:1–2 to reject all critical and paranoid and judgmental thinking. To paraphrase it, 'Do not condemn, do not judge, do not criticize.' These are the very words in the form of commands that Yeshua commands us to behave. This is in regards to both mental and verbal criticism, condemnation and judgmentalism. We must also keep from forming false imaginations. False imaginations or figments are based on dwelling our thoughts on the past, our presumptions, and assumptions along with our erroneous projections for the future. We must learn to base our thoughts only on facts, which is what I call the true imaginations. Also, we must keep a check on any projections for the future. The Apostle James makes this clear when he says, 'Go to now, ye that say, Today or tomorrow we will go into such a city, and continue there a year, and buy and sell, and get gain: Whereas ye know not what shall be on the morrow. For what is your life? It is even a vapor that appeareth for a little time, and then vanisheth away. For that ye ought to shay, If the Lord will, we shall live, and do this or that'" (James 5:13–15).

"We must make every effort to follow the Holy Spirit, helping us to practice these most intense disciplines of virtues and by replacing our bad attitudes with the Be-Attitudes."

"Thus we, who want to comply with Yeshua, need to practice the good mental habits such as submission to GOD and resistance to the enemy of our soul."

"James gives us these instructions," Marvin went on, "Which I will call Spiritual Disciplines, not techniques." Turning to James 4:7, he read, "Submit yourselves therefore to God, Resist the devil, and he will flee from you."

"From these instructions what does submit mean, Murray?"

Marvin, waiting for an answer said, "Go straight to GOD. Tell Him whatever it is that you feel. Is it fear? Is it worry? Is it grief? Is it the unexpected death of a loved one? Do you doubt the Word of God?" Marvin continued, "I could go on and mention every kind of fear or worry, but this should give you the idea. Bring it to GOD first. Then resist the devil. It means do not give in to your human nature. Then second we must hold onto our reasoning powers that GOD has given us. Then resist means when any one of our vain thoughts cross our minds, we must stop them. Don't remunerate them over and over. We must not permit it to stay in our mind. Put the red light up and stop it! We must put up a fight and the way to do that is to stop it. Ask the Lord for a verse that you can use to replace any lie or doubt or deception that you should use with your sword, the Word of GOD. Did not Yeshua Himself use this discipline of the mind when the devil tempted Him? Well, He is our example. Let us make every effort to obey Romans 1:2, '... But, be renewed of your mind ...'"

"Philippians 2:5–8 says, 'Subordinate your thoughts to God.' Stop all vain thinking; complete self-emptying."

"Luke 12:25 says, stop worrying. Resist worry. Instead pray to GOD and exercise faith in GOD and His help, especially with any stubborn spots we may have. Have confidence that He will see you through."

"Matthew the 5th, 6th and 7th chapters say, stop criticizing, judging and condemning people, Christian and non-Christian, both mentally and verbally. Practice these three chapters in cooperation with the leading of the Holy Spirit. He will assist you in this transformation of the mind. It takes discipline of the mind. It is not easy. It takes all the strength of your inner life. All of this incorporated means to love GOD with all our heart, all our mind and all our strength."

"The Lord's Prayer instructs us do not have hatred or seek revenge. Hold no grudges, and do not be spiteful."

Suddenly, an ear splitting noise filled the room. A tremendous jolt shook the walls, books fell to the floor and a fissure formed on the ground right before their eyes. People were screaming. Panic filled the air.

Marvin quickly said, "Moshe stay with me. Murray, Barry and Joel, check all rooms. Barry, Joel and I will put into action a security alarm that we practiced with all of the people in the underground with them."

Next, they assessed the damage. There was none. And best of all no one was hurt. In a short time calm was maintained. The only damage was the fissure formed in front of the library.

Barry, Joel and Murray returned to Moshe and Marvin with the good news.

However, the sound kept getting louder and louder.

Moshe said, "It sounds like the noise of a trumpet."

In an alarming state of excitement, they wondered, "What would come next?"

Chapter 6

The Boomerang— The Last World Government

"Evil has its physics. It is a current that passes through the world and through the human heart. It often manifests itself sometimes in violent acts. It often makes itself invisible like an electron magnetic flow, of a daring humming force field. Evil is much more active and surprising than gravity. But, like gravity it is mysterious. It may hide itself in deep ancient caves."

~Larry Morrow

Strange as it may be, I was always called an ideaphoric, boomerang baby. I entered the laboratory, housed in a stately, tree-studded building. Leaving my personal bodyguards at the door, I greeted the security guards standing guard in the foyer of the building. Removing my coat and jacket, carefully folding them and laying them across my arm, I walked through the long empty hall. You could hear my shoes clicking as they echoed throughout the marbled hall. With each step I made, my legs grew heavier and heavier. The white marbled walls lacked decorations, creating a tranquil atmosphere. It somehow helped take the edge off my nerves.

It was just as poignant that after six thousand years of recorded history, no one in the world of the present moment, in real time knew that Fillmore, Benny and I were in the process of a worldwide genetic breakthrough. We would be the first to produce an army of 200-million human clones, the first in modern molecular biology. We would raise clones and mobilize an indestructible army.

"This army is one that would break all previous world military records, including those of impregnable Rome!"

As I approached the glass-lined elevator, a strange smell filled the air. Ringing the buzzer, the elevator doors opened. I stepped inside and pressed the buzzer for the fourth floor lower basement level. Lifting the telephone receiver, I dialed our secret code. Benny picked up the receiver on the first ring.

Benny asked "Is that you, Felix?"

I replied, "Yes, I am on my way down. See you in a minute."

Landing on the fourth lower level of the building, the elevator doors opened and I greeted an excited Benny.

"Come in, Mr. Prime Minister. I am ready to begin Chondriana production. Follow me." Lifting his hand Benny pressed a red button on a small panel on the wall. Behind the panel there was concealed a large hidden door which appeared. It looked like it was a part of the wall. The odor I smelled when I first entered the building grew stronger as I entered the laboratory. It made me sick to my stomach. I felt dizzy and my breathing became labored. Benny noticed and asked me, "Are you all right, Felix?"

I replied, "What is that odor? I feel like I can't breathe. It's suffocating and putrid."

Benny responded, "It's a combination of ether and other chemicals needed to promote the breeding process. Here, put this mask on. It will help you breathe more easily."

With my eyes I stared at Benny and gave him an exasperated look. Benny knew what this look implied. He could almost read my mind.

Before I could open my mouth, he said, "Felix, once production of fifty thousand is complete, I have arranged for the Chondriana to be transported. One out of every fifty is programmed with the ability to drive a truck and transport them in groups to Dimona, a nuclear fuel depot, described in the past as the Old Textile Factory. Another group will arrive at Tirosh, south of Tel Nof Airbase off Route 4 just South of Tel Aviv. Another group is scheduled to arrive at Hirbat Zekharzah, a Missile Base in the same area. The remaining group is scheduled for bunkers at Palmikhim Air Base, home to Israel's version of the U.S. Doomsday plane."

Benny went on, "They will enter a series of caverns where the same drivers will instruct the others on how to erect their own bunkers."

Once I put the special mask on I found I was able to breathe more easily. "Benny," I asked, "Are there enough supplies for 200-million?"

"Yes, Felix, I personally checked all supplies. And you will see how each Chondriana once he is completed will open and put on his own packet of camouflage suits, shoes, cap, rifle and uzi."

"Benny," I asked, "Is security tight enough? Will this activity arouse any suspicion on the part of our enemies?"

"Felix, over the past year we have been stockpiling large amounts of materials in all of our underground locations. All during those months up until now, we have received no activity from other governments in cryptic intelligence from the Mossad or our stringers stationed in other nations. So far, we are in the clear."

Benny and I left that section of the laboratory. We walked down a long corridor, turned left, walked down another long corridor and turned right, approaching a dead end. This was a part of the building I had never seen before. Benny pushed in one of the white tiles on the wall. Two glass doors appeared and opened to expose another elevator. Benny said, "We will be going to the sub-level ten. It's another part of the lab you have never seen before."

I looked at Benny and said, "You're a real wizard, not at all the rounder everyone thinks you are. Tell me how long did it take you to set all of this up?"

Benny replied, "Long enough."

Hitting the button for the tenth level, the elevator descended. I was dying for a smoke, but too many chemicals were around. So, I did not want to chance it.

The elevator came to a smooth stop and Benny and I exited the tenth sub-level of the building. Immediately we entered a large room with a dome top, surrounded by several rooms. All the rooms were made of special, almost indestructible plastic, which looked like clear glass.

Smiling, Benny stepped over to a large wall lined with scans and computer coders.

Excitedly Benny said to me, "Felix, this is it! Once I hit this start button, life will never be the same for anyone."

Apprehensive, I nibbled on my upper lip wishing that it had a cigarette in it. I began to sweat. My body went limp. Frightened but cocksure, I knew this was the only way to stamp out the terrorists forever.

"Sit down here, Felix," Benny said, pointing to a plush black leather chair.

My legs and feet felt like lead. Gratefully I sat down, easing my large frame into the luxury of the recliner that had a footrest. Benny stared at me. His eyes glazed with excitement. No doubt thrilled and intoxicated by the power we were about to unleash upon the world. Lifting his right hand he pressed a red button with his index finger, revealing large paneled doors that slid open. These led into a room full of computers. Benny walked over to one of the computers, placing his finger on the keyboard of what looked like an ordinary computer. He keyed in the name Chondriana. Suddenly a cold chill ran up and down my spine. I could not believe my eyes. What started out as an infinitesimal pre-cell, multiplied and took the form of a man.

Within a minute, it started to multiply so rapidly thereafter that I could not follow their rapid acceleration, or keep count. Benny, sure now that everything was running as planned said to me, "Felix, I need some sleep. I will be in the room here on my left. I'll be sleeping for a few hours. If you need me buzz me on the intercom. I'll answer you quickly."

"Fillmore," Benny went on, "Should be arriving at about eight tonight. If I am not awake by then, ring me immediately. If you get hungry there is a small refrigerator behind the desk. It is filled with prepared foods for our short stay here."

Benny pushed one of the tiles into another secret compartment in the wall. He said, "Behind this wall is a microwave and all utensils and eating supplies you may need. If the replication gets to be too overwhelming, click this green switch and a canopy will roll down over each replicating room."

I said, "Benny, you were always sharp as a tack! I knew you would never let me down."

Benny grinned and said, "Thanks. I am going to take a much needed rest now." And with that he left the laboratory, entered the room next to the lab and settled down on a large open futon. He undressed, always sleeping naked. Wrapping himself up in the luxury of the silk sheets and a soft down quilt covering the bed, he fell fast asleep. Alone for now, it was quiet enough to hear a swishing noise. It sounded like the waves in the ocean.

I looked up and into the plexiglass rooms and decided to close them with the canopy. It kept the noise down and it helped keep the putrid odor of the chemicals to a minimum. Several times throughout the eight hours I spent on watch, I felt the pangs for a cigarette. I was dying for a Camel. No smoking, but let me see what there is to eat. Rising from the chair, I stood up and placed my hand on the tile in the wall, pushing the tile in with my hand. A door opened revealing a coffee machine and supplies, so I brewed some coffee instead. The smell of brewed coffee helped drown out some of the heady smell of the chemicals. Bored, I used my cell phone to page the security guards, seated at the foyer's entrance to the building. They were about to change their shift.

The security guard, Sam, answered the call. "Yes, Sam here," he replied.

"Sam," I said, "It's almost eight o'clock, Fillmore should be here any moment. Tell the next shift he will be arriving shortly."

"Yes, Mr. Prime Minister," Sam said and hung up.

I was getting restless now. It was time to eat. I had put it off long enough, trying to control my appetite. I opened the door behind the wall and picked out a container from the refrigerator marked "Tongue." Well, I was not expecting this, I mused to myself. I also took out a bottle of cold Borsht. I placed the container inside the microwave, setting the timer for three minutes, adding some sour cream. Then the sound of a large buzzer startled me. It was the sound coming from a monitor on the wall, indicating someone had entered the building. I pushed the monitor button in and said, "Yes, this is Felix."

"Felix, it's Fillmore." I accessed the code and let Fillmore in, instructing him how to get to the sub-tenth level below.

Fillmore arrived, choking. He said, "My throat feels sore and scratchy, like someone just pepper sprayed me. The smell is like burning rubber or hot tar." Fillmore asked me, "Felix, what is that horrible smell?"

I replied, "They're the chemicals used in the production of the Chondriana. Fillmore, I assure you, to keep the smell down I already have closed the canopies to each proliferation room. You probably never noticed the odor during previous experiments. Now in mass production this is what you get. Here, take this mask and put it on whenever you need it. It will help you breath easier."

Fillmore gave me his usual smirk. Grabbing the mask out from my hand, he quickly put it on. Then he asked me, "How are things coming along? Are they what you expected?"

185

"Fillmore," I replied, "Everything is going so precisely I can hardly believe it myself. Just to bring you up to date, Benny has each individual Chondriana outfit himself with military clothes, a rifle and an uzi. He also programmed one out of every fifty, making them the designated drivers of trucks scheduled to reach Dimona, Tirosh, Hirbat Zekharyah and Palmikhim Air Base. Once they reach their destinations the same leader will instruct each one to set up their own bunkers in each location."

Fillmore asked me, "What about enemy surveillance?"

"I've received up to the minute intelligence from our Mossad. They report that there is a chance of detection due to the large numbers of transports, but if the Chondriana are inadvertently detected, I believe it's more for our enemies to fear. If they do count to 200-million, they will be more than willing, I am sure, to negotiate a deal. This is a real non-zero sum. A lose-lose game that we will win by not playing."

Fillmore said, "Felix, you have surpassed yourself! I am proud of you, boy. Darn proud."

My nerves grated every time Fillmore called me boy. But, rather than pick a fight over it during this critical stage of processing the Chondriana, I put a lid on it. Then I rang for Benny. Benny heard the ring, quickly dressed and entered the lab. Excited, like a little kid receiving his first bicycle, Benny said, "Fillmore, let me show you our masterpiece."

Hitting the control button on the computer, the canopies rolled up. Fillmore stood there astonished by what he saw. Fillmore said, "Top speed. Superior my boy, superior. Benny, I always knew you would outclass yourself. You are a true maverick!"

Benny basked in the compliment.

Fillmore said, "Benny, what are your next plans?"

Benny replied, "To make sure production is contiguously uninterrupted. For that, Felix has already taken an eight hour shift and you, Fillmore, will take the next eight hour shift."

Then Benny said, "I am headed for Dimona now to check on things there. I should be back in about an hour. If things are going as expected there, then I'll make a stop. And I'll check on how things are going at Tirrosh, Palmikham, and Hirbat."

"Then Felix," Benny said, "While I am gone orient Fillmore to the facility. Then Fillmore can take this shift while you rest."

Handing Fillmore a card he said, "Here is my cell phone number. It is secured. Call me should any problems or questions arise while I'm gone."

Benny left the room and entered the elevator, exited the building, headed for Dimona. Quickly, I showed Fillmore where the food, drinks and other necessities were located.

186

"Fillmore, I'll be in the room next to this lab. I am going to shower and take a rest."

I was grateful that Benny had the foresight to have a shower conveniently located in the room.

Fillmore said, "Fine, go ahead."

I entered the room, undressed and entered the hot shower. Washing my body I thought to myself, hell, I feel like I am taking a shower for two people instead of one! I was always disgusted with my tremendous size. However, thoughts about my body brought back memories of the only one who did adore my body, Felixovna. Sometimes they even joked about me being as big as a bear, one she could hug and feel safe and secure with. Her great beauty was indelibly fixed in my memory. Her tanned skin made her icy blue eyes sparkle. Clearly I remembered how with her height she towered over everyone but me. She stood six feet tall, was large boned with a delicious hourglass figure. It was so vivid in my mind, it seemed as if she were there with me at this very moment.

Felixovna was a career officer who served in the British Secret Investigation Service (SIS). Later she made a career change and entered the Israeli IDF. I had met her right after I was told that during a fire fight she was found in a ditch, single-handedly holding off a band of infiltrators. Officers and enlisted men alike would covet guard duty in order to get a closer look at her. Whenever she entered a room, all eyes would be fixed on her. Exiting the shower, I sat down on the bed, grief stricken. Thinking about her, brought tears to my eyes.

My heart broke once again into a million pieces. I felt as if a strong water current was pulling me under. Then a smile crossed my face as I recalled how in the short time she had given me, it felt like it had been a life of unspeakable delight! No one could ever replace her. I never wanted anyone else.

Sad, I thought, that she had been declared missing in action and would never return.

Socially, living alone without a woman led some to think that I was androgynous. Although I knew that rumors and gossip had it that I might have homosexual tendencies or they were heard to say, "Why doesn't he have a woman? He's always with men only."

Never one to listen to gossip, what I felt was my own affair and I let it go at that. Still I kept hoping I would hear news about her soon. Hours of waiting to hear from her had turned into days and my days into weeks. Hours filled with emotional turmoil I had never dreamed of having. By now the bitter winds of the lonely winter had past and spring burst forth with flowers blooming and birds singing, easing my anxiety and despair over her whereabouts. Somehow a semblance of hope leaped into my heart.

Grabbing a towel, I quickly dried myself. Running a comb through my thick black hair, reminded me of how she thought that was one of my best features. Checking the chest of drawers in the corner of the room I found some pajamas, finding a soft silk pair in my size. Agilely I slipped into them.

All the while thinking to myself that Benny, a perfectionist, had thought of every detail. Satisfied with Benny's performance, I hit the bed. I thought, at least I can dream of her. Moaning softly to myself, I knew that I would never stop thinking about her. Her perfect face was etched in my mind forever. Pulling the soft sheets over me, I fell fast asleep.

When I woke up I felt like I was living in a dream. Thoughts about her streamed in once again. Life seemed so unreal without her in it. A strange emptiness fell over me every time I thought about her. It was painful heartbreak. It was as if someone had stabbed me in the heart and left the knife there, tormenting me while I was still alive.

Meanwhile, Fillmore took a seat, putting his feet up on the desk and marveled as he watched how the Chondrianas wildly replicated. Used to the smell of the chemicals now, there would be no covering the Chondriana up for Fillmore. He wanted to watch. All the money in the world could never stop him.

Meanwhile, Benny had gone and now returned to the laboratory. Entering the building, he passed through security checkpoints. Finally reaching the elevator, he entered sub-level ten. His feelings were in such a maelstrom. He could not explain it. He felt as if he was enveloped in a dark cocoon.

Upon entering the lab, he looked at the remaining replication of the Chondriana as they continued to multiply and mobilize themselves. His fear recurred as he watched them replicate themselves.

Glibly he said, "Hi Fillmore, hi Felix," as he quickly fumbled with his finger, he pressed the green button letting the canopies drop down over the plexiglass rooms, cutting out the visibility of the Chondriana. He was white as a sheet. His mouth curled up so tightly his face must have looked like a mask. His eyes fixed into a stare and glazed over as if he was walking in a trance. These feelings were worse than any nightmare. He put the canopies down so fast, Felix and Fillmore didn't know what was going on.

Fillmore spoke first and said, "Benny, you look like you have seen a ghost. Are you okay, boy?"

He could not answer Fillmore yet. He reached for the bottom drawer of the desk and pulled out a bottle of Cognac. His hands trembled as he poured it into a glass, drank it and asked, "Felix, Fillmore, care for one?"

Both said, "No thanks. It's too early."

Fillmore said, "What in heaven's name has happened to you boy? Why have you closed the canopies?"

He replied, "Give me a few minutes and I'll explain."

Finally, Benny said, "Felix, Fillmore, even though it was as much as my creation as yours, it turns my stomach to watch the procedure. Fillmore, on the other hand I know felt just the opposite. Feeling invigorated, lively and quite jovial, not minding in the least. Is not that true, Fillmore?" Fillmore grinned, but did not make a comment.

So he went on, "After traveling some forty miles I arrived at Dimona, eight and a half miles from the town by that name, and some twenty-five miles from the Jordanian border between Beersheba and Sodom. As you are both aware, there are twenty-five hundred employees who work there, but only 150 are permitted access to the Machon, two nuclear reactors and our 200 nuclear weapons. No one exhibited any suspicions about what was going on in the caverns below, in sub-level ten where the Chondriana secretly set up their bunkers and living quarters, having entered through an undisclosed tunnel. God where would we be without tunnels?"

"So, entering the building, I passed through the security check-points without any difficulty."

"As I entered sub-level ten, four levels below the reactor and nuclear weapons, I saw the Chondriana had already completed setting up their bunkers. This was my first look at more than one of them in action. Even though I knew that cloning the Chondriana would work, I never envisioned or even experienced what it would be like seeing all of them together at the same time, in real time. It left me feeling strange and overwhelmed. It surprised me to feel this way."

"Not knowing what to expect, I was riddled with doubt. It was as if it were possible that the Chondriana would or could act independently, or become confused and may unexpectedly even attack me. During the few seconds I spent lost in my thoughts, the Chondrianas all stood up at attention. They were staring at me in a strange frightening stare. It was a weird feeling. Waiting for my first interaction with them, I stumbled over my thoughts. What would their first words sound like? In the awesomeness of the moment I felt a sudden fear and dread. My life seemed to flash before me. I had mastered fear but not this, fear of the unknown. My body began to shake. My hands trembled, and I felt a spine tingling icy cold go up and down my spine. The hair on the back of my neck stood up on end. The saliva in my mouth dried up. My tongue stuck to the roof of my mouth, like it was glued together. I felt as if I was all alone in a barren dessert without water. My body felt like a fragile piece of china, ready to fall to the ground and break at any moment. Never one to be at a loss for words, I remained momentarily mute. Stunned by my own creation, I felt dazed, bewildered and afflicted with a sudden onset of cataplasia. My body frozen to the spot."

"I was too frightened to touch them in any way. Gradually I inched my way back toward the door. I said to myself, keep it simple, Benny, keep it simple. Bracing my emotions, I began to regain my composure. Fear and dread left the maze of my thoughts. Like a robot, I replaced the kaleidoscope of my thoughts, changing them with deeper and chillier sensations into thrills and excitement. I was exhilarated as I caught a vision of our enemies being filled with electrifying fear once they too came face to face with the Chondriana as I did now. The real shock came when one of the Chondrianas broke the ice and spoke to me first. As if to read my mind it said, 'We are all here. We will advance by your order.'"

"I felt dizzy. My head was spinning. I finally managed to speak. I said, 'I need fifty of you to accompany me to the President's Residence. Twenty-five of you will accompany me to the War Room there. And twenty-five of you will guard the outside of the Residence. The rest of you will remain here in your quarters until I return with final orders.'"

"Simple words. I could not believe I finally got them out. Quickly as I could, I exited the cavern. My hands still shaking as the Chondriana followed behind me. Yet, I was relieved that my very first verbal confrontation with the Chondriana was over."

"When we reached the transport truck, I spoke to the Chondriana. 'All fifty of you can load up by sitting in the back of the truck. I'll take one of you who already has been designated the driver. I will accompany you to the Residence.'"

"Leaving the building and sitting next to the Chondriana driver made me feel like hell. It was a truly surreal encounter. I felt I was in no shape to drive myself. I instructed the driver to make a stop at the laboratory before going to the Residence. Arriving back to the laboratory, I instructed the Chondriana to remain in the truck until I returned. I entered the building, greeted the security guards and commenced walking at a fast pace. I went through the halls and on into the elevator."

"Fillmore," Benny said. Then he hesitated growing quiet for more than a minute. Benny finally blurted out, "Fillmore, Felix, here is what happened. I arrived at Dimona without any interruptions or problems. The only outstanding event was an eerie feeling I felt while I watched so many Chondriana all at one time."

"I felt overwhelmed. I hate to admit it but I was downright frightened out of my wits as they all stared intently at me, waiting for me to speak. When one of them, as if reading my mind and sensing my fear finally did speak, I almost fell apart. I quickly gathered my composure. And since everything was going smoothly as planned, I told them I needed fifty of them to accompany me to the President's Residence with one of them driving. Twenty-five of them were to assist the guards outside. And the other twenty-five were to follow me into the War Room to protect you, Felix, and all those in the Military War Room. I then instructed the rest of them, there in their quarters, to await further orders. I then made as quick an exit as I could, but I am still shaken by the awesomeness of the whole operation. One thought though kept me going though," Benny continued, "And that thought was, what would it be like to see the reaction of our enemies once they witnessed seeing the Chondriana for themselves?"

"Well, my boy, you have done bloody well, yes, bloody well, I must say," said Fillmore.

"What is your next move," I asked Benny?

"First, Felix, I am going to have another drink, then I'll be on my way to see if things are going as smoothly at Tirosh, Palmiklim and Hirbat Zekharzah. After checking them I am going to stop off at my home and pick up some extra food to nosh on."

Fillmore always one for comfort gave Benny a quick smile and said, "Hurry on, boy. Hurry on."

Benny fixed himself his drink feeling the warmth of the liquor, helping him to calm down. He was ready to hit the road now and face his demons.

Finishing his drink, Benny washed his glass out in the sink, dried it and put it back in the drawer along with the bottle of Cognac and said to Felix and Fillmore, "Help yourselves at any time."

Fillmore stared intently at Benny and said, "Sure, sure, go ahead now, boy, stop dallying."

Benny left the room.

I told Fillmore, "I guess he needs some more of his fashionable digs too. You know him. I am surprised he does not have a woman stashed somewhere in here."

"Come now, Felix," Fillmore said with a chuckle. "Hold your tongue boy. He has done brilliantly and if I must say so myself, so have you! Yes, my boy. You have not disappointed me. I am exceptionally pleased."

My jaw nearly fell to the floor. In jest I said, "I wish I could say the same about you Fillmore," I blurted out! Then with a growl, I said, "And would you stop that pain in the ass boy stuff!"

"Now b-b-b—," he stuttered, stopping himself. "Now Felix, my son," said Fillmore, "Hold your horses. Now is not the time to quibble over my most cherished vernacular."

"Yes, yes, okay," I retorted!

Fillmore changed the subject and asked, "How about some tongue? Is there any left for me?"

"Yes, if you push this white tile in on the wall it opens up to the refrigerator, a microwave and anything else you might need. Help yourself," I said, anxious to get him out of the room.

"I will b-b-ba," he caught himself again. "I will, Felix. Thank you my b—," and dropped off not finishing his favorite word for me.

Meanwhile, I put in a call to all intelligence for up to the minute reports using my cell phone and settled down in the black leather contour chair. What I read in the reports made me sit bolt upright, almost breaking the lower panel of the chair. "Damn, damn, damn!"

"What in heaven's name is wrong," Fillmore asked?

"Daura, our private intelligence mole, has wired me that the new Ten Arab Coalition of Iraq and their allies are ready to wipe us out next!"

"Fillmore, quick," I said hurriedly, "Page Benny while I notify the military to meet us in the War Room. You stay here to cover the remaining production of the Chondriana. When they are completed close up the lab, leave the security guards in place and meet me at the Residence in the War Room.

"Yes, Felix, will do," replied Fillmore.

"Then, I'll put in a call to the Shinbet Israelis' Internal Security ordering a high level emergency meeting with several military commanders. Then notify the security guard, Maurice, that we will be arriving shortly."

Paging Maurice, Maurice answered, "Yes, Mr. Prime Minister, Maurice speaking."

"Maurice," I said, "We have a code red. Notify my bodyguards. We will be meeting at the Residence in the War Room."

"Yes sir, immediately, sir."

Then I put in a call to internal intelligence, the Shaback, and external security, the Shinbet.

Within minutes, twenty ultra-magnificent Mossad agents, each armed with a twenty-two Caliber Berretta pistol stormed the building. I met them in the lobby.

"Gentlemen," I said, "I have set up an emergency meeting at my Residence. I need you to escort me there as quickly as is possible."

It was ten in the morning by that time. Surrounded by my bodyguards and the entourage of Mossad agents and the stationary security guards brandishing semiautomatic rifles, along with the 25 Chondriana with their uzies, I entered the large columned President's Residence.

Filing past them, I entered the entrance hall. The entrance hall was very spacious with fresh flowers and eucalyptus filling the air with its pungent aroma. Luxurious Indian Madras rugs donned the walls and marble floors elegantly set throughout the hall running through the entire Residence. Several ottoman chairs were scattered here and there.

After my arrival, then one by one, my military commanders came filing in. I led the way and entered the library. Hidden behind a bookcase was a hidden panel. I entered a coded number and the bookcases opened up to reveal an underground passageway. They descended several steps that were carved from natural rock lined with wrought iron railings. As they continued their approach towards the War Room you could faintly hear the sound of water flowing.

For those who had never come this far, I said, "About a quarter mile from the War Room is a natural underground spring. Once we pass it we will enter a newly developed, rock-hewn War Room, with modern up to the minute monitors and computers. Some of you have been here and know what to expect. You can fill in those who have never been here before."

Once everyone was gathered together inside the War Room they were introduced to several military personnel responsible for up to the minute events, secret intelligence information and tactical plans for warfare.

"Gentlemen," I said, "Due to the current crisis, our Tsiach (annual meeting of military and civilian Israeli intelligence) scheduled for next week has been moved up to today. While Jordan is not a gulf state as such, it had reportedly offered ship supplies from the port of Aqaba to Baghdad. Jordan, many of you may well know, has for years made the pretense of a State of War with us. Instead secretly sharing in our security arrangements, commerce, industry, banking, joint agricultural projects and water conservation as well as across the border trade. However, now that Iraq has taken over Amman, the capital of the Hashemite Kingdom of Jordan, also known as the City on Seven Hills, I have already set in motion a plan approved by our foreign minister to smuggle out the 30,000 Jews in Iran, the 6,000 still in Syria and those in Yemen and others in North African countries."

"We have, gentlemen," I continued, "Survived the Arab propaganda with their yarns and conspiracy theories, even insisting that some of our own Mossad are secretly converting to Islam so that we can corrupt the Iraqi Nations' youth. They believe that Israel is evil. But, they are, in my book totally Psycho-Semitic! They refuse to heed the Title Deed directly given in person to our patriarch, Abraham, by God Himself. The Title Deed lies in the documentation in the Tanachs many scriptures including the Psalms, a permanent gift to us, the Jews. The Arabs are instigating ignominious defeat upon themselves because they teach and practice hatred of the Jews. Even their own Koran describes us as aggressors, and instructs them 'to kill them wherever you find them.'"

Felix went on, "Results of a concealed vote taken by the Knesset in response to this crisis is that from this day forward we will retain a direct election of the Prime Minister and eliminate the requirement that the Cabinet be supported by a Knesset majority. The Cabinet will serve a fixed term and legislation will be passed as the result of debaters and merits, and not any deals which could topple a coalition. In addition, of a sixty-one seat majority has been secretly voted on, which means I now have the majority needed to remain in power and retain power. All Arab MKs have been outlawed. Now those !@#$% terrorists will finally have to reject the Palestinian Covenant created by Hamas."

"Permanent Peace they know cannot exist unless they reject its original principles that as you all know calls for our destruction. Reconnaissance planes have been deployed. In addition, up to the minute reports from our intelligence have uncovered where Hamas' new leader has hid their funds, known by most governments of the world to be hidden in secret accounts all over the world, also known as the Hamas' insurance policy. Therefore our discovery of this special insurance policy can no longer protect him from being destroyed by Hamas as well as some of his own supporters, who by the way have an assassination plan against me, in effect to take place at any moment. And we will deal with Hamas."

"Now, General Jack Gold will brief you on weapons."

Jack, a fifty-five year old career Army officer, formerly head of the small Center Party, explained, "Gentlemen, ever since 1937 we have faced the threatening term created by our enemies, weapons of mass destruction. There has been a possible apocalyptic event, creating a global crisis. Bombs that destroyed Hiroshima and Nagasaki, both implosion bombs. This bomb has led to Mutual Assimilation Destruction, in addition to the weapons inventory of all major and minor governments. You have already received my handouts. These are updated copies of weapons in Israel's inventory. You will notice that twenty-four percent of Chinese troops and ordinances are based near the Korean border. We, however, have replicated an army of 200-million cloned male humans. Twenty-five who have arrived and are guarding us here. Our Israeli National Military Army will be their back up."

"These man-made life forms are now being housed in three of our vast subterranean bunkers. They proliferate at speeds beyond human comprehension. They are super-intelligent, indestructible and preserved on a disc, thus immortalizing their national DNA blueprint! They are fully armed with AK 47 semiautomatic and automatic rifles, flamethrowers, rocket launchers, and 9mm uzi submachine guns and rocket propelled grenades. We also have along with the non-lethal Sabra Laser, Stinger grenades, the Body Optical System mounted on our Military Hummers, to capture snipers, which has the combat-alert signal ready to charge Jordan, Iraq and its newly formed ten member group of Arab nations."

"They are joined by China. We therefore, outnumber them three to one! The 1967 six-day war involved only three Muslim countries. That was kid stuff in comparison to what is going to happen now! Israel will overwhelm the whole world!"

General Gold continued, "Main battle tanks, artillery armored vehicles and multiple rocket launchers total a round figure of thirty-thousand, led by robotic unmanned Land Warriors and Robot scouts. These are exclusive. Robotic surveyors are able to survey an entire continent in one day. Our upgraded night-vision gear is capable of seeing five-hundred yards through dark or gloom. This gear also let's commandoes confirm enemy camps without getting too close, while satellite gear uploads what each team member sees to a command center. They also carry a laser viewing system which can identify buildings, cars and people from miles away. This along with our Howitzers will light up the night sky like daylight!"

"We also have fifty new Interim Fast Attack Vehicles. These four wheel drive, five-cylinder turbo diesel rugged off-road vehicles are small enough to fit into helicopters, with six seats, two more than a jeep. They sport mount assorted machine guns and grenade launchers, and a snorkel that will keep air flowing to the engine in thirty inches of deep water. Our commandoes can confirm terrorist camps without entering too close while satellite gear uploads what each team member sees to a command center, each equipped with a GPS receiver and satellite equipment that can pinpoint locations of every member of their unit. They also carry third generation night vision gear, also capable of seeing five-hundred yards, even through gloom or fog. Additionally, this laser viewing system can identify buildings, cars and people from miles away. We have Sabra Lasers that are non-lethal weapons that can take control and incapacitate. We have Boss. They are photo light bullets propelled by Laser guns which function as a battlefield observation mounted on top of our Hummers. We have mobilized guns called Metal Storm that eject one-quarter million bullets a minute! They are aptly called Silent Assassins, unmanned and it can never jam. We have Bunk Busters and Traveling Grenades that travel four-thousand miles a second! Also, we have Multiple Launch Rocket System with its guided GPS. It detonates on impact, striking its lethal target."

"The Arial weapons of our IAF, Israeli Air Force, have Super-Hyper and Trans-Sonic airplanes which can be compared to Britain's GL Links Helicopter, which reaches speeds of hurricane velocities which are ready and on standby alert. At our fingertips when ordered is Electric-magnetic Pulse. With its appropriate use we can destroy all electronics, including immobilizing all vehicles, including tanks over an entire city. Our inventory," he continued, "Includes surface to surface missiles numbered in the thousands, with four-hundred additional F16 aircraft which have been added to our arsenal of fifty Global Hawks. These unmanned aerial airplanes use covert surveillance that can scout terrain without human risk. Their sophisticated radar equipped satellites can map terrain, finding and following moving targets as well as listening in on communications. Our GPS cruise-missiles can now reach their targets in any weather. A unique feature is that they can distinguish a tank from a tractor and hit the right one, enabling them to reach any target, anytime, making it a seven-twenty-four hour war. More on regarding targets."

"We also have in our possession now and ready for use, a startling new future weapon called Brilliant. Its action when ready to impact and the target is not there, it will wait!"

"Not to be outdone, in addition we have twenty-five unmanned RD-1 Predators and seventy-five unmanned missiles, armed with fifty micro-air missiles. We have overhauled one hundred Hunter DAV unmanned air vehicles. Newly developed unmanned Copter Vision. Weapons, similar to the Helicopter. In addition, we also have an arsenal of six-hundred stealth Tigre helicopters, three-hundred Apache Longbow helicopters with digital intelligence and twenty of the Tilt Rotator helicopters. We have already at our disposal, the recently developed F 22 Rapture, Space Age Stealth Fighters. These are virtually invisible and can fix themselves. We also in our arsenal have ten Bibendum missiles, each capable of holding one nuclear bomb and ten TACAMOs (Take Charge And Move Out), each one loaded with a nuclear warhead, twenty times the power of the bomb that struck Hiroshima. Our Navy, has upgraded three of our fleet. These ships feature advanced sensors, warning of impending attack."

"They are very quiet and very versatile. They are capable of responding to air, sea or subsurface strikes. Its twin thirty-thousand horse powered engines will propel the ships at thirty-three knots. They were built without armaments. We also have five Ballistic Submarines that can wipe out an entire continent in one hour. Gentlemen, Israel will win this war."

General Gold went on, "In response to nuclear terror we have also implemented a swat team called NEST, similar to the one in the U.S., Nuclear Energy Search. It consists of an elite organization of passionate, diverse, intelligent and creative scientists, engineers, nuclear weapons' experts and technicians who are prepared to respond to any nuclear emergencies, including hidden bombs. They fly in especially designed helicopters that can detect radiation sound from the air. They also go on the ground in hot spots in mobilized labs loaded with equipment disguised as delivery vans. On foot they blend with backpacks wired to pick up radiation sources. They are on-call twenty-four-seven, three hundred-sixty-five. These are followed by our military units who are equipped with the new science of electromagnetic fields to produce relaxation for those men who are fatigued by the war." He finished speaking.

Standing up I said, "Thank you General Gold. Now I ask, is the current situation really an existential threat to us? Or is this a bluff? Can this conflict not be settled by military means, but negotiation? Is our nuclear status strong enough to give us the victory? Will the hammer and the sickle strike us? Can 200-million Chondriana come and boomerang a two-hundred million man army approaching us? Gentlemen, my answer is yes, we can win, but is it possible at this point to think about negotiation?"

Several officers began to speak all at once.

"Gentlemen, gentleman," I barked, "Let me finish, then I will take your questions."

General Cohen spoke up and asked, "How can we stop them?"

I responded, "In addition to my earlier statement, the NEST, as we call them, will infiltrate and some have already done so. They will pour liquid nitrogen over them. This will freeze their bombs' mechanisms, or they can also use small explosives around the nuclear material. They can also disarm them by a remote control robot."

General Robbins, the only half breed of the generals, who had a Jewish mother but an American father, asked, "What about their dirty bombs?"

197

I replied, "When these are found we will kill their dirty bombs by what we have devised. It is a cover, a nylon tent. The nylon tent is then filled with thirty thousand cubic feet of foam. When the bomb explodes, the force will absorb the radiation."

At that moment Benny arrived at the President's Residence. Exiting the truck, he instructed the Chondriana to follow him. With twenty-five armed Chondriana already on guard surrounding the building, the other twenty-five exited the truck and followed Benny into the War Room.

I was interrupted as Benny entered the War Room, followed by the twenty-five armed Chondriana.

Benny, his heart racing faster than a stock car going full speed, addressed everyone, "Gentlemen, these are the additional Chondriana, our genetically altered fully armed human male clones, twenty-five of whom are on guard outside the Residence. Twenty-five are armed and assisting our guards outside of the Residence, and these twenty-five will stand guard outside the War Room. The remaining are ready for combat and poised to strike on my orders."

I gave each Chondriana an up and down stare while everyone else sat riveted to their seats, stunned by their appearance. Their bodies were muscular and looked human, like the build of someone who was six foot tall and weighing in at 250 pounds.

Even their heads were the shape of a normal man's. But, the queerest thing of all was that they all looked alike! It was terrifying to say the least!

Exasperated, I said, "Benny, we are contemplating negotiation. Have a seat."

I watched as Benny sat down on one of the stiff but comfortable maroon leather chairs scattered throughout the room. He looked bewildered, he pulled his soft silk suit jacket together, his hand brushing against the bulge of what I knew to be his pistol tucked snugly in its holster. Hidden from view, he caressed it, as if giving him a real sense of security.

Ignoring my reactions of my military's appearance of the Chondriana, I gave Benny a hard look for his interruption. Irritated, I said, "It appears that Bertrand Russell possibly had the answer. To quote him, 'Science has made unrestricted national sovereignty incompatible with human survival. The only possibilities are now one world government or death!'"

Then turning my head and looking into the eyes of every officer present and giving Benny the hardest stare, I asked him, "What then? What's your decision, considering that with Chondriana we have the upper hand? Or should we go for one world government with our nation at the helm?"

Benny almost fell off his chair. This was the first time he heard me mention what could wind up and boomerang us! However, Benny pulled himself together and spoke up, "Release Chondriana information to world news media and see what results."

One by one, by a show of hands, all agreed, this would be a good step to take.

Immediately I released the information to all intelligence agencies worldwide.

"Gentlemen," I said, "It is now midnight. This release will take a few hours to reach everyone. Therefore we'll take those few hours to get some much needed sleep. I have secured several rooms available here in the Residence. I'll have my aide show you to your rooms. We'll resume strategy at six in the morning. The Chondriana will stand guard outside the War Room Residence overnight. That concludes this meeting. Goodnight, gentlemen."

Then I paged my aide and asked him to escort everyone to the assigned bedrooms.

Benny sat glued to his chair, waiting. He wanted to speak with me alone. After everyone except for the Chondriana left for the night, I invited Benny up for a nightcap.

"Felix," Benny said, "Are you sure you want to proceed with negotiation?"

"No," I said. "I want to bide my time. We have Chondriana. We are on top as far as I am concerned, but world power could resolve our insecurity over national existence."

Pouring out a shot of Scotch over the rocks, I said, "Is this okay?"

Benny, usually happy to get his hands on any liquor right now said, "Sure, sure Felix."

I said, "I plan to keep everything and everyone on alert status, including the Chondriana. Let's see what the world has to say once they hear about the Chondriana. Indubitably, no government in the world has ever had to face off to this type of challenge."

Benny said, "Felix, there is no doubt in my mind that we have the upper hand. But, all of a sudden, you're interested in leading one world government? Sounds kind of absurd."

Changing the subject, I asked, "Benny, have you seen Fillmore since all this happened?"

Benny replied, "No, but I plan to go back to the lab now to see if all the Chondrianas have stopped replicating."

I said, "His shift has been over an hour ago. See what has delayed him and brief him on what's transpired here in the War Room and see if he would like to come to the Residence and get some sleep."

Benny gulped down his scotch and asked, "Where do you want me to stay for the night?"

I said, "I have a room for you and for Fillmore, so you might as well stay here considering the emergency. I'll have three of my Mossad agents accompany you. Check on things at the lab and lock it up."

Benny excused himself, exiting the War Room. Hesitant at first, he walked up the stairs through the hall out of the library. Three Mossad agents approached him as he exited the War Room.

"Benny, my name is Jay. I will accompany you to the lab. I've been instructed by Felix to escort and return you and Fillmore to the Residence."

"Fine with me," said Benny, "Let's go." Approaching the truck driver parked outside, Benny told Jay to stay put. "The others will continue to maintain security until I give further orders." The driver turned his head towards Benny. Benny stared back, his pitch black eyes concealed his pupils.

As a bizarre grin came across his mouth, his hands grasped tightly on the steering wheel of the truck, he responded to Benny, in a deep bellowed voice and said, "I will relay your command to the others."

With that Benny walked past the front door of the Residence, ready to enter the car with the Mossad when suddenly he felt a strange feeling come over him once again. His body started to tremble. Benny took in a deep breath, relieved the Chondriana were not following him. His hands were wet and his face dripping with sweat the size of a pearl. Benny let out a sigh and entered the car with the three Mossad agents. He instructed the driver to head for the laboratory.

Wiping his face with his handkerchief, Jay asked, "Are you alright, Benny?"

Benny gave Jay a smirk and said, "Yes, nothing I can't handle. But, thanks for asking." Arriving at the laboratory, Benny instructed the Mossad agents to wait for him in the foyer. Briefing the security guards to continue their watch, Benny instructed them to seal and lock all the doors except for the main entrance and that they were not to let anyone in without his prior approval and the use of the password Achor. Benny walked swiftly down the hall, entered the elevator and paged Fillmore. Benny blurted out, "Fillmore, my God, wait until you hear what has transpired!"

"Go on, go on, speak up! And what is Felix planning to do," asked Fillmore?

"He is thinking about the World Federation Parliament, One-World Government, controlled by Felix, with Israel at the helm."

"What," exclaimed Fillmore! "What makes him think we have what it takes to do it?"

Benny replied, "With Chondrianas we will have an indestructible army. Felix and I feel that with this army we will outclass all the armies of the world. And this will give us the upper hand."

Benny went on, "Fillmore, no one has what we have. Plus we have all the money now to do it! Our Valley of Achor will turn the tide for us. It will no longer be called the Valley of Trouble, but the Valley of Hope! I say this regardless of the fact that Ahmed has overtaken Jordan."

Fillmore couldn't wait for Benny to shut up! He was bursting inside. In full throttle he said, "Preposterous, absolutely preposterous. Why he's bordering on the insane. I must get to him immediately."

Benny said, "Hold on, Fillmore. I have a few things to pack. Felix wants us back at the Residence for the night. He has already released the information about the Chondriana. He knows it will take a few hours to transmit the information worldwide, so now that Chondriana production is over and they are ready for an altercation, he feels we had better get a few hours of sleep. He's scheduled a meeting to resume for six in the morning."

"Oh my God," Fillmore belched out! "He's really going to go through with it! Benny, my boy, hurry, hurry, and don't waste another moment!"

"Fillmore," Benny said, "A set of fresh clothes are in the closet for you in the bedroom behind the lab."

"Quite right, my boy. With all the hurrying, one cannot fit into his normal routine and where would I be without a change of clothes. Thanks, my boy. I'll be with you in a jiffy."

While Fillmore gathered a clean set of clothes, Benny paged the building security guard, Sam.

Sam answered, "Sam here."

"Where is Maurice," asked Benny?

"We just made a shift change, Benny."

Benny said, "Okay Sam. I am posting two of our Mossad agents to guard the building. Within the hour I will send a garrison of IDF soldiers to secure it. I need you to stay alert. One of you can go into my office, fix some coffee. I will keep you posted on the latest events. Page me immediately if anything suspicious or out of the ordinary happens to come along."

Benny quickly packed some extra clothes for himself while Fillmore packed his. Now that Chondriana production was completed, Benny locked up the lab on sub levels six and ten.

Wrapping things up, he and Fillmore took the elevator to the main floor. All the while Fillmore was mumbling under his breath, using expletives over his frustration with Felix. Benny instructed the security guards to stay at their post. Benny said to Sam, "Everything in the laboratories on level six and level ten are locked up. No one is to enter this building. Page me first with all visitors and I will give you a password. If the person knows this password, you can admit him to the premises; if not, bar whomever it is and keep them under house arrest."

"Yes sir," replied Sam, "Will do."

Benny and Fillmore exited the building. A strong wind was blowing. The sky was overcast and gray. The three Mossad agents were in a car waiting to escort Benny and Fillmore to the President's Residence. Jay, the driver, a burly man with a cropped beard greeted them as they both entered the car.

Benny and Fillmore knew Jay and engaged in some small talk. Fillmore, always clean shaven, thought Jay's whiskers made him look like a Notting Hill bum and not like an intelligence agent.

Benny instructed two of the Mossad to remain on guard in the building and that the IDF would be arriving soon and to let no one in without the password he had previously given them. Using the narrow back roads that were less notable, Jay drove on. An eerie silence filled the streets. Passing by the U.S. Consulate next to the YMCA, they reached the President's Residence. Once they arrived at the Residence, Benny hurriedly exited the car and up the steps, past security and into the house, with Fillmore following right behind him. Seconds later a horrific downpour of rain pelted the Residence.

"Well, my boy," said Fillmore to Benny, "That was close. I hope this is not a portent of what is to come."

Felix's aide, Jay, the young ambitious sort was on hand to greet them.

"Hello gentlemen. My name is Jay. Come this way."

Fillmore asked Jay in a derogatory tone of voice, "Where's the Prime Minister?"

"Asleep, and my name is Jay, if you please address me as Sir Jay."

Fillmore ignored the remark and went on a tirade about Felix. "Preposterous, absolutely ridiculous," mumbled Fillmore. "At a time like this, how can he sleep? Where is his room? I'll wake that boy!"

Before Jay could even answer, Benny interrupted him.

"Fillmore, let it go for now," said Benny, feeling tired himself. "Tomorrow will bring out enough hell. Let's have a nightcap."

Jay said, "This way to the study. I'll fix one up for you. Will that be Scotch on the rocks, sir?"

"Yes, fine," replied Benny.

"And what will you have, Mr. Fox?"

Fillmore replied, "I'll have a Brandy. Thank you, Jay."

Jay, giving Benny a hard look and with a grin turned to Fillmore and said, "You're quite welcome, sir."

Entering the study, Jay opened up the curio and took out some brandy. "When you're ready, just take the stairs, and turn left. The first and second rooms are available. Goodnight, gentlemen, see you in the morning at six sharp."

Finishing their first round of liquor, Benny poured another nightcap then settled down onto a Chintz sofa and propped a pillow under his head. A fireplace still kindled, giving the room a warm glow and soon Benny fell fast asleep. Fillmore, still awake and agitated, headed up the stairs and into the bedroom. He had no pension for sleep.

Not usually one given to insomnia, Fillmore tossed and turned the whole night. His nerves a total wreck. He couldn't wait to let Felix have it.

It was five o'clock. The sun filtered through the blinds on the windows causing me to awaken. Opening my eyes I got up from bed, quickly showered, shaved and dressed. Immediately I checked in with intelligence. I then descended the stairs and headed for the dining area. Several Israeli commanders were in the dining area ready for breakfast. Benny had already joined them. Fillmore, spry as ever, was already up and seated. When he saw me ready to enter the room he jumped out of his seat and pulled me aside before I could even say good morning to everyone.

"What the hell are you thinking about b-b-oy," he caught himself. "Felix, are you insane? What is all this about this old cliche, One-World Government?"

He was trying to berate me for considering this as an answer to their immediate crisis.

Quickly, I distanced myself from Fillmore and said, "Don't scold me like I am a six year old! You'll hear along with everyone else what my reasons are. Now let us join the others for breakfast. I'll be there in a minute."

No one, nor anything, not even this colossal crisis could set me on edge. Only my father could do that to me. Fillmore was livid. His face turned beat red. His nostrils flared. Even the white of his eyes turned bloodshot.

"Be sure b–, I will be heard!"

Shooting dagger slit eyes at Fillmore, I clenched my teeth and said, "Don't think you will pull the rug out from under me. Remember who the Prime Minister is and don't you forget it!"

Fillmore, his anger strong, left the room, slamming the dining room door behind him. He sat down for breakfast. Entering the dining room, I gripped the chair and sat down. Everyone ate a hasty breakfast and then covened on the War Room. Benny and most of the commanders overheard the roar between Fillmore and I. Not having time enough for private discussion they would have to save their questions and voice their opinions and objections later.

The War Room was a technological tangle of computers, game boards and a newly installed three-dimensional table map. The room smelled musty, no doubt from the underground stones. The lighting was so bright it could pass for sunlight. Outside the Chondriana secured the room. Then, one by one the commanders took their seats.

I began, "Gentlemen, because of the urgency, I've issued a Presidential Priority Directive to establish Marshall Law."

Dumbstruck, Fillmore's eyebrows shot up, deep furrows on his forehead bulged out. Benny, sober for once, almost fell over in his chair and the military present sat, stunned by my statement of action. Continuing I said, "From this day forward we will retain a direct election of Prime Minister and the requirement that the cabinet be supported by a Knesset majority has been eliminated. In addition, the cabinet will serve a fixed term and legislation will be passed as the result of debates and merits and not party deals to topple a coalition."

Fillmore spoke up, his voice echoing a slow simmer, "Mr. Prime Minister, your idea for a One-World Government with our nation at the helm has made the survival of Israel in a hostile Arab world no longer relevant. And what about our nuclear opacity, no checks or balances on Israel's Doomsday nuclear weapons? Is the current situation really an existential threat?"

Bellowing my words, I replied, "Our survival is relevant. And we are ready to establish auspices of the United Nations. The following will be a nonce. United Nations Emergency Forces and the United Nations Truce Supervision Organization are also on alert on our side."

"The new age of Globalism will now enter the world's future society. In route to global occupation, I am calling Iraq's threat a bluff. In response to our release about Chondriana, ciphers have come in from all over the globe, astounded by the possible march of a 200-million man-made, indestructible army. Fear of nuclear extinction was also echoed. In accordance I have scheduled a UN meeting within the hour. The world will no longer be attached by the isolationists who do not believe in world cooperation or by the perfectionists who think they have the perfect system."

"Gentlemen, should our session at the U.N. hit a downward spiral, I will abandon them and relegate them to irrelevancy. Do I have your complete approval to release Chondriana?"

Everyone present gave a vote of approval. Continuing, I said, "I'll brief the Knesset subcommittee and issue a Code of Silence, impending release of nuclear weapons. Now we have to deal with the men responsible for the Iraqi coup who have taken over Jordan and who are ready to attack us."

"It's reported that Ahmet Harambi, the new Iraqi leader, the Dictator who has replaced the deceased Saddam Hussein in that capacity strangely enough had an Iraqi father, but his mother was a Sabra. Born in Jerusalem in 1945, shortly after the Arab League was formed. He was later educated in the U.S., graduating from Harvard Law, of all times, in 1967."

"Powerful, dynamic and obstinate beyond all bounds, with a truly undisciplined intellect and moved by a malevolent spirit, he is an incurable madman. For several years he has kept close ties with Russia, working with agents in a counterintelligence with their Federal Counter Intelligence Service, FCIS, formerly the KGB."

I continued, "Ahmet's weaknesses: his fear of the Evil Eye and his use of his immense riches gained from the sale of illegal drugs, money laundering and his own habitual use of the big "H," heroine, also used by many of the members of the Rizadh, whom are frequent guests at his wild weekend parties reported in our national dailies, as well as television and radio media whom have kept tabs on Abdul and his chief army officers' drug connections and money laundering, many times even going incognito and becoming a member of the International Narcotics Research Club. Gentlemen, Ahmet Harambi may be viewed by some as brilliant, but he is nothing but an impudent oddball, a pernicious villain with sadistic tendencies and one who loves torture. It also goes without saying he loves danger. He loves it so much, the satisfaction is like eating elegantly prepared gourmet food. Even his own people consider him a control monster, rude, inconsiderate, belligerent, hostile and devoid of all the good virtues and human emotions. He is an eccentric extremist whose stream of thought runs his weird fantasies and false imaginations about world dominance. He holds the belief that the Koran's Sura 5:50, advises him, to take neither Jews or Christians for your friends. Nothing or no one can shake his concrete fixation on Shira (Muslim Law) that the Jews are the aggressors and he has made it known publicly, that he intends to follow the letter of that law."

"In his wanton desire to eliminate us, he believes that by doing this, it is a service to God! He wants to chase us into the desert and hopes to drive us into the Dead Sea and the rest of us into the Mediterranean. However, I believe the non-Muslim world looks upon Ahmet Harabi and his newly formed Ten Arab Nations as though all of them are sociopaths and schizophrenics. I want you to know I don't intend to turn a blind eye to him or his newly formed coalition as war crimes!"

Interrupting me, General Abrams full of pride said, "Felix, the military agrees with you. And we have good news. We have just this moment received a report that nature is on our side. If I may go ahead?"

I said, "Yes, by all means."

General Abrams continued, "Our up to the minute report tells us that all escape routes from Jordan, Saudi Arabia, Iraq, Yemen, and the United Arab Emirates are blocked. A terrific sand storm, a Genie, is holding the Chinese army from marching through the dried up Euphrates River. Ahmet Harambi, we are informed, has received your dispatch to release the Chondriana Army against him. His aides report that when he read your report that his hands fell helpless by his side. Obvious pangs of terror have gripped him by now. We now, therefore, have the upper hand. There is a consensus among our military seated here that support your decision to go ahead and release the Chondriana."

With that General Abrams said, "Felix we are headed for victory!" He then sat down, applauded by everyone present.

"Gentlemen, not only is nature on our side, but I have more good news. I have located the Ark of the Covenant and all of the Second Temple Treasures!"

A shout rose up from everyone, cheering me on. Some with looks of incredulity on their faces.

"Gentlemen, please hold all or any of your remarks or questions until you have read a copy of my print-out listing every recovery I have made."

Silence filled the room. You could hear a pin drop. Egos ran high as I handed print-outs featuring a list of my personal discoveries, as follows:

1. Second Temple Treasures
2. The Tabernacle (Mishkan)
3. The Curtain that covered the Holy of Holies
4. The Holy Candelabra

5. The Ark of the Covenant
6. The Golden Plate that the High Priest wore on his head
7. The Breast Plate worn by the High Priest
8. The Silver Trumpets
9. The Cherubim on top of the Ark of the Covenant
10. The Golden Altar (upon which the incense was offered in the daily service)
11. The Outer Curtains
12. The Golden Table (upon which was placed the showbread)
13. The Veil that covered the outer entrance to the Mishkan
14. The Copper altar (upon which the daily and seasonal sacrifices were offered)
15. The Holy Garments worn by the High Priest in the Holy of Holies on the Day of Atonement
16. The Bells and Pomegranates that were on the bottom of the coat of the High Priest
17. All the other Holy Vessels that were used in the Mishkan (too numerous to mention specifically)
18. The Staff of Moses that he used to bring the 10 plagues on Egypt
19. The container of Manna

"This concludes the list of Second Temple Treasures," I said.

Excitedly, General Abrams spoke up, smiling from ear to ear, he inquired, "My God, Felix, how did you find it? And where did you find them?"

I replied, "As some of you know, I take a late solo night ride. Then I get out and take a walk to many different locations, observing as I go. One night atop Mt. Nebo, about eleven miles away, I looked and saw a blue glow emanating from one of the caves just above the Valley of Achor. The gold and silver, along with the veins are located in The Valley of Achor, known to most of us as The Valley of Trouble, beginning at the Arabah stretching from Aroer at the edge of the Arnon River Valley to Mt. Hermon. It includes all of the Arabah east of the Jordan River between the Dead Sea below the slopes of Mt. Pisgah. It is four miles from north to south, centered on the Wadi Qumran between the outlet of the Wadi Kelt to Beit Arabah. A division comes between the Valley of Jericho on the right. Ten miles south is the Valley of Achor on the left. It lies between the original borders of Judah and Benjamin. It was the place of Acan's stoning, recorded for us in Joshua 7:24–26 and 15:7. This Valley of Achor was recorded by the prophet Hosea 2:15 as a symbol of fruitful hope. It lies just twelve miles south of Jerusalem."

"In one of the caves, I located another copy of the Copper Scroll. Once I deciphered the code it clearly created a map, telling me exactly where these secret treasures were to be found. I will brief the Knesset's subcommittee along with all of the authorities in Israel, with an immediate report of our decisions and actions. I will issue and sign the necessary directives for all the commanders present of the twelve army divisions, the navy, air force and special forces. The Chondriana will be taken off of alert status and instructed to march into action. We will reconvene today at four this afternoon in the War Room. You are dismissed."

Meanwhile, Fillmore had been sitting through Felix's bombastic speech, mute. Not one for being silent especially when it came to Felix's decisions and subsequent actions. He felt like the wind had been blown out of him. He sat astonished and flabbergasted that Felix had kept him, as well as Benny, in the dark about leading us into a One-World Government.

Shocked by Felix's directives, his temples pounding, he felt like someone had hit him over the head with a jack-hammer. This was one of Felix's surprises he had never bargained for.

The military left the War Room, leaving Benny, Fillmore and I alone with the Chondriana on guard outside the door.

Before Fillmore could get a word in, I spoke up, quickly flicking my lighter as I lit up a Camel. They, next to liquor were very calming, and I needed that more than ever. Then turning towards Benny, I said, "Benny, take the necessary steps to mobilize the Chondriana. Then join me at the United Nations by noon. Fillmore, you accompany me."

Benny said, "It will take a few minutes to get the Chondriana in motion, but I'll be able to make it to the U.N. by noon today. See you there."

Then Benny left the room, turned his back and facing the Chondriana, he said, "You twenty-five continue to guard the Prime Minister, Fillmore and the Residence. I'll be back here at the President's Residence, in the War Room, later this afternoon." With that said, Benny left the premises, his mind working in a labyrinth filled with doubts and questions. Would Chondriana perform as he expected? Or would they splinter and become confused?

To beef up security, I notified the Mossad that I was leaving the Residence, and headed for the United Nations. I instructed them to send for my bodyguards. Together, with the Chondriana, they helped secure my safety.

As for Fillmore, I knew he was elated to be with me, for no reason other than he would be able to keep a close eye on me. Fillmore was always for peace. He always felt that war and bloodshed were insane, but agreed that sometimes it was necessary. And what of the future generations, he wondered. Many in the prime of life would die if the madness did not come to a halt.

However, Fillmore was excited and proud, thrilled to a tee that Felix found such vast treasures. And the money they would accrue would be phenomenal. Thinking back, I recalled the financial intrigue when the International Monetary Fund (IMF) was established and the birth of the World Bank back in 1944.

"Felix," Fillmore said, "What can we expect will happen at the U.N.?"

I replied, "Well, my speech will be very brief, but as to the nations gathered one will have to wait and see. I will call for a summit conference of nations and go from there."

Chain smoking, I was annoyed with Fillmore as he led the Chondriana behind them. Exiting the library, we left the Residence and had the Chondriana enter the truck parked out front. Benny had left instructions with the Chondriana driver to follow Felix and Fillmore. Surrounded by the Mossad, we entered the limo and headed for the U.N. headquarters located now in Jerusalem. It seemed like only yesterday the U.N. was officially established in San Francisco, California also known as the City on Seven Hills in 1945.

I recalled how Fillmore briefed me on the first meeting of the U.N.'s General Assembly. It was in London. Later, on November 29, 1947, a most courageous and collective General Assembly voted to divide Palestine between two states, one Arab and one Jewish. However, the Arabs failed to take up the option, causing untold bloodshed and terrorism even up until this very day. It had always made sense to me that Jerusalem would be a United Nations capital.

Knowing that I had brought it about, closing the deal, I felt I was making a move in the direction of complete redemption. A strange warm surge came over me. I felt totally secure surrounded by the supernatural power of the armed Chondriana, the Mossad and my own personal bodyguards.

The last time I had appeared before the U.N. was when the United States appealed for intervention by the U.N. to sponsor a plan that would give the PLO guerrillas the chance to evacuate Palestine, dispersing them to any Arab country willing to accept them. The plan failed just like Oslo and the U.N.'s Millennium Summit had came to a dead end.

The U.S. was no longer in its glory days. Its descent, slowly deteriorating, was drenched in moral decay and going into a deep financial depression.

Even when expectations had run high when the U.S. had moved their Embassy from Tel Aviv to Jerusalem. As if out of nowhere Fillmore jumped in, shouting in a shrill tone of voice, "Felix! Will you stop smoking those damn Camels?"

Breaking my train of thought, I blew up shouting back at Fillmore. I said, "You old rascal. Is that all I can hear from you during this crisis?"

Fillmore hissed back bellowing, "Felix, you may not care if your life is shortened by smoking those cancer sticks. I don't care who you are, you overgrown ox! I will not tolerate secondary smoke in such close quarters!"

Angrily, I died my cigarette out in the limo's ashtray. Then turning towards Fillmore, with my eyebrows arched and my eyes full of daggers, I said, "Fillmore, you can nag more than most women! Why I should give you an Oscar for the part."

"And I would accept," Fillmore retorted, giving me a steely glance.

Then I retorted, "Fillmore, knock it off. I am piecing together my speech before the U.N."

Fillmore snickered, his eyes a fiery red. Turning his nose up into the air, he shook his head from side to side and said, "Don't be naughty b–," catching himself, he stopped short of saying my much hated word, boy. Totally disgusted with me, he closed his eyes and laid his head back against the limo's seat.

Our sleek black limo entered the garage of the U.N. building. Leading the way were the twenty-five armed Chondriana. Coming to a halt they exited the truck guarding Fillmore and I entering the auditorium, with a forty-four Magnum strapped to my waist. Surrounded by the Chondriana and twenty ultra-magnificent Mossad agents, each one of them armed with their twenty-two caliber Barettas. I was not the first one to address the U.N. General Assembly wearing a pistol. That position was held in November of 1974 by the now deceased Yasser Arafat.

In the General Assembly, dozens of Presidents, Prime Ministers, Foreign Ministers and Ambassadors were present. Members of the Israeli Knesset and other Israeli leaders rose from their seats, applauding as I made my entrance. The U.S. Ambassador was present in absentia. Nodding my head in approval, I glanced all around the room, eyeing each person in the General Assembly. Taking my seat on the podium, my entourage stood guard behind me.

The applause died down and the U.N. Secretary General, Ives Thoran of Swedena, approached the podium. Formally he addressed the

Israeli statesmen and scholar, David Solomon Cohen. A round of applause filled the room, but tensions were thick with worry and fear which filled the faces of those in the audience. Speaking extemporaneously, the Secretary General formally recognized each nation present.

He went on into a litany of praises stating that I had proved myself to be an absolute master of the U.N.'s activities, both in the Political and Social Sciences, praising my expertise in International Law, especially those involving U.N. treaties, the environment and its economic statistics, International Economics, Trade, Industry, Agriculture, Communications, Transportation, Engineering, Construction, Public Administration, Science and Technology, just to name a few.

Then he introduced me. He said, "I now give the floor to our new Chairman, Prime Minister, Felix Sebastian Fox."

Taking a slow bow, I mouthed a thank you to all those in the audience.

Applauding Felix, the members of the General Assembly stood confused by those clones standing guard over Felix. Who were they? Where did they come from? They recognized the Mossad and bodyguards, but who were these strange men who all looked alike? These were questions the members whispered among each other.

Felix looked stunning, surrounded by the strange looking Chondriana and the elite Mossad guards. It was time for him to gloat. After all, for years Israel had been the only nation ever denied a seat on the U.N.'s Security Council. And now emerging as a world leader, all television cameras were focused on him as news reporters from around the globe flashed cameras and took notes.

Fillmore was seated next to the General Secretary. The General Secretary turned to give Fillmore a smile, but Fillmore just glared at him, his eyes cold as ice, to which in return the General Secretary gave him an exasperated smirk.

Ignoring the formal acknowledgments of the dignitaries present, I said, "Gentlemen, may this day go down in infamy as every tribe and every nation gathers together to pursue peace among all in the Global Community. The United Nations fulfills the great words that are pinned on the outside of this building. Its motto taken from the writings of a well-known Jew, named Isaiah. In the book written by him and bearing his name, I refer you to Isaiah, chapter two verse four, 'And they shall beat their swords into plowshares and their spears into pruning hooks.'"

"Let me say in response to this current emergency, the U.N. Security Council has distributed to every one of you the reaction and action to be taken against Ahmet Humrabi's Coup, usurping Jordan and setting up in its place a ten nation Arab government, thereby isolating themselves from the global village. His take over of our third Temple has succeeded. They have killed all of our priests. But, now the Temple is under siege, under our control."

"In response to their threat to wipe Israel out we have taken emergency measures in defense of our borders. We will show that we have what it takes to be the core of the U.N. peacekeeping force. Towards this end, we have produced, in addition to our own military, the Israeli armed forces, we have cloned an emergency Task Force of 200 million Chondriana soldiers. These soldiers have been programmed to defend us. Twenty-five who now stand guard here by my side. This action however is not an experiment nor is it to be considered a premature action."

"It has been established by reports we have secured that Iraq has not only taken over Jordan and set up its own coalition during this coup, but they have also assassinated all of the Jordanian Royal Air force, and arrested and imprisoned the Royal Family."

"Iraqi Military have set up a new government in Amon Jordan, the City on Seven Hills. This new government has succeeded in drying up the Euphrates River, with the intent to march two-hundred million Chinese soldiers, who at present have become their allies. They have joined ranks with this new government, with plans to march against Israel and take over Jerusalem. Their plan is to go through the dried up Euphrates River to reach us more quickly and easily. Their plan has failed. A severe sand storm, a Genie, is keeping them at bay."

"In addition to overtaking Jerusalem they also plan to take over the United Nations!"

"It is our resolve to shield this very body of nations represented here today and to safeguard our people and our nation from this intended destruction by meeting brute force with brute force."

Whispers spread throughout the various members as they sat on the edge of their seats stunned by their own responses towards the Chondriana and the tremendous impact of my speech.

I continued, "Today, before this body I submit the results of a Title search. The documentation you have been given declares that Israel and only Israel holds the Title Deed to all the land from the river of Egypt, Jordan and the Northern part of Iraq. This is taken from Leviticus 35:42 and Genesis 15:18."

Total silence filled the auditorium. Members sat dumbfounded as I went on to present exactly how I would finally destroy this government and take possession of all of its territory by force if necessary. Seven years since the original peace treaty was originally set up with them when they first took power was about to end. (*See Notes 3.)

Over the next thirty minutes I spoke informally, revealing to the U.N. that Israel was now under Marshall Law with scheduled evacuation of its citizens.

Then addressing the Arab world in absentia, I said, "Today, gentlemen, the ten nation Arab world, its allies and all the nations present here today, let it be known to you that Israel is ready to establish a World Constitutional Parliament under my direct control. Any person serving the U.N. peacekeeping force must relinquish his or her own nationality and become a World Citizen. Should any government threaten Israel from this day and forward, I put them on instant notice that if they do not comply they will be immediately exterminated."

As I continued to speak, fear gripped those present. "Mr. Chairman," I said, "I would like to request a two hour recess for lunch and to give everyone time to think over their vote when the session resumes. This concludes my speech."

A recess was called. Two hours whizzed by.

On our return to the General Assembly a vote would be taken. Whereby all the members present ratified by the World Constitution, global government to be called, "The Federation of Earth." This excluded the United States. They abstained from entering a system of global government, having barely survived its own internal corrupt power and its downward moral spiral along with the worst financial crisis since the 1929 Depression, they were on their way out as a leading world power.

I stepped down from the podium, closely followed by the Mossad and the Chondriana. Leaders from the World Constitution Parliament Association, WCPA, founded in 1959 approached me.

"Mr. Prime Minister, the World Federalist welcomes you and your leadership."

"Thank you," I said as I moved through the crowd. All eyes were fixed on Fillmore, the Mossad, me and the Chondriana whom were still behind me.

Other leaders of the Rainbow Coalition, the Council on Foreign Relations, the Club of Rome and several prominent members of the secret society and world powerhouse, The Bilderbergs, shook my hand in hearty approval.

As I turned to exit the auditorium on the left, from the corner of my eye I spotted Daura and Felixovna. My heart dropped in my stomach. My body started to tremble. I felt faint and my mind went numb. I could not believe my eyes. Both of them were holding hands, revealing possible signs of intimacy. I thought she was dead. Daura never did get back to me on the search he had requested to find out what had happened to her.

After my initial shock, a sense of disdain and disgust took over. I immediately had my bodyguard, Bruce, to check the reason for their presence.

I began to chain smoke. Getting into my limo, my hands trembling, I sat down next to Fillmore and instructed the driver and the truck with the Chondrianas to wait for a few minutes before they would take off for the Orde Wingate Building.

Meanwhile, Bruce proceeded to network, found a few mobile agents, asked a few questions. Then he headed back towards me with the information he had gathered.

I saw Bruce approaching my limo. I hand motioned Bruce to get into the limo.

Bruce opened the door to the limo, stepped in and sat next to me.

Noticeably upset, I said, "Fill me in, Bruce. What did you find out?"

Bruce said, "Have your driver take us to the Residence where we can take this up in private."

I said "Driver, to the Residence please."

Meanwhile, exiting the U.N. building Felixovna headed towards my limo. According to rumors I had heard, she did not show any visible signs of being pregnant.

Immediately I said to my driver, "Stop the limo!" The driver quickly brought the limo to a halt!

Felixovna approached the door of the limo. I lowered the window. Felixovna glanced at me and our eyes locked. It was in sweet agony.

Brazenly she said, "Felix, how delightful to see you!"

My face must have turned red, my insides boiling in desperation and anger.

Hesitantly I asked, "Would you join me for lunch? I am headed for lunch at the Orde Wingate Building. I'll be there in a few minutes."

Smiling she said, "Great, I'll see you then."

She then took off by herself, leaving me to wonder, where in heaven's name did Daura disappear to?

The limo took off, passing the limestone and concrete buildings on the jutting hills. The limo driver took the back roads to avoid the Military action, passing the Dome of the Rock. First I headed home. The driver pulled up. I passed the fleet of Chondriana protecting my Residence.

Once inside, I said, "Fillmore, take a seat here in the Library while I instruct the Chondriana."

Fillmore complied and I instructed twenty-five of the Chondriana to stand guard around the building and the other twenty-five to stand guard outside the War Room.

They complied.

Bruce, paced the hall until I approached him and led him to my office. Upon closing the door I instructed Jay, my office manager, to put a hold on all calls. I wanted no interruptions.

"Okay," I said, "Bruce, what have you found out?"

"Well Felix, Daura is not only a Mole, but a triple-crossing Mole. He is a Bagman for Iraq, Russia and our government as well."

I asked, "And what about Felixovna?"

"Are you sure you want to know?"

"Yes. This is a case of National Security."

"Felixovna is a double-crosser, a spy for Iraq. And reports have it that she is also no longer a nulligravia."*

"Whose is it," I asked?

"Its a by-child," answered Bruce.*

"Why didn't she abort it," I asked Bruce?

"Word has it," said Bruce, "That she is going to use it to broker a deal for world power."

I didn't know weather to laugh or cry. Is it possible, I wondered, could the child be mine? Or did she broker a deal and clone an embryo?

Then I asked Bruce, "What was her link to Daura? Do you have any information about the status of their relationship?"

Bruce replied, "There are so many rumors. I cannot tell you which were true or which were lies. I cannot give you an accurate answerer to that. That is all I know for now Felix."

"Thank you, Bruce," I said.

"Be sure she gets to the club. That will be all," I said. Shaking Bruce's hand I led him to the door. Somewhat puzzled, I lit up a Camel and went over to the Curio and poured myself a Scotch and Soda. Then I sat down. The jolt had shaken me to the core of my being.

Could the child be mine, or was it Daura's? It had only been about six weeks since I had lost track of her.

And Daura, a triple-crossing Mole? How had all this escaped me? Where was intelligence? How could I have been so naive and unaware? It was so unlike me. I thought about that old cliché, love is blind!

Anger rose up in my heart, a kind of anger that was a stranger to me. Oh, I had known anger before, anger over my mother's untimely death, anger against Fillmore and his incessant nagging. But, this anger made me sick to the very pit of my stomach. The reality that Daura was a triple crosser and a thief, robbing me of my only true love. This betrayal pierced me like a knife had been plunged into my heart. I was astonished by my own lack of suspicion towards her and Daura. Strangely I never even sensed or felt an evil foreboding during and even after our relationship had dissipated. Besides, once again, where was intelligence?

What if it was mine, I thought. If it was mine why would she keep it from me?

Then a sudden calm came over me. I sat silently, puffed on my Camel, toying with the thought of their execution.

I quickly freshened up. I was filled with anxiety. It was an anxiety that even world politics could not stir in me.

I had so many unanswered questions. I hoped I would soon have them answered. Then I paged my driver.

"Sam," I said, "Have the limo and my guards ready. I'll be out momentarily."

Sam replied, "Sure, Mr. Prime Minister. I am on it now."

"Sam," I instructed, "Take me to the Orde Wingate Building."

Sam glanced back while I entered the limo, accompanied by the Mossad and my bodyguards.

When the limo arrived at the Orde Wingate Building, I instructed Sam to wait in the limo and for my bodyguards, I instructed them to wait in the lobby. I said, "I'll page you if I need you."

I entered the building. Blinded by my passionate love for her, I threw all sane protocol and caution to the wind, leaving my bodyguards behind me in the lobby. I headed for the mezzanine where private dining rooms were available for lunch.

Apprehensive I thought she might be a no show.

Just then Bruce entered the room.

I asked Bruce, "Is she here?"

"Yes," Bruce replied, "But she has company."

"Are they her bodyguards?"

"That's the assumption for the moment," replied Bruce.

Entering the dining room I saw her sitting patiently, surrounded by several bodyguards.

Disappointed that she was not alone, I asked her, "Are these necessary?"

"Yes, Felix, they are," she replied. "You see," she said to me, "You are now under house arrest!"

Caught off guard I started to shake. I wondered how could I have walked so blindly into an ambush? Never the one to be without bodyguards, now I foolishly had them waiting for me in the lobby.

"This is an absolute outrage," I shouted out at her. "What a fool I've been for allowing myself no cover."

Boom-boom-boom-boom-boom! The sound of a large explosion, possibly at the entrance of the building. Without any further warning, a piece of duck tape was drawn across my mouth and someone handcuffed my hands behind my back. The men mounted their rifles and exited the building at the back exit, unnoticed, with me in tow. The bomb no doubt used as a diversion to block anyone from following us.

Then I saw Daura. What was Daura doing here? Where was Bruce? Where were my bodyguards? Where were the Chondriana? Had they been killed in the explosion which had occurred a few seconds ago? Left in the dark, I passed out.

Chapter 7

Catastrophes Of A Third Class—Collapse—The Last Stages Of Civilization

"Therefore I will make the heavens tremble and the earth will rumble from its place."

~Isaiah 13:1

"And the foundation of earth will quake ... the land will totter like a drunkard."

~Isaiah 24:17 & 20

It was too late! Daura did not get the chance to tell me that he had never been intimate with her.

Before he knew it, a gun pointed at Daura, shooting thirty rounds a second, traveling more than two thousand miles per hour velocity. A two-twenty three bullet pierced the air, hitting Daura in the heart. It was a dead center hit. The rank smell of gun smoke filled the room.

Quickly, my bodyguards succeeded in releasing me from my captors and uncuffed me. The Mossad agents and the Chondriana present stopped the blonde vixen dead in her tracks.

They grabbed the stunned conspirator, Felixovna, as she stood clutching her chest, trembling. Seized by panic, her heart pounding louder than her high-pitched ear shattering scream. She knew she was next. The price for her treachery was a grizzly death by guillotine! Suddenly, the ground began to crumble under her feet. Her world turned black as pitch. I felt like my insides were being sucked out! How, I wondered, could I have given myself so completely to her? How could I have breached my own security? Why had my usual sense of danger failed me? How could I have been such a fool? The whole affair disgusted me.

Instantaneously, I brushed aside my egotistical thoughts and immediately summoned my emotions, freeing me from the vacuum that had for so long left me empty.

It took every ounce of my nerve to keep me from picking her up from the ground. Slowly my bodyguards picked her up and carried her to an empty room for interrogation.

Blindfolded and wreathing with pain, someone began to pull out her fingernails, one by one. Her very own screams bringing her in and out of consciousness. I could barely watch.

"Who," her tormenter asked, "Who is behind the Prime Minister's assassination attempt? Who has bewitched you? Who has planned to destroy us?"

Hours went by but Felixovna did not submit. In agony, she blacked out several times. I could no longer watch and left the room. Raw, bleeding and in pain she finally gave in.

"It was," she said, "Ahmet and his ten nation government who set me and Daura up to assassinate the Prime Minister and take over the world." Then she lost consciousness for the last time.

I was notified of her death. Would I ever find out if her unborn child was mine? Gruesome as it seemed, I ordered an autopsy and a DNA test on the fetus.

I could not stand the pain. Hearing of her execution by the Kidon, the operational arm of our Mossad, made me shudder. I felt as if my heart was broken into a million pieces. The pit of my stomach felt like it was tied into knots. I went into dry heaves and finally vomited.

After cleaning myself up, I put in a call requesting all of my generals and chiefs of staff to meet me at the U. N. building. Once my generals, chiefs of staff and the Chondriana, still on guard duty, arrived, I made arrangements with the U.N.'s General Secretary and was given an emergency meeting. Not wasting any time, the General Secretary notified everyone. Once everyone was seated, he took the liberty of giving me and everyone present an informal greeting and introduction.

I walked to the podium and spoke, saying, "Gentlemen, a plot by Ahmet to assassinate me has been uncovered and has failed. The culprits have been interrogated. Gentlemen, in addition we are gathered here to address the following reports: the military plot of Ahmet and his ten Arab nations out to destroy Israel has boomeranged! I have launched a massive counterattack on all of their cities, plateaus and valleys in the countries surrounding us. They have been destroyed by release of our Stealth Tiger helicopters. Iraq has fallen like a drunkard! And to our good fortune, a horrific sand storm, a Genie, holding back China, their allies, from marching through the dried up Euphrates River, bringing their march to a complete halt!"

"World War Three is now in progress as I speak. I have released a nuclear bomb upon Egypt. Right now it is being demolished, leaving the tongue of Egypt totally obliterated. No one will be able to live there for forty years! Reports show that the Chondrianas are stationed by the banks of the Arnon River and state that Ahmet has been completely wiped out."

"Gentlemen, we shall recess. Time for everyone to absorb these events. We will then reconvene in an hour here at the U.N." As if out of nowhere I felt an eerie chill go through my body. Anxious, I lit up a Camel, poured myself a brandy, then calmly waited out the hour. Then I cell phoned Benny.

"Benny, this is Felix. Where were you? The U.N. emergency session is about to resume. I want you here now!"

"Felix," Benny said, "There are plans being laid to destroy the Chondrianas."

"By whom," I asked Benny?

"Ahmet and his allies," Benny replied.

I asked, "Does he know about BLCZ?"

Benny said, "I have not received any intelligence to that effect, so I'll say no."

221

Benny arrived at the U.N. building.

I saw Benny approaching. He walked up to me and said, "Greetings, Felix. I wanted you to know how relieved I am that the assassination attempt by Ahmet has failed. Our bug escaped their clean sweep. And by the way, my condolences on Felixovna."

I winced at the sound of her name. Ignoring the comment, I moved on, totally dismissing my burning emotions for her.

"Yes," I replied, "Thank God no one has found the bug we planted. We are still ahead of their every move."

Benny went on, "Felix, a brief press conference is scheduled to be held in the Rotunda prior to the return to the U.N.'s emergency session. My god, Felix, what is going on?"

"You'll know the answer to that in a few minutes," I replied as I swiftly walked past Benny and entered the Rotunda.

Upon entering the U.N.'s Rotunda, the U.N. Secretary General, panic stricken, grabbed me by my arm. His face drained of blood, he said, "Felix, we thought about your successful attempt in forming the World Constitutional Parliament and the seven year peace treaty with Iraq and its members. We need you to unite our devastated globe and restore the peace treaty destroyed by Ahmet. Please step up to the press box and fill us in."

Giving the Secretary General a cold stare, I said, "Calm down old man, calm down!"

The Secretary General then gave me a smirk, resenting the fact that I had called him an old man.

"Gentlemen," I said addressing the members of the press and U.N., "In view of the overwhelmingly tragic events, the planetary emergency and the resulting chaos, I have set in motion a plan to settle what is now World War Three. In addition we have wiped out Egypt, destroying her before she could destroy us. Her threats to annihilate us were real. I have sent a rapid directive to all nations that are still in existence and able to function, suspending all international tensions, in order to prevent utter failure, confusion, and some which appear to have been obscure. However, to avoid a potential perpetual holocaust, I have taken control of the U.N.'s military operations. I have rescinded the eight member command units and dismantled the Rapidly Deploy Mission Headquarters (RDMHQ). And I am putting in a call to arms with the standby U.N. Army. However, these men will not wear the U.N. uniform nor don the U.N.'s blue helmets. Also, all non-military police are to maintain civilian order against a magnitude of violence and upheaval never before known to man."

"You have seen the Chondriana. I am holding them at bay, pending a truce, whereby the Hammas guerillas must evacuate those Palestinians who are still alive. These will be resettled in the remaining Arab countries that are still in existence, who have agreed to accept them. From this moment on, nationhood will be made obsolete and all states will recognize Israel as the single global authority."

With my hands trembling, I lit up another Camel. I felt as if my face was on fire. I said, "I wish to inform the press and the U.N. members that an assassination attempt upon my life by the harlot, Felixovna, set up and backed up by Ahmet, his Ten Nations and their allies in a coup to take over Jerusalem have both been unsuccessful. The culprits, Felixovna and the triple crossing minion, Daura, have been executed. It has been another three and a half years since they broke our original seven year peace treaty. Soon they will all be dead."

Hearing myself echo those words made me feel dead too, but I went on. "In addition an order for the arrest and execution of all opposition, including Messianic Jews has gone out. A search for their hiding place is ongoing. Some say they are hiding out in Petra. Others say they have disappeared from off the face of the earth. In addition to Egypt's total obliteration and all of the Jordanian Royal Air Force, parts of Saudi Arabia and the entire army in Damascus no longer exist. Fire is burning and has destroyed all of Iraq, but their government is still intact. The few people who are left in Iraq and Iran are in panic. The Chondrianas have successfully surrounded Iraq and Iran in all directions. Gentlemen, it's a blitzkrieg! Globally we are the world's future! The rest of the world is more than ready now to accept Israel's World Constitutional Parliament, thus to rule the world, fulfilling the Jewish prophet's words found in Isaiah 2:1–3. His words have come true. I will now read it to all of you. 'The prophecy of Isaiah son of Amos, concerning Judah and Jerusalem: It will happen in the end of days: the mountain of the Temple of Heaven will be firmly established as the head of the mountains, and it will be exalted above the hill, and all the nations will stream to it.'"

Members of the press sat astonished, while members of the U.N. sat trembling in utter horror as I went on with my uninterrupted pronouncements. No one was in more agony than Fillmore. I could see his heartache and his head no doubt throbbing.

Addressing the press, I concluded the interview and walked back to the podium. Addressing the session I said, "Gentlemen there is another emergency not on the agenda. One that threatens those of us who remain in this strategic location. Gentlemen, what I fear is about to come true. An immanent disaster is headed towards the Jordan Valley. There exists in this valley a major geological fault line known to most of you and today's geologists as The Great Rift Valley. This fault line runs from Lebanon all the way down to the Dead Sea, the lowest point on earth's surface. It also runs through Israel, parallel along the entire length of the King's Highway." Pulling down a wall map of the area, I pointed to the south border from the shore of the Dead Sea, fixing my laser pointer on the map to a place called the Arabah, a trough east of the Jordan River, between the Dead Sea and The Great Rift Valley, below the slopes of Mt. Pisgah. "According to my specks," I continued, "We can expect a massive earthquake to register as an unheard of ten and a half. That is more than the maximum ten on the Richter Scale. In conclusion gentlemen, Civil Defense is executing massive evacuations. In addition, I am implementing Marshall Law to prevail."

Glancing at my watch, the U.N. Chairman rose to his feet. His body visibly trembling and his lips quivering, he said, "This takeover by you, Mr. Prime Minister, smacks without a doubt of pulling off the twenty-four steps of a Jewish conspiracy to control the world as indicated in the Protocols of the Elders of Zion. In protest, I therefore withdraw myself as Chairman of the U.N."

Outraged, I felt my face flush and my mouth curl up in contortion. I responded to this vicious accusation, "I accept your withdrawal as Chairman of the U.N., but in your reference to my takeover as leader of the newly formed World Constitutional Parliament relating to me fulfilling The Protocols of the Elders of Zion, I have this to reply. In the past these writings were thoroughly investigated by several political governments and found to be unauthentic, a hoax, a fraudulent work of fiction. Originally they proved to be written by the Russian Secret Police who were dead set to wipe out the Jews."

"This work of forgery originally entered the political realm prior to World War One. It was at that time used by that fiend, Hitler, as a death warrant during World War Two to justify the genocide of six million Jews! It therefore has no place in these proceedings and will be ignored in the written minutes and deleted in the world press!"

Quickly I concluded the emergency session, "Gentlemen, due to the impending emergency this concludes our session. Evacuation is necessary. You are thereby dismissed. Hopefully, if all media forms are still functioning, you will be contacted with the date, time and location of our next session." Then escorted under heavy guard by the Mossad and the Chondriana, Benny, Fillmore and I safely headed back to the Residence. They were to remain with me in the underground headquarters of the President's Residence.

Immediately, the press sent out a montage of news reports to all of the remaining media that was left of Saudis Al-Watan and the

224

global Cabernet in their various languages. Second Coming headlines would read, "Ahmet's Ten Arab Nations wiped out! United Nations now defunct! Israel's Prime Minister will lead us by the World Constitutional Parliament."

Soon thereafter, Benny, Fillmore and I settled in the War Room of the President's underground headquarters. The security contingent made up of the Mossad and Chondriana stood guard outside the door.

Intelligence reports were being received from around the world by fax. Sifting through them, I started to shake, breaking out into a cold sweat and leaving me almost mute and frightened by what I read. Fillmore, usually silent, grumbled and in a rapid fire voice he asked me, "Well, my boy, what is it?"

Almost stumbling over my words, I replied, "The fax I received and which I am now about to read to you is from the Royal Observatory. Fillmore, Benny, both of you had better take a seat."

Benny and Fillmore, were both startled by what I read. I spoke with a shaky voice with a sense of impending doom. "Benny, Fillmore," I repeated, "As scientists we know that the moon is the climate regulator of the earth. This is something that will be hard to believe. It has to do with the United States of America. This fax states, due to previous huge changes in the weather we have precipitated a prolonged famine in the U.S. Indications are that NASA scientists, have today, implemented a plan to counteract their problem. The plan, though dangerous, is an operation led by the U.S. Government. NASA scientists have proceeded to send three nuclear rockets to blast the moon apart, which at this time is in its perigee and they plan to totally destroy it. Their purpose in sending these nuclear rockets to rip the moon into pieces in order to totally destroy it, they say they expect its debris will disintegrate into the upper atmosphere and not into the Pacific Ocean or on land. Since the moon creates earth's twenty-three and a half degree axis, their plan is to move the earth from off of its normal twenty-three and a half degree axis. This would re-establish earth's spin rate onto a ninety degree axis. This new rate of the earth's axis they say would cause the sun's rays to shine directly and evenly onto the whole surface of the earth. This will cause the earth to slow down, making the days longer, thus creating an eternal springtime. Planting and growing food would increase and thereby eliminate famine forever! Their goal in doing this is to create a permanent change in earth's climate, leaving the entire globe to bask, as I said, into its eternal springtime! The bad news is that their operation has failed!"

Fillmore cried out, "Why this action borders on insanity! Are you sure this fax is not a hoax, Felix?" Fillmore was petrified, glued to his seat, mentally now drawing a blank. However, he managed to blurt out several questions.

He went on asking me, "Were NASA's calculations correct? Do we face another global holocaust? My God, man, who or what will be left?"

Exasperated with Fillmore's outbreak of onerous questions, I said, "Fillmore, I have not finished reading. The answer will become clear as I finish reading all the faxes."

Continuing to read, I said, "This time I will read from the Heidelberg's Observatory Report." As I read I felt all my blood drain out of me. What I read left me in a state of shock. I held my breath for a few seconds, astounded. Finally I managed to say, "It gets worse! The information from the Heidelberg Observatory reports that NASA's plan has not only failed but it has backfired! Our scientists tell us that they failed and that this operation may even cause the earth not only to slow its spin, but it may even cause it to come to a complete stop! Science has come a long way since the Near-Shoemaker Spacecraft's first landing on the twenty-one mile asteroid EROS (named after the Greek God of love) whose materials are even older than our own planet. But, the real threat is the asteroid 1950 DA is headed this way!"

"Benny, Fillmore, we are about to witness another emergency, a worldwide catastrophe. This event of epic proportions will end the sciences of astronomy, geography, meteorology and humanity forever!"

Fillmore blurted out, "My God, Felix, is it possible that the earth will come to a complete stop and will it be able to restart its new spin rate?"

"Yes," I replied. "However, there is a strong potential for the global extinction of man. In addition, we can expect to shortly see an increasingly abhorrent celestial phenomenon, a global commotion with the possibly that no one will survive!"

Hesitantly I went on, "Scientists in the field of astronomy say here that a perturbation has occurred in the rotating movement of the earth. This report states, due to an electrical discharge caused by an immensely strong magnetic field generated by eddy currents interacting with the top layer of the earth's crust and slowing down the rotation of the earth, the moon not only has disintegrated, but a more serious catastrophe has erupted."

"And what the hell is it," growled Fillmore?

"Well," I replied exasperated, "The earth's orbit will shortly change its global axis. It will reverse its current direction! Let me read out the details, some of which you both as scientists are familiar with."

I continued to read on, "This fax states that the outer shell of the earth's crust will rotate west, while its inner core or magma will rotate in the opposite direction. The earth's spin will then gradually slow down. It will then start to violently wobble back and forth. Then, faster than the blink of an eye, the velocity of the earth's rotation will come to a complete halt! Immanently, this will be felt all around the entire world, leaving the West Coast and the East Coast of the U.S., and all of Europe and parts of Russia buried under ice. All of the people, all of their culture and their respective governments will no doubt be totally wiped out!"

Fillmore's teeth began to chatter. Hardly able to speak, he stuttered and said, "Felix, this means that the U.S. and most of Europe will be entering an ice age doesn't it?"

Tersely I replied, "Yes! NASA's miscalculations have triggered an ecological catastrophe, the Big Chill. It will change all of the northern latitudes. This polar flip action will bring about colossal destruction on a scale never even conceived of in all of man's history."

Fillmore, turning grayer every minute, managed to say, "Felix, if the poles are reversed that means that we can expect a shift in the poles electro-magnetism, leaving many other continents buried under ice. My god, man, the underpinnings of earth will lose their grip, loosening it from its regular rotational spin, leaving earth's strata totally deranged."

Benny, silent all this time, was shaking all over. His body grew weak. He let out a deep sigh and said, "Felix, Fillmore, it's going to be more than a horrendous global catastrophe."

In sheer terror I said, "Yes Benny, it will be a global catastrophe. And you are right, that's not all. I am almost afraid to read this fax from the Royal Astronomical Society."

Almost in a state of shock and barely able to speak, I felt as if someone had blown all the air out of me. Speaking in a low tone of voice, I went on to read the report in almost a whisper. "Their report states once the polar shifts begin, we can expect tempest gases to be carried along by a spontaneous lack of oxygen. This will cause fires in our atmosphere. Then once the poles have reversed, all latitudes will be displaced. Seaports of New York, London, Tokyo, Singapore, China, Hong Kong, South America and Sydney will have collapsed. The results will be that millions of people will die by asphyxiation or electrocution in certain areas. And there are indications that some fragments of the moon that did not totally disintegrate from its impact by the nuclear weapons will orbit the earth, ending up with a ring of its leftover debris, similar to the rings of Saturn and the phenomenal Asteroid Belt."

Fillmore, struggling to gain self-control of his fear asked me, "My god, is there any good news?"

I had been speaking in a low voice, now I spoke in a hushed tone. I said, "Well, Fillmore and Benny, one thing in our favor is that the polar flip will not affect our continent. I am grateful that the U.S.'s Super-Volcano, in their Yellowstone National Park, didn't blow. Their Super-Volcano would be ten times the eruption of their Mt. St. Helen's in their state of Washington. It would be more than hell because if it were to erupt it would fill the global stratosphere with sulfur dioxide leaving all of the seas, all sea creatures and end all agriculture. Yes, Benny and Fillmore, we knew about it, but we did not believe it."

Fillmore, rasping now, said, "Well isn't that just dandy. The polar flip will not affect our continent, but will we enter a volcanic winter?"

Benny started with a nervous cough and said, "In our favor too, is the season. It's early spring and even if it were summer we could still have a good harvest that would give us a good food supply, an adequate one to meet our current crisis. However it will knock out the growing seasons all over the rest of the world."

Somewhat surprised, I heard my pager ring.

Answering I said, "Prime Minister Fox here, whom am I speaking with?"

The voice on the other end said, "This is General One, Mr. Prime Minister. I have horrifying news to report to you. Millions lie dead here in the Valley of Achor, most of them Jordanians and Ahmet's ten Arab nations and their allies. What is our next move?"

"General One," I said, "These are your instructions. Summon the troops, gather your battalions and send out your men in groups of ten and proceed to retreat. Go to the George Allenby Bridge, cross over and start catastrophic burial proceedings of the dead. Bury them quickly before plague or disease should kill those of us who remain alive. I will contact you within the hour via GPS. Copy that?"

"Copy that, Prime Minister Fox," General One replied and then hung up.

Suddenly, without warning, in under a split second, the ground under Fillmore, Benny and I shook. High-speed electrons passed through the earth and the earth came to an unprecedented stop!

My body slammed against the wall and I landed on the floor. I almost fainted as I watched Fillmore hit the floor. And Fillmore's eyes bulged out of his head while he watched Benny disappear, buried under falling rocks, stones, metal and other dangerous rubble.

Fillmore pulled himself up from the floor, then gave me a hand. But, we could not find Benny.

The earth started to wobble back and forth and the earth's rotational spin rate reached absolute zero, causing earth shocks no doubt felt simultaneously around the whole world!

This was a great blow for all the physicists whose calculations had failed. They could hardly believe that they would be witnesses of the change in the earth's tilt take place, let alone see it to the point of arrest in its orbit, coming to a complete dead stop!

Parenthetically, miraculously, deep below the underground tunnels in the Valley of Achor everything remained intact. Strange, one could not believe one's eyes, ears or senses, but there were no injuries or fatalities among the Messianic Jews hiding there below.

However, it goes without saying that in their human nature they were frightened and a few were almost torn out of their wits when they heard the rumble of the earth and its spin come to an abrupt stop! People and things were strewn about, but thankfully there were no serious injuries or damage to the tunnel walls or their foundations. Only a layer of dust blanketed the tables, chairs and the dirt flooring of the tunnels and the caves. But after the dust cleared, it was obvious that a miracle, by the finger of God, had protected them.

Moshe spoke up first and said, "We do not know the fate of those above us, but it's a great relief to know everyone is safe down here."

Barry chimed in and said, "Praise the Lord! We have not suffered any casualties either!"

Marvin entered the room which had been previously hewn out of a cave and said, "Gentlemen, the word down here is that we are safe and have had no casualties or injuries from the catastrophic event taking place above us. Even our food storage rooms all remain intact!"

David, a former Mossad agent and intelligence gatherer, came running into the room. Almost out of breath, he said in alarm, "Moshe, brothers, I received news that NASA, backed by the U.S. Government, has created a geologically instantaneous cosmic blunder."

"Sit down, David," said Moshe, "And have a glass of Magen, David. It will help calm you down. Now what has happened?"

David swallowed a few sips of wine, put his glass down and said, "They, that is NASA backed by the U.S. government, put into operation a plan to end their perpetual famines of late. They have sent three nuclear rockets, all carrying warheads to destroy the moon."

"Their predicted expectations were that its rubble would disintegrate before reaching earth's atmosphere. Thereby preventing any fears of its debris from crashing into the Pacific Ocean without incident. With the moon gone they envisioned the results would bring about eternal springtime, one that would envelope the whole earth, thus evading their frequent famines forever and other world famines. But, their plan has backfired. It's hard to believe that in their genius they had not anticipated such an obviously elementary scientific subtrahendtion. What I further gathered from our Ham Radio is that the impact of the explosion of the moon created radical changes in the earth's electro magnetism, causing the earth to slow down, then causing it to come to a full stop!"

Moshe interjected, "Why that must have caused our disarray. We felt the earth jolt us down here, but we suffered no casualties, injuries or damage to the tunnel walls."

"It gets worse," said David. "Not only has NASA's operation backfired, but it has resulted in causing a polar flip. This disaster has buried all of the East and West Coasts of the U.S., Europe and parts of Russia under ice. In addition to all of this tragedy, some of the moon's debris has entered the Pacific Ocean, and some of its debris is now circling in an orbit in the earth's upper atmosphere. This could block out the sun for several months, which means trouble for those parts of the world. Their people will face even more severe and deadly famine. The only wonder is that the U.S. government is still functioning."

David, went on breathlessly. Breathing out a deep sigh, he went on, "I know our continent is out of danger and for that I praise God. We are all okay down here and we have enough food in storage to last us for several years or more. But, we have no news about the condition of our brothers and sisters still living above ground."

Moshe, who had been sitting by silently and almost speechless, now spoke up.

Addressing them all he said, "David, brothers, we have called for a general meeting. We want to let everyone down here know about these events and what has happened to cause the deadly sound and the violent rumbling and rocking of the earth we felt so strongly here below. The rocking back and forth of the earth did frighten most of us. We have scheduled a special meeting in the atrium and will explain what has actually transpired. We will start in a few minutes. Let's head that way."

****

In between time, right before Benny disappeared under the rocks, stones and rubble from earth's terrifying halt, he anxiously had tried to page his prognosticator and an avid Kabbalist, Bruce Allen. Bruce was not by the way a biological Jew, but he had always been his liaison within the three hundred companies who used him as an astrological tool, one who was able to peer successfully into the future of the world of finance. He was quite a phenomenon, strange but brilliant.

But, he wondered, was Bruce dead or alive? To his great surprise, Bruce answered the page.

Barely able to speak, he managed to say, "Bruce, this is Benny."

"Benny," he said, "I am surprised you were able to reach me during such a desperate hour."

"Bruce," he replied, "I am at the Res ..." His voice trailed off.

These were the last words Bruce heard him say, against a background noise which sounded like an explosion. His phone then went dead.

Laying in the dirt and rubble for what seemed like an eternity, Benny wondered, had the world come to an end?

Tons of rocks, large ones about the size of truck tires and smaller ones, the size of a baseball, exploded along with dirt splattering everywhere. Hideous snakes slivered out of the cracks in the rocks along the walls of what he thought must be a cave. Freeing his hands from the soft dirt, he was able to clear enough of the rocks surrounding him. Struggling, he finally managed to set his legs free.

When he went to stand up, he felt a sharp pain go through his right leg. He saw that it had a deep gash in it and it was bleeding. Hoping to keep the wound covered, he tore off a piece of his shirt and wrapped it around his leg. He was alone. Looking for an exit in the debris, he saw one. Shaking the dust and dirt off his clothing, he decided to see where the opening would lead. His mouth held the taste of dirt and dust kicked up by the explosion. He was dying for a glass of water.

Grateful that he had no broken bones, he stood fully erect and started to walk, haltingly.

Small pebbles and debris filled his shoes. He stopped, took them off and shook them out.

With his shoes back on he began to follow the opening in the wall that had collapsed around him. He wondered what could have happened to Felix and Fillmore.

It was dark. He had only a small cigarette lighter to light the way. He took the rest of his torn shirt and wrapped it around a piece of wood and lit it. He hoped it would last long enough for him to escape from what could turn out to possibly be his burial ground.

He saw an opening in a wall that at first looked like it came to a dead end, but as he cleared some stones and rocks away, he was able to follow a path through several tunnels. It seemed he had been walking through the tunnels for hours. Then he approached a wall which had crumbled in a tunnel that looked familiar, as if he had walked through it once before. The tunnel led to a room. Looking around he saw rows of bookcases filled with books. This must be someone's library, he thought to himself. Glancing around the room it appeared to have recently been inhabited. He picked up a book that was lying on the table. It was a New Testament Bible written in both Hebrew and English. This was the first time he had seen such a New Testament. Leafing through it, he found a small tract inside one of its pages. Curious, he read the heading of the tract, which read: You Can't Escape Death!

He was ready to jump out of his skin! The large bold words pierced him as if someone had shot an arrow through his heart! He started to shake. Shivering with fear, but still curious he continued to read: And it is appointed unto men once to die, but after this the judgement. Hebrews 9:27 was the source of this profound written statement. He was almost ready to put the tract down, when his eyes fell upon these words: What if you died today?

"Oh God, what if I do die today," he thought. "It was after all a close call. Where would I go if I died today? Is there really a hell," he wondered, "awaiting me? But, I've never felt as if I had ever done anything real bad, no drastic sin during my lifetime. I am not a criminal either."

Turning, his focus went back to the tract. He read John 11:25. As he began to read these words, simultaneously, he heard an inward voice read it for him. "I am the resurrection and the life: he that believes in me though he were dead, yet shall he live. And whosoever liveth and believes in me shall never die. Believe thou this?"

Intensely startled, he stood spellbound. He could not move. He was hearing a voice, but he did not see anyone. He wondered to himself if he was going crazy.

Trembling and shaking in his shoes, he managed to ask, "Who are you?"

Not really expecting an answer, he heard the same voice say, "I am Yeshua, your HaMashiach. For, whosoever shall call upon the name of the Lord shall be saved."

Barely able to speak, he whimpered out a weak, "What would you have me do?"

To his astonishment the voice answered him! "Read what is in your hand and listen to the men who will shortly arrive into this room."

Unexpectedly, he started to cry out loud. His tears now were not tears of fear but tears of pure unadulterated joy!

"It is true! It is real! Yeshua is HaMashiach! He is alive!"

Then he heard people laughing and talking. So, he turned toward the entrance and he saw a group of people enter the library.

Upon entering the room, one by one, Moshe and the other leaders with him could not believe their eyes. The wall that they had repaired had partially fallen down with a hole big enough for a man to fit through. Here was the man, standing with tears streaming down his face. In his hand was a copy of the Hebrew/English translation of the New Testament, also known as the Delitzsch.

At first, bruises, dust and dirt on his face and body disguised his identity. However, he did not slip by Barry, Marvin or Murray. They knew the government position he held in the Knesset.

Moshe, with a puzzled look on his face, spoke up first, not knowing who he was. "Sir," he addressed him, "My name is Moshe Rosen. Who are you? How did you arrive here?"

"My name is Benny Stein. I am the Minister of Defense for the state of Israel. Your men here know who I am. In reference to your question, how did I get here, well, for security reasons, I was kept protected and secluded in the President's Residence until a cosmic catastrophe hit the earth. I fell, buried under rock and debris. My only escape was following through a series of tunnels, beginning at the President's Residence and leading me here to this very room."

Moshe said in a hurried voice, "Murray, go quickly and get the first-aid kit and some fresh drinking water for our unexpected visitor."

Murray said, "Sure, I'll be back in a flash, Moshe."

Barry then interjected and asked him, "Why the tears?"

"I just found out who Yeshua is! He is my HaMashiach! He spoke the very same words I had begun to read from this tract, which I found in this copy of the New Testament." Benny was holding it in his hand. "In between its pages my eye caught the words in the tract, 'You can't escape death' and 'What if you died today.'" Then, he read, "For that which is corruptible must put on incorruption, and that which is mortal must put on immortality."*

"Terrified, I suddenly heard a voice speaking in my mind, saying, 'I am the resurrection and the life. He that is dead and believes in me shall rise again and he that is living and believes in me shall never die at all. Do you believe this to be real?'"

"Without having to go to the Greek, Hebrew or Aramaic, I knew this was God Almighty speaking to me! I then asked Him who He was and He answered me and said, 'This is it! I am Yeshua, I am God! I am your HaMashiach.' Tears welled up in my eyes and I started to cry. Then I realized that in the past I had always believed that our nation, the nation of Israel, was the source of my redemption. I had even gone so far in my desire to be eternal that I joined the Immortality Club. But, now I know that only God can give this blessed gift from God, Himself!"

Exuberantly, he said, "Now I know that Yeshua HaMashiach is God Almighty and that He is the true Son of God. He knew my belief system was confused so He personally deprogrammed me! Then He reprogrammed me with the truth about Himself and myself. I found out who I was and where I would be going when I leave this body of mine behind!"

Moshe spoke up and said, "Benny, what you have told us that you have experienced is very rare. It is called a Christophany. This is so rare that many of today's Christians may look upon what you experienced as a figment of your imagination, or they may even say you're psychotic. So, be prepared and be careful who you relate this experience to."

Benny said, "Moshe, I know that if I were to tell my friends and the people I work within our government, they would classify me in that category. For a few minutes I thought I might be going crazy myself. Maybe even brain damaged from my fall."

Moshe asked me, "What do you think of your experience?"

Benny replied, "After such an awesome revelation, I know I am not crazy."

Moshe said, "There will be some who think that your experience is not for today or that you are psychotic if you hear voices. Notwithstanding, I will say this, when humans communicate, we do it by sound, but what you heard was done by what is called telepathy and I believe it is possible that God spoke to you, in scientific terms, by way of neurogenic transmission. No doubt He related to you by radioactive propagation, a non-acoustic medium."

Benny was flabbergasted by Moshe's highly scientific and spiritual insight into his experience.

Benny said, "Now I know I was not crazy or psychotic. And I believe no one can take it away from me!"

Curious and concerned about his safety and that of the others he said, "Let me ask you, are you aware of the new legislation set by our government that death by guillotine has been made into law against anyone who tries to evangelize the Jews to convert to HaMashiach?"

Sadly, Moshe, in a soft-spoken humble voice replied, "Yes Benny, we know. Although we have been hiding in these caves, we know that our government has passed legislation into law that condemns us to death by guillotine. We also know about the Chondriana."

"Do you know, too," he asked in an emotionally excited tone of voice, "That it is impossible to permanently kill the Chondriana? Did you know that they are immortal and that they have an indestructible molecular structure? And that if you do kill them at first it would look like you were successful, but after three days they will resurrect themselves! They come back to life!"

Before Moshe could respond to that profound statement, Murray walked in having returned to the library with the water and first-aid kit. He handed Benny the glass of warm water. He rinsed out his mouth, and then washed his face and hands. Then he sat down, remaining pensive, still in awe over his profound and personal experience with Yeshua.

Murray then gently treated and wrapped the gash in his leg and tended to his other scrapes and bruises too. Remorseful, he said, "Murray, I want you to forgive me for nicknaming you a rock head."

Murray said, "Benny, that is all water under the bridge. Let's start fresh."

Benny said, "Yes, let's start fresh."

Then he asked, "Did you know that Iraq, Egypt, Saudi Arabia and Jordan are all wiped out by the start of WWIII? It was started by Ahmet and his ten Arab nations. To top it all off an unprecedented earthquake, a ten and a half off the Richter Scale, has hit the very area where we are now standing?"

"Yes," answered Moshe, "But notice how protected we all are here in the Valley of Achor? I might add by God's Divine Providence."

Then he asked Moshe, "Then what about the end of the world? It looks to me that the world we know of is coming to an end."

Joel, who had just walked in, overheard his question and he spoke up.

"Benny Stein, my goodness, how in heaven's name did you get here?"

Surprised that now he was easily recognized, he replied, "Well, it's a long story, which I presume I will soon be sharing with everyone down here."

"Yes," Moshe said, "Let's save your testimony for tonight's general meeting."

With his thoughts reeling, Benny stood, shocked by how easily he fell right into the Yeshua HaMashiach jargon.

Joel went on, "Benny, I could not help but overhear your question about the end of the world, such a profound statement. But, Yeshua spoke of it during His first appearance, indicating that the last and final stages of civilization will not come to an end until after the tribulation, which is now going on above us. Here I will show you what He had to say about this topic. It is all written here in Matthew 24:29–33."

Joel opened up his Bible and approaching him, he turned to those verses and read, "Immediately after the tribulation of those days shall the sun be darkened, and the moon shall not give her light, and the stars shall fall from heaven, and the power of the heavens shall be shaken."

"Now Benny," Joel continued, "I know that you are a scientist. What possible cosmic catastrophe can describe those conditions?"

Startled by what Yeshua described, he stumbled over his answerer and said, "A few things come to my mind. About three thousand meteorites bombard the Earth every year, but they are small and harmless. However, this could be the future killer asteroid ready to strike the Earth. Just before my journey down here, the scientific community received news that an asteroid followed by a comet ready to hit the Earth was imminent. It could even include a volcanic eruption, the largest one being in Yellowstone National Park in the USA. In fact that area, the mid-west USA, is the only land left unaffected by the polar flip, which has buried the East and West coasts of the U.S., Europe and parts of Russia."

Moshe said, "Yes, Benny we are aware of all these things. Yeshua predicted all of these cosmic events to occur would signal His visible return to Earth."

Benny was surprised to find out that the Bible indicated current scientific facts! "But how do you know all this?"

Moshe replied, "The power of the Holy Spirit is our teacher." Quickly turning to the Bible's book of John 15:26 he read out loud, "But when the Comforter is come, whom I will send unto you from the Father, he shall testify of me." And in John 16:13, he continued to read, "Howbeit when He the Spirit of truth is come, He will guide you into all truth: for He shall not speak of himself; but whatsoever He shall hear, that shall He speak: and He will show you things to come."

"So, Benny, the Holy Spirit makes sure we keep abreast of what is going on above us. This, he knows, will give us a sound sense of security, no matter what horrors may or may not befall us, now at the present time or in the future."

Benny quietly, he received the salutary succinct words spoken to him. He felt so renewed. His mind was clean and in perfect peace. Why, he thought to himself, had he been so blind all these years? What had he been afraid of? Was being ostracized by his family, friends and the government itself the real reason? If it was, then he had surely been a fool. Who among them could offer him such a healthy mind and spirit? Who in fact was powerful enough to grant him to have all his sins forgiven and give him the gift of immortality? And most of all the deep joy and happiness he had just found along with his true identity with the Godhead? And give him what he always longed for, eternal life? Somehow he knew there would be more questions that would arise

236

inside of his new sense of awareness now imbedded in his conscience. But, at least for now he knew he would get some of the true answers.

It was midnight. Everyone was asleep when he was awakened by what sounded like a distant triumphant march, followed by the triumphant sound of an orchestra usually played for the entrance of approaching royalty. The music grew louder and louder.

Suddenly, Benny found himself ascending towards the sky. With amazement, Benny looked up and saw that there were rows and rows of people in front, rising together with him. They formed together, shoulder to shoulder, in a narrow space about one hundred feet wide. And they were all rising, going up as if they were on the stairs of an escalator. His body was somehow different. He noticed from his hips down he was making a side-to-side movement, making a swishing sound, making it possible for him to fly into his place on the end, on the left side of the row!

Rapidly behind him the very next row of people formed another row and on and on. He did not see an end of the rows because suddenly he heard loud excited voices saying, "They're here! They're here!"

Astounded and excited but fearful, he said to himself, we are going up to heaven! He wondered if the Lord would let him look at those who were so happy to see us.

Glancing upward, he saw a large throne situated in front of the rows and rows of people. And the one seated on the throne nodded His head in an up and down jester, replying to him, "Yes."

He did not see His face, just His form. But, he knew it was okay to turn and look. So, he very slowly turned his head towards the left. As he turned, he saw what looked like a bright star and from inside the brightness he saw what looked like someone smiling, grinning from ear to ear. He could see no form, but once he looked, he heard the words, "There's Benny!" Excited beyond belief he thought to himself, it must be his angel! This must be the rapture Moshe showed him would take place, written in the New Testament! We're going to heaven! The olam haba, where there is no time or space! How profound! How beautiful, the wonder of GOD!

This must be the seventh trumpet that he read about. For Revelation revealed the events of the first six trumpets: nuclear war, the USA and NASA's destruction of the moon and its failure to bring about an eternal springtime, great hailstones and super-volcanic eruption seen with his very own eyes. He saw what came to pass.

It is glorious for us. We enter heavenly bliss with Yeshua, but greater woes will no doubt bring hell on earth.

Chapter 8

Catastrophes Of A Third Class Mingled With Catastrophes Of A First Class—A Crescendo Of Cataclysmic Catastrophes— The End Of The Last Days

"Immediately after the tribulation of those days ... there shall be signs in the sun and the moon, and in the stars ... shall the sun be darkened and the moon shall not give her light, and the stars shall fall from heaven ... and upon the Earth distress of Nations with perplexity... Men's hearts failing them for fear and for looking after those things which are coming on the Earth: For the powers of the heavens shall be shaken."
~Matthew 24:29 and Luke 21:25–26

"The end of all life on our globe, the death of the planet, the ultimate phase of the phenomenon of man ... The end of the world defies the imagination."
~Teilhard de Chardin, The Phenomenon of Man

The press, though limited, was making headlines. As for me, I found myself on the floor of the War Room. I was shaken and realized I must have been knocked unconscious. I picked myself up from off the floor. When I surveyed the room I noticed that all but one exit was blocked by fallen rock.

Burgeoning questions filled my mind; questions as old as the philosophers and mystics who made them.

But I wondered, was the polar shift a sign of the end of the last days? Did I just witness the eve of the apocalypse? Was the philosopher Philo right in believing that the end of the world would not enter a state of nonexistence, but rather that it would only form a new arrangement? Was Antony Milne correct when he proposed the theory that there are or will be a periodic cleansing of the Earth? What then, I wondered, did the biblical prophecies predicting the end of the world really mean the extinction of all humanity? After all, these were biblical prophesies put forth by my very fathers and the prophets of Judaism itself. Was it possible that their prophetic predictions of a coming cataclysmic-geologic convulsion of Earth was really true? Were these events meant to happen in real time or were they just fables?

When I glanced at the fax machine I saw that new faxes had come in. No doubt they had come in while I lay unconscious. Anxious, I quickly scooped them up. One was a report that had come in from the still functioning British Astronomical Association. Their headlines read, "Celestial Phenomena: Meteor to impact Earth in 12 hours. Most of U.S. & Europe Under Ice!"

This fax was followed by another fax. Amazingly the darned thing still worked! This fax was from the Royal Observatory. It issued a civil defense warning among the remaining citizens not yet evacuated. Imminently, an asteroid followed by a comet will impact Earth by the most dangerous asteroid in space. Or was it Eros? Was the comet Temple One that had left the Ort Cloud ready to impact the Earth? The comet and the asteroid were both classified once by Sir Isaac Asimov as "Catastrophes of a Third Class." The asteroid would be followed by the comet. It would pass by the astral belt. Both will enter Earth's elliptical path. It is to be considered a ten on the Torino Scale! They will be classified as an "Extinction Level Event!"

Beads of sweat rolled from my forehead, down my cheeks and onto the faxes I held in my hands. Trembling I read the following report from the Heidelberg Observatory. Its headline read, "Catastrophes of a Third Class and First Class Catastrophe now headed toward the Earth. The comet will follow the asteroid. An impact extinction level proportion is now approaching Earth's elliptical path. Issue an immediate global evacuation toward the southern hemisphere."

Rummaging through my thoughts, I wondered, even though I had received more than one report, were these deep observations and perceptions by the scientific community true valid warnings? Or were they a miscalculated error? Had the Space Guard Survey missed the detection? Was this a real nightmare bound to come true? Did a comet follow an asteroid on the brink of colliding with Earth? Would it be after all an extinction level impact? Quickly I put in a call to the Israel Meteorological Station. I was relieved to hear someone answer the call, grateful it was still in existence.

"This is Prime Minister Fox. Whom am I speaking with?"

"This is Dr. Cohen, Mr. Prime Minister."

"Dr. Cohen, I have received several faxes stating that Catastrophes of a Third Class are impending to impact Earth. They report that the Asteroid 1950 DA or Eros, followed by a comet, is going to impact Earth. I am asking you, Dr. Cohen, are these observations by the astronomers and cosmologists accurate? Is this event going to be the end of civilization as we know it?"

Dr. Cohen replied, "Accurate. However, we have another threat."

"Oh."

Dr. Cohen, a Paleo-Seismologist, said, "Seismic readings indicate that a series of earthquakes will shortly strike the Middle East."

Pensive, I asked, "Is it volcanic or tectonic?"

"Both," replied Dr. Cohen.

Hesitant I asked, "How big?"

Dr. Cohen warned, "Brace yourself! The first one will be approximately 6.5 on the Richter, but the next one will be a Catastrophe of a Third Class, the worse global event, a Mega-Thrust Earthquake. It will be intense due to the fact that the magnetic sphere will affect it. It will reach to a 10.5 off the Richter Scale!"

In a state of near shock, I went mute. Bracing myself, I asked, "When can we expect it to hit?"

Dr. Cohen replied, "Within the next twenty-four hours."

"Dr. Cohen," I said, "Find a place of safety quickly. I'll marshal what is left of Civil Defense and the Chondriana immediately." Sweat from my hand covered the telephone receiver. Wiping it clean with my shirt tail, I hung up.

Immediately I put in a call to Civil Defense headquarters, all the while wondering why Sky Cam had failed to pick up the approaching asteroid and comet.

Mike answered the call, "Mike here."

"Mike, this is Prime Minister Fox. I need an update on evacuation."

Mike replied, "We are already headed south. Evacuation is at a decent ninety percent, sir. All but what is left of essential services has been evacuated."

I said, "Mike, evacuate all of essential service employees too. In their place I will have the Chondriana desist from all burial procedures so that they can handle all essential services. Therefore issue a total evacuation of all police, firemen and medics. Issue a warning for all remaining evacuees to get to the highest ground possible and try to head south. Then get back to me within the hour."

Mike replied, "I will take care of this immediately, sir."

Next, I contacted my generals. The first to respond was the Chondrianas' General known as General One.

I contacted him and said, "General One, this is Prime Minister Fox calling. Where do we stand on the war?"

"Mr. Prime Minister, a Genie (furious sand storm) is on our side. It is so severe particles of sand are rising fifty feet above the ground, holding back the march of our enemies across the dried up Euphrates River. It is keeping all of our remaining enemies at bay. Geographically, nothing is left! Even if they were to try and march through it, the landslides will stop them."

"What is the status of the Chondriana," I inquired?

"Sir, we have stayed the course. We have surrounded what little is left of Jordan, and Ahmet's massive armies are all dead."

"General One, we are headed for several deadly Catastrophes of a Third Class, mingled with Catastrophes of a First Class. Desist from performing burial procedures. Instead, place half of your units to replace all essential services and have the rest of your men assist all remaining evacuees and head south with them to seek safety and shelter onto higher ground. Help as many survivors as you can find. Once all evacuations have taken place I will discontinue all human essential services at which time I will release that half of your contingents. Organize them into groups of ten. As you travel south have them maintain order and have them perform whatever essential services whenever and wherever they are needed and get back to me within the hour." With that, I hung up. Attempts to reach all of my other generals failed.

Frantic, it was time I paged my father to see if he was okay.

Successfully reaching him I asked, "Fillmore, where are you? Are you okay?"

Fillmore quivered and said, "Felix, I am trapped outside the War Room but I am okay, simply shaken. I'll see if I can make my way to you. Where are you?"

I replied, "I am in the War Room. I am okay. I have no injuries. However, all exits to get you out appear to be blocked."

Fillmore asked, "What about Benny?"

I replied, "Fillmore, I am sad to say, I don't see him anywhere. He could be buried under the rubble."

Swallowing my pride and in an emotionally charged voice, I said, "Dad, I am glad you are safe. I want you to know that."

Fillmore said, "Felix, my jaw just dropped. It was the first time in ages that you have called me Dad. Thanks, Felix, thanks. I needed to hear that from you."

"Dad, can you manage to remove enough rubble to clear the door?"

Fillmore said, "I'll try. And thank God the cell phones are working."

After successfully removing the rubble around him, I was grateful that Fillmore had eventually made it safely inside the War Room.

I decided to warn my father of the coming catastrophic events headed toward the Earth.

"Fillmore," I said, "Please have a seat."

"That bad, huh," replied Fillmore?

Solemnly, I replied, "Yes Dad, it's alarming and horrifying news."

Curious, I asked Fillmore, "What about the Chondriana who were guarding the War Room door? Did you see any of them?"

Fillmore, stumbling over his words replied, "Felix, if they are still alive they must be buried. I did not see any one of them. All that is in front of the War Room has been buried under tons of debris."

I said, "Well, Dad, perhaps this is the test to see if they will manage to escape death and pull through to resurrect themselves in three days."

Fillmore said, "Let's hope they do. We need their protection."

Fillmore then asked me, "What about communications? Are any still up and running?"

"To my astonishment the fax machine is still operating. I have received several faxes from the astronomy societies. They tell us that astronomers and cosmologists say calculations are correct and they indicate that an Asteroid-1950 D.A and/or Eros followed by a comet is headed towards an Earth impact. In addition they warn us to expect earthquakes, one that is likely to register off the Richter Scale!"

Anxious, Fillmore asked, "My God, Felix, what about our financial outlook?"

I replied, "Financially, I am checking what is left of the global markets."

Stunned, Fillmore yelled, "What do you mean what is left?"

I replied, "Television, radio and other media are not in working order, but phone and fax lines continue to function intermittently. Even the written press that had been severally limited, has come to a sudden halt! But, the Internet continues."

"It was from these sources that I have learned of global financial catastrophes which have already taken place. The return replies from the worldwide stock exchanges trickled in. First the NASDAQ read, 'In one day, the performance of the NASDAQ crumbles.'"

"Brace yourself, Dad," I said.

Not surprised, I read aloud, "The failure of the New York stock exchange and the NASDAQ have totally failed to perform due to the tragedy of the polar flip which occurred on both the East and West coasts of the U.S."

"Then, one by one, fax reports came in from the global markets of London, Sweden, Norway, Tokyo, Amsterdam and Brussels, Paris, the Euronet and even the Deutsche House exchanges have ceased. All global utilities, commodities and equity markets have reached the Zero margin! Economic death has ushered in a worldwide depression."

"In one day the stock exchanges of the entire world have died! It was 'Doomsday!'* I can hardly believe it, Fillmore. Gone are the industrial, electronic, digital and microchip revolutions of the world. Soon, the World Wide Web will cease."

"Cities and nations have collapsed like fallen dominos. Whole continents have become land sacked. Global mayhem has followed."

My hands were shaking so hard. I could hardly give Fillmore the rest of the global economic report. It was death to Fillmore.

I wondered was Anthony Millner's statement true that "periods of regeneration start at the beginning of a new era and often end with a destruction tale."

No sooner had my thoughts about the end of all things, when suddenly the ground shook violently under my feet. Structures around me continued to move. Dust filled the air, while ear splitting sounds rumbled and the sounds of mighty winds of a fierce squall arose. The Earth erupted right before our eyes. The Residence started to topple, tossing Fillmore and I back and forth like ping-pong balls. I fell, hitting my head against the corner of the table, but I remained conscious. To my utter horror, as I felt like my eyes were almost ready to bulge out of their sockets, I watched Fillmore fall into a deep crevasse, burying him alive. The vast global upheaval disturbing the forces continued to create cosmic whirlpools of dense dust. Dust so thick that I could just about see my hands in front of me.

I called out to Fillmore. "Fillmore, are you okay?" There was no response. Terror stricken, I managed to pull myself up and made my way toward where I had seen him fall. I wondered was he still alive.

Immediately, I began to remove several rocks. Then I saw my Father. His eyes were open. I reached out to touch him. His body was already stone cold. He was not breathing!

I felt for his pulse. There was none! My attempts at performing CPR were unsuccessful. I had to face it. My Father was stone cold dead! Stunned and in shock, I held back unexpected tears. I was crushed by having watched my Father's death. I wiped the dust from his face and hair. Silently, I gave a brief eulogy as I covered him with my own jacket, "Goodbye, old boy." And with that I closed his eyes.

Brushing myself off, I did a quick body check on myself. I was grateful none of my bones were broken, but my mouth was dry and taught. My lips were so parched I could hardly let out a sound. Taking a few halting steps through the debris, I found a water cooler still standing. I bent down and put my lips to the spigot, turning up the leaver, drinking as much as I could to rinse the dirt from out of my mouth. Feeling the cool fresh water, I then rinsed the dirt from off my face and hands using my handkerchief as a towel. I could hardly believe I had survived and escaped becoming a victim of Earth's tragic and abrupt violence.

Glancing around the room, I looked to see if there were any openings to make way for an escape from what had now become a hell hole. Could I escape from what otherwise could at any moment turn into my own burial grounds?

I had successfully escaped Ahmet and his rule over most of the then known world. Even escaping Ahmet's attempt to take over the U.N. Even establishing my World Federation. Even recovering the stolen code to deactivate all of the Chondriana. Unbelievable, I thought to myself. Even beating Ahmet and his ten Arab government.

I surveyed the room, what was left of it, and noticed a small opening leading to a passageway into an underground tunnel. Despite frequent rumblings of the Earth beneath me I made my way, removing some of the debris I found in my way. Totally alone, I forged ahead.

Then I came upon a maze of tunnels, all of which I had never come upon before. I kept going through tunnel after tunnel. Some of the tunnels were blocked by fallen debris, rocks and large stones.

I wondered if I would ever find a way out. Or would this really turn out to become my final resting place?

245

After walking and sometimes stumbling for what seemed like hours, I came upon a series of tunnels that were graded on steep inclines. I began a gradual climb up several of the elevated grades. I continued to climb, hoping this was the way out.

My hopes were high as I got up from one set of steps. Yet, this led to several more tunnels that were also on an elevated grade. It had numerous steps too. There were so many I climbed that I lost count of just how many grades and steps I had already climbed.

All at once a bright light lit up ahead came shining through the tunnel.

Finally I saw the sky! There was an opening above me. An exit at last, I thought out loud as I pulled myself up over a large rock. I saw that I had reached the top surface of a plateau that looked like Mt. Nebo. It had a prominent spur of the Abarim mountain range. I was elated. Almost out of breath from the climb, I breathed out a sigh of relief. I was not going to be buried alive after all!

From this unobstructed vantage point I could see the magnificent, unparalleled view of all of what was left of my country. I estimated I must have traveled some ten to fifteen miles through the tunnels.

Then I scanned the landscape below. Highways had erupted with asphalt cascading like waves in a heavy sea surge, pouring it into the Red Sea. Numerous vehicles blazed from the fires caused by ruptured fuel tanks of cars, trucks and other vehicles. Others had been tossed into the air, hanging from buildings, completely destroyed. Unparalleled devastation was to be seen everywhere!

Turning to look at the West Bank, Judea and Samaria, usually half buried with dirt, now lay completely covered with dirt. Reaching all the way from Egypt to Damascus were no longer visible. They lay completely buried. Nablus Road, once the crossroads of the ancient world with its highway, was gone.

The destruction was even more profound as I saw Jordan's side of the West Bank. It was thoroughly obliterated! Gone were its buff hills, white towns and lush green valleys.

Strange, it was surreal! It seemed so unbelievable that I was witnessing it all for myself.

Here I was, a witness to what eschatologists only spoke of, read or wrote about in the Tanach by our prophets of old.

Yes, I recall the one time I even had read about it on the pages of our prophets, but I didn't believe it would ever come true! To me it was like reading Science Fiction.

And now here I was hearing all the sounds of violence and seeing it all happen right before my very own eyes!

Then, in the blink of an eye, as if out of nowhere, I heard blood-curdling screams fill the air.

My God, I could hardly believe it! What looked like a river turned red was really a river of human blood! The stench was full of the smell of death warmed over. I read about this too! I remember precisely reading in the last book, the Revelation, that the blood would run for a "distance of two-hundred miles long and reach as high as the bridle of a horse!" In unabashed horror I witnessed biblical prophecy take place. As I looked south of Aman, Jordan, what was left of it, down toward the Aquaba, I saw the Earth start to split some two hundred miles away. Its path crossed the Negev desert highway. It followed the old railroad path through the entire length of the Kings Highway. It wiped out all of Amman, Jordan, known to many as the "City on Seven Hills." This ferocious earthquake also wiped out all of Moab and Edom, sometimes called by travelers as, "The Enchantment of the World." Yet, it left me on top of Mt. Nebo still standing.

When I turned my head toward Qatif, I saw what I thought to be impossible. Another immense earthquake zipped through the Gaza Strip, wiping out the Gaza Ez ARISH Railroad, totally destroying the entire coastal highway next to it. Spiraling south, the earthquake continued to rip the ground open. Ripping open the ground and tearing the sixty mile Med-Dead Sea pipeline apart, ending on the southwestern shore of the Dead Sea at Ein Bokek and pulverizing and wiping out the Med-Dead Sea hydroelectric power plant.

I remained spellbound. To think that in one brief span of time, in one cataclysmic instant, I watched, petrified by what I saw.

It could not be, but it was. As another major earthquake erupted, moving the waters of the Mediterranean sea at ten miles per second, creating a tsunami. A three-mile high mountain of water came crashing down, splitting Haifa, ripping open all along its port, all the way through to En-eglaim and Samaria. Snaking its way down the now dried up bed of the Jordan River, taking with it what remained of the West Bank and dumping it into the Dead Sea, the epicenter of the earthquake and leaving Tyre, Sidon and Beruit, Lebanon, completely disintegrated by the rush of the fierce tsunami, barely missing me, but destroying all of the people who had not heeded evacuation orders. I knew this earthquake was of such tremendous proportions that it turned out to be one that had never been witnessed in all of recorded history. To my amazement, the sky above me suddenly turned black as pitch, though it was still daytime.

Without warning a blazing white thunderbolt struck the Earth beneath my feet. Peals of rumbling thunder filled the air. It missed hitting me by mere inches. What I thought was a thunderbolt turned out to be a comet, releasing scathing gases as it passed near Earth, causing Earth's internal heat to blaze, which in turn created electrically charged winds. Grey clouds burst asunder replacing the pitch-black sky, casting off beams of red, pink and silver colors of light shining in all directions.

I fought to hold onto a nearby tree, hoping to escape the hurricane winds as they swept the Earth and seas that now were no doubt rushing over all the continents of the Earth.

All I could do was let out a soft groan, while my eyes remained transfixed on the sky. What I saw almost defied description. I could hardly even ever dream of seeing such a cataclysmic cosmic event. I watched as the hydrogen from the comet's tail mixed with the oxygen of Earth's atmosphere as it formed its gases into a chain reaction, igniting the atmosphere, making it toxic.

I felt like I was turning into stone as the celestial phenomenon of the comet followed Earth's elliptical orbit. Its motion was rapidly spinning like a giant wheel. Then, it went into a zigzag movement, getting closer and closer in its fierce descent. Unexpectedly its head projected itself into the direction of the sun. Thunderstorms, premonitory to more earthquakes, rocked by rain driven winds burst into torrents of rain. Landslides followed everywhere my eyes could follow. The comet's gravitational pull triggered massive violent lightning attacks, filling the sky with black waves, igniting what was left of forests, fields and cities, while earthquakes and tidal waves raised havoc all around the globe. Its gases enveloped the Earth, creating huge, powerful tornados and enormous sky fires precipitating violent and continual electrical discharges that collided between the Earth's atmosphere and its terrestrial atmosphere. The comet's tail whipped up great winds of thick dust, gases and ice, blotting out the sun. Days of darkness were sure to follow, creating climatic repercussions and worldwide famine. Bread, if you could get it, would have to sell for no less than twenty dollars a loaf! Its discharges complete, the comet freed itself from its cosmic convulsions, leaving Earth as quickly as it came, finding a new orbit. But the scientists must have miscalculated, for the comet had already arrived. Would the asteroid follow it instead? Now a horrified spectator, I faced the harshest environment of my life. I wondered why the USA's Cosmic Eye of the NEAT, Near Earth Asteroid Tracking System, built by NASA had failed to capture and give an advance warning to the people of the Earth. Not to mention the out right failure to destroy the moon and Earth's hope for its Eternal Springtime project. Instead, they, along with global warming, triggered mainly in the U.S. an unending drought and famine.

Where had the Earth Simulator, the largest super computer in the world, gone wrong?

I collapsed. As I lay supine upon the cold wet Earth, raging rain sent chills through my body, almost cold enough to turn my blood into ice. Stone boulders, scrapping against my skin all along the rock strewn plateau, sucked in my body. It was my worst nightmare come true. Unexpectedly, the hurricane that sent cold torrential wind driven rain came to a halt. Blasts of intense heat waves instantly dried my rain soaked clothes, warming my near frozen body.

Once again the Earth shook violently. A powerful volcanic eruption had just occurred spiraling my body into the air. I landed near a small disheveled garden, some fifty feet from a small church, set near the edge of the plateau.

Pulsing pain pummeled against my entire body. I managed to pick myself up.

Looking eastward I could see as far away as what used to be the city of Jerusalem. Towards the west of the city I watched, horrified at what I saw. It was simply incredible! With my eyes glued to the spot I saw the Earth move. It was another mighty earthquake! The impact split what still remained of the Mount of Olives, splitting in two, creating a great valley in between. I saw the Earth move half of the mountain, pushing it toward the north and the other half pushed toward the south, pushing rocks and filling the chasm left by the earthquake, altering the entire landscape. Running eastward beneath the remains of the Temple Proper. The ground swiftly passed towards the right of what was the Altar of what was our third Temple. On the south side of the eastern passageway, swallowing up the Temple Mount, the Dome of the Rock and the Mosque called Haram-Al-Sharif, second only to Mecca, a holy Muslim shrine. From there running parallel along the entire Rift Valley fault line it destroyed the entire Hejaz Railway. Then it ran into the Gulf of the Aqaba on into the Red Sea and on into the eastern part of Africa causing the edge of two tectonic plates that frequently rubbed against each other to rupture.

As I grappled with such immense seismic changes and the changes occurring in the lithosphere and the hydrosphere of Earth, tremors shattered rocks and whipped me back and forth like a boxer being pummeled in the ring. I could not help but wonder what was keeping me from entire physical collapse. With all that was going on around me, what was keeping me alive? Why was I being protected when all around me was death?

To my astonishment, the earthquake that had created the tsunami that had split the Haifa's port, shifting the Earth, opening it once

249

again. Beginning at Haifa it rippled open the Earth, piercing through the cities of En Glamin to the springs of the En Gedi Reserve. Opening wider into an even wider chasm, gushing waters from the Mediterranean Sea formed a double river right before my eyes. It left all the land from Geba to the North border of Jordan to Amnon (Rimmon), also known as The City on Seven Hills, disintegrating all that remained into dust. While on its southern border, it completely obliterated what used to be the International Hotel, once the site of a luxurious Arab Hotel and ancient Jewish Cemetery. It totally demolished what was left of the Dome of the Rock, leveling the hill, upon which it once stood, producing an eerie lunar landscape, spinning the weather out of control, changing the sea and river currents, rearranging the shoreline, the soil and the complete environment and no doubt the entire globe.

Yet, I still held onto my life. But, this was a very different earthquake, in that it created powerful aftershocks. Usually aftershocks would last from seconds to possible minutes. Instead these aftershocks lasted the whole day!

I gasped at the scene while aftershocks destroyed the coast of Lebanon. Traveling at speeds which looked to be over five-hundred miles an hour. Vigorously it cast large blocks of asphalt to float into the Red Sea, the epicenter of the previous earthquake.

The heavens were not to be outdone by the Earth's upheavals. Immediately following these destructive earthquakes and the comet that had left Earth's elliptical path, I saw what appeared in the distance to be an asteroid.

Clutching my arms around one of the stone columns of the tiny church, I remained safe.

Checking my pockets, I found them full of gravel and dust. Fumbling through my breast pocket I pulled out a pen. It was the one Felixovna had given me on our first date. Struck by a curious insight I felt like someone had pierced my heart with a hot poker. I proceeded to take the pen apart. Inside I found a transmitter. What a fool I have been! And even a bigger fool for failing to maintain basic security measures with her. How had I been so insipidly in love? Why did my love for her blind me to the point that I ignored all security protocols? It was so unlike me to be so totally naive, letting my heart rule my head. Was it true love or was it perhaps obsessive infatuation? This thought made chills run through my body. Then I quickly dismissed this stinking thinking of my past from my mind.

In an instant, without any preemptive warning I heard the profound sound of silence. Everything around me grew quiet. The winds had ceased and the rain and the heat had dissipated, although earthquake aftershocks remained continuous.

My mind swirled with thoughts of the pending major seismic pulse announced earlier by our own Geological Society. Would it strike at any moment? There had been, at the time, a strong sense that the predicted tectonic earthquake would be followed by a volcanic earthquake. Would that be next? What or where had the appearance of an asteroid gone?

Then, unexpectedly, for no apparent reason I saw the asteroid appear, but it missed hitting the Earth, disappearing out of my view. For the first time in my life, I thanked God!

Then out of the corner of my eye, however, I saw something else. It was heading toward Earth, coming from the west, but I could not make it out.

My ears were ringing from the death sounds now silenced below. I collapsed, but remained conscious.

My head pounded like a hammer. Questions filled my mind. Was there another asteroid? Were the astronomers correct? Had they written their square roots and geometrical figures, speaking in algebraic terms, correctly? Had their calculations of an asteroid predicted to impact the Earth by a mega-thrust hyper velocity of fifty thousand miles per hour been accurate? Would this impact then trigger a series of more volcanic and tectonic earthquake eruptions? Would these Catastrophes of a Third and First Class cause its tremors to spread ash and lava to scorch what would be left of the Earth? And an even more drastic question filled my thoughts, one I dared not to think, yet I gave way to it. Would it be an extinction level event? Or could it be another near miss and explode and then vaporize into Earth's atmosphere, left to disintegrate there? Would this explosion cause fragments to hit Earth starting more fires and tidal waves?

I had to stop these questions. If I did not let them go they could send me over the edge.

Then out of the blue, in one unexpected, unpremeditated, synchronized instant, all of the material world, the entire world of appearance grew strangely quiet. All sound ceased once again.

Though my clothes and my flesh were torn and tattered, I happily joined in with nature and grew very quiet too! I was grateful for the gifted ability to clear my mind of all thoughts, opinions, assumptions, presumptions, suppositions and projections of the future. I became intensely focused, going into a deep state of consciousness. As I set about to decipher my thoughts, I was astounded. I believed I had entered the Alpha state.

Listening intently, I could hear what sounded like the faint blare of a trumpet. It grew louder and louder. Although I could hear it, like an

251

electromagnetic force, I could not see it. Then in sheer terror I slowly turned my head up toward the sky and saw a bright light. It looked like a ball of fire was approaching Earth headed right at me! As it drew closer and closer I saw it suddenly take the shape of a man. It was a Hazazoh.* However, I was able to comprehend that what I saw had come from another dimension. What happened next almost defied description. Through no mental or physical action of my own, I entered this dimension. It felt like I had entered some field of time I could only describe as being in a place where all was constant. It was stupendous! But, how could that be? I was still physically in real time! It was obvious to me as a scientist that somehow my perceptions had entered a new dimension, one that surpasses the boundaries of space and time.

I wondered and was almost certain that this experience was the paradoxical dimension that I was taught about when I was Bar Mitzvahed. This place is where the future is behind us. Known to some in the rabbinical world as Achor. And it is also known to them as the olam haba in which there exists neither time or space. So, this is it! Oh they may have known about it, but here I was, able to comprehend this unique experience. This was the cosmological constant, a world that existed in a dimension surpassing, not even existing in time and space. Had I really entered infinity, the perfect constant?

In a flash, I heard a great-unsolicited voice speak inaudibly to me. It was a calm, male voice speaking. He was speaking to my mind, just as one holds a telephone to his ear and hears the voice that is on the other end of the line, but the person is not physically present or visible. It was without a doubt, a voice independent of the antecedent, independent from my own thoughts. Old paradigms broke down in me signaling a mind-blowing breakthrough, entering a whole new dimension and deeper world of thought.

Facing a new horizon, I experienced the most awesome paradigm shift. My mind was sensing an unsolicited alteration in my perception. I felt this experience expanded my state of spiritual awareness. I sensed my own consciousness enter a state of ecstasy, one I never knew or felt before. What I can say is that I was receiving this voice and this communication neurologically. Listening to what the person behind the voice had to say. Transmitting it to me telepathically. Perhaps, was it being transmitted by means of some form of undiscovered radiation propagation, similar I would say to the cell phone in modern day use?

Was it possible or even probable that I had the capacity to really enter into a rare form of the mind, a true reality? Was it at all possible, I asked myself for the whole of humanity to have the same subjective ability and the capacity to enter into it while still existing in real time? Or was the transmission possibly transmitted by cosmic rays? Could it be transmitted perhaps by ultra violet light rays? Or could it be by infared light rays? Or perhaps radio waves transmitted by the so called dreaded gamma rays? What if transmission is by means of some form of chemical communication?

I continued to ponder in flashes of thought as He spoke to me personally and contemporaneously, speaking to me in my own vernacular, the English language. When the voice spoke to my mind He inaugurated in me an unexpected, whole new reality and burgeoning true imaginations.

Frightened, yet awed I asked, "Who are you, sir?

The voice complied and identified Himself saying, "I am that I am. I am Yeshua, your HaMashiach. This is it! I am Yeshua. I am the God of your forefathers."

Jolted and still in this new state of expanded spiritual consciousness and at the same time experiencing an ecstatic abnegation, I recalled what Carl Jung once wrote about this synchronistic phenomena I found myself in. I realized that the knowledge was not abstract, but absolute. Knowledge not mediated by the sense organs, where the conscious activity and sense perceptions are suppressed. It was, I felt, a perception independent of space and time.

It was a communication that was subjective and not known to or discovered by the whole of humanity. I acknowledged that this must mean the term I always had hated to hear, born-again. Now I understood it to mean to be given a fresh new start into the world of the supernatural. All of my doubts and thoughts about the manner of this communication vanished, when the voice spoke to me again. Speaking to me in a very even and calm voice without any tonal inflection, the person behind the voice repeated, "I am the Way, the Truth and the Life. No man can come unto the Father but by me. I am the Resurrection and the life. He that believes in me, though he were dead, yet shall he live and he that is living and believes in me shall never die."

In an epiphany, I recalled that my very own Jewish Fathers wrote what Yeshua was now speaking to me in Holy Scripture. It was a genuine validation of this experience. It is something so profound to experience I can hardly articulate it.

Yeshua continued to speak saying, "I will pour upon the house of David, and upon the inhabitants of Jerusalem, a spirit of grace and supplications ... They will look toward Me ... they will mourn over him ... like the embitterment over a (deceased) firstborn."* The voice continued, "It will happen on that day, the prophets will be ashamed

... His feet will stand on that day on the Mount of Olives which face Jerusalem on the east, and the Mount of Olives will split open at its middle, east to west (forming) a very wide valley; half of the mountain will move north and half of it to the south."

Remaining transfixed, I gasped and fell to my knees of my own accord. What Yeshua once said would happen at the end of the world, I had just witnessed with my very own eyes.

The constant whirlwind of catastrophes pummeled against me. The tremendous beating left my clothes torn and tattered. My skin was rubbed raw and covered in dirt. My body was aching and racked with pain. When all of a sudden I found my body become pain free! No more pain! I felt like I would burst with unutterable joy! Tears filled my eyes and rolled down my face in buckets.

Remorseful, contrite and humbled, I realized that this could be no other than Yeshua HaMashiach. My people's long awaited HaMashiach, who was speaking to me directly. Transformed and converted, I did feel like I was a newborn baby. It was then that I was able to comprehend that yes there are many gods, but only one Yeshua that you can have a personal encounter and relationship with. For this was certainly a one on one paradigm shift, an epiphany.

A spiritual awakening, the invisible inner light which had jolted my intellect and moral consciousness, so profoundly that I had to conclude that the natural world, although it consists of the whole world of appearance, is not the whole world of reality! I realized I had made a complete a volte face! In this rare encounter with HaMashiach I had also acquired all new attitudes!

This explosion of new concepts transformed and broke all, usually unseen, chains of all my doubts and fears, and gave me a new spiritual consciousness.

In what seemed like a split second I experienced the unusual faculties of the intellect, intuition, true imagination and spiritual perceptions. These were so powerful and strong that it would control all of my life forever! After a swift period of intense introspection, I could scarcely contain the sense of reverence and awe that filled my entire being.

I could hardly believe I had let go of all logic and made my mind up. Not the mind we think rationally with, but the mind that is moved by the heart, the seat of our emotions.

Emotions that do not express themselves verbally, but rather conceive of and make a decision to receive Yeshua HaMashiach as my own personal Lord and Savior. I was so overcome with love, I felt as if I would explode with joy. It filled me with an intense desire now to become holy and to lead a holy life.

This was a radical departure from my own orthodox and I might say scientific views and ways of thinking. For a brief second I questioned myself. Doubts crept into my thoughts, rearing their ugly heads once again. Am I crazy? Is this really true that Yeshua HaMashiach is the embodiment of all truth? But just as quickly as doubt reared its ugly head, I realized I had just experienced and comprehended true intelligent, spiritual revelations. This was a subjective, unseen explosion of new concepts, transforming my conscience, breaking the chains and setting me free from any and all falsehood.

This was to me, knowledge of God independent and outside of reason. It was experiencing a deep innate, intimate union with God Himself! It was a transformation through the very real presence of God. God was no longer an abstract being to me.

For the first time in my life I uttered a spontaneous prayer to God the Father, calling to at the same time a prayer for erroneous utterances found in the Tanach that I had memorized as a small boy in the Synagogue.

Then in my own words I prayed, "O Hashem, God of my Fathers, I ask you to forgive my sins against You and against Your Son Yeshua HaMashiach whom I now ask You to come into my mind, my heart, my soul and my spirit. I ask this heavenly Father in the name of Your Son, Yeshua HaMashiach."

I closed my eyes for a few moments. Then the preaching of the two witnesses three-and-a-half years ago came to my mind. How wrong I had been, and I wondered how can I ever face those Jews whom I sent to their death? These thoughts pierced my heart like a knife.

And the Lord heard me and to my grateful heart and much to my amazement He said to me, "Felix, I died for those sins too!"

This dynamic interaction filled me with a magnitude of pure bliss and an ecstasy that were not and could not be an occult or psychotic experience. Much to my shame that is exactly what I myself had accused Murray Andrews of that time not so long ago. It had happened on the eve of the Jerusalem Day celebration at my condominium. I realized what a fool I had been. Opening my eyes I turned once more to look towards the east. What I saw was unbelievable. A dazzling site appeared. Filled with indescribable passion, feelings of joy and love, I watched. It was no longer just a bright light or the figure of a man. It had to be Yeshua! As I continued to gaze up at the sky, this brilliant regal being came down from the sky and His feet touched down upon the Mount of Olives. Even though I was seeing it, I could hardly believe I had been chosen to see such magnificence!

It was then that I realized it was my own Jewish Prophet, Zachariah, who foretold that which I now was able to see in real time!

Now all that I had learned about the Tanach began to make real sense to me. Further enlightened, I no longer steeled myself off from God emotionally and I was no longer bewildered by the infinite and dazzling order of my mind and its new sense of spirituality. I found unexpectedly, that I suddenly had perfect recall of what the Prophet Daniel had to say. I was able to repeat it word for word in my mind. "I was watching in the night visions and behold with the clouds of heaven, one like a man came; he came up to the One of Ancient Days, and they brought him before Him. He was given dominion, honor and kingship, so that all peoples, nations shall serve him; his dominion would be an everlasting dominion that would never pass, and his kingship would never be destroyed" (Daniel 7:13–14).

I burst out into uncontrollable tears, tears of gratitude that surpassed all human wisdom and understanding. With a clear head and a clean heart I had a Savior and a message to bring to those who had survived. One that was no longer mysterious. It is the end of the last days.

NOTES

1

1. The Bilderber Group. The Invisible Power house. www.LaRouch.com. and www.Paraciceioe.cin/mx/artical/Bilderberss.htm. P. 17 & 29.

2

1. Jesus Messianic Prophesies and Their Fulfillment (The First Coming.) Christ for the Nations, December 1979. P. 208.

2. Science and the Bible. Messianic Prophesies and Mathematics. P. 123–127.

3. The Case for Christ. Lee Strobel. Zondervan Press. 1998.

4. Thompson Chain Reference Bible. Condensed Cyclopedia of Topics and Texts. P. 695. 2007-2013. 2890. B. B. Kirkbride Company, Inc. Indianapolis, Indiana.

3

1. The Tanach. Isaiah 53. Hebrew/English Translation, The Art Series, Mesurah Publications. 1996. P. 189.

4

1. By Way of Deception. Victor Ostrovsky and Claire Hoy/ Glossary of Terms 1990. P. 154.

5

1. The Old Testament Pseudepigrapha, Pocalypse of Daniel. City on Seven hills. James Charlesworth. Duke University. Doubleday and Company, Inc. 1983. P. 761.

2. Pop Trivia. Seven Up. Francis X. Lambdin. Catholic Digest. March 1996. NOTE: There are three geographical locations that stand out as being The City on Seven Hills. The Seven Hills of Rome: Avebtube, Caelian, Capitolline, Esqiline, Palatine, Ourirnal, Vunina; The Seven Hills of Jordan: Jebel Aman, Jebel-Al-Welbdeh, Jebel Hussein, Jebel Quala, Jebel

Ashrafieh, Jebel Nadhif, Jebel Nadhif, Jebel Al- Welbdehb, Jebel Al-Taj;
The Seven Hills of San Francisco: Original Home of the United Nations:
Nob Hill, Twin Peaks (North & South), Telegraph Hill, Russia Hill, Potrero
Hill, Mt. Gutrol, Mt. Davidson. 1996. P. 299.

6

1. Searching For The Ark of the Covenant Intensifies. Randal Price
Publisher. Messianic Times. Spring 1993. P. 11.

2. The Search For the Lost Ark. Harold A Severner. Chosen People
Publisher. March 1982. ISSN 164-5323.

3. The Gospel Truth. Southwest Radio Church Publisher. September
1982. Volumn 22NO10-L292.

4. Is The Ark of The Covenant In Ethiopia? Ephriam Iaac. Biblical
Archeology Review (BAR). July/Aug. 1993.

5. Did The Ark Stop at Elephanttine? Bazale Porten. Biblical Archeology
Review (BAR). May/June 1993. P. 219, 225, 230.

GLOSSARY

Albedo—Reflective function of snow.

Alpha, Cosmic—The beginning point. Invented by Sir Isaac Newton.

Allegory—The use of ideas by stories, symbols, or figures of speech. Deeper meaning of Holy Scripture intended by the divine Author, than what is written by man. Use of the imagination over deductive reasoning.

Alpha state of mind—When the mind relaxes and reflects. The ability to release the mind from all of its prejudices, worries, opinions, assumptions, presumptions suppositions and projections.

Allegory—To explain or teach something by telling a story or illustration.

Amnesia—A crisis of memory. Confusion in deliberation. Loss of direction. Spiritual blindness caused by doubt induced amnesia triggered by either spiritual rape or when a person is presented with an apparent contradiction between his religious beliefs. An individual deprived of memory who as a result becomes disoriented and lost. Arthur Schlesinger, Jr.

Amphibological—Ambiguity of language. A phrase or sentence ambiguous because of its grammatical construction. Capable of more than one interpretation.

Androcentric—Male centered mind set.

Asteroid—It is an Earth grazer. Icarus, a Meteorite discovered in 1948 has an eccentric orbit. At one end of its orbit, it passes through thee Asteroid Zone. At the other end it approaches the Sun even closer than Mercury Disk. It passes Earth four million miles apart.

Anthropomorphic—Humanization of God. Attributing human characteristics to God.

Anthropormorphism—An interpretation of what is not human or personal in terms of human or personal characteristics.

Apocalypse—Universal Revelation.

Anti-Christ—Against Christ, opposed to his authority, (1st and 2nd John). Those who deny that Jesus Christ came in the flesh, (1st John 2:22; 4:3. Many deceivers) (Anti-Christs 2nd John 7.) The man of sin, (one person to stand out.) The Antichrist. 2 Thessalonians 2:3–8 and Revelation 13:1 describes him as a east, and a blasphemer who will make war with the saints of Jesus Christ. He will command worship by people, tongues and nations for himself, and he will be worshiped by all the world as if he were God Almighty. He will control all people by being able to perform miracles and give life. His identification code is 666 (Revelation 13:18). Down through the centuries he has been identified in the Middle Ages by Pope Innocent, The Third as Mohammed. Later on he was identified by The Reformers as being the Pope himself. Note these identifications are not Biblical. However it can be noted that the Muslim's Koran does have 6,666 sentences in it. In more recent times he has been identified at Napoleon then Hitler.

Anti-Semetic—Against the Jew and the Jewish Nation of Israel.

Antitype—A meaning of Holy Scripture conveyed through a person i.,e., Adam and Christ (Romans 5:14), an action (the flood waters in the time of Noah and the waters of Baptism A(1st Peter 3:20–21), or thing. Type is the thing, i.e., the sacrificial Lamb of the Passover celebration by the Jews were not to break any of its bones. The antitype is Christ sacrificed for us, to pass over our sins, while on the cross not one of his bones were broken. The Literal sense must be determined before the typical (also called spiritual sense) or fuller or deeper meaning, in so far as they are fulfilled at a later period in the dimension of time.

Apocalypse, "Unveiling," "Revelation"—When the Lord Jesus Christ comes for the second time to the earth. He comes first for his body of believers, then unveils and reveals himself to the entire world, all at one time to act in divine intervention to save the planet of Earth from complete destruction, due to catastrophic events, there ushers in the new age.

Archeology—The study of ancient cultures.

Asteroid—Numerous rocks consisting of Metal, Iron or other debris. Revolves in the Asteroid belt.

Atmosphere, Cosmic—The mass of gases that surrounds the earth and is held by the force of gravity; the air. An odorless, tasteless and invisible mixture of Oxygen, Nitrogen, Argon, Carbon Dioxide, Hydrogen, small amounts of Neon and Helium. Vapor. In Physics; a unit of pressure equal to 14,699 pounds per inch.

Axis, Earth—Never moves more than 24.5 degrees or less than 22 degrees.

Bibliography—References. Also known as Citations.

Biosphere—The region surrounding the earth that can support life, including the lithosphere, the hydrosphere and the atmosphere.

By-child —A kinder word for "Bastard."

Calculus—System of calculating advanced mathematics, using algebraic symbols to solve problems dealing with changing quantities.

Calculus, Cosmic—Using calculus mathematics in Astronomy. Started by Nosttrodomus.

Catastrophe—A sudden, widespread or extraordinary disaster. A tragedy that usually brings ruin and or death.

Catastrophes of a Third Class—Isaac Asminov's classification of Cosmic disasters affecting earth and the lives of humans. The bombardment of the earth by Extraterrestrial objects; Comets, Asteroids, Volcanos, Earthquakes, including Earthquakes created by Plate Tectonics and Continental Drift.

Catastrophes, Biblical—Predictions of Cosmic disasters called, "The End of the World."

Catastrophes, Cosmic—Disasters by collisions on earth by asteroids, comets, meteorites and other heavenly bodies.

Catastrophes, Geological—Natural disasters by volcanic eruptions, earthquakes, floods and tidal waves.

Chemical Communication—Communication by means of radioactivity transmission, communicated by chemicals at the speed of light (186,000 miles per second) using alternating currents. A process as yet undiscovered.

Contemporaneously—Events occurring all at the same time period.

Comet—A heavenly body with a starlike center made up of ice rock and an iceberg tail that melts. Sometimes collides with earth with disastrous consequences.

Delusion—A false belief about the self, person or object outside a person. Self-deception. Believing a lie which a person thinks is true. Error, or faulty reasoning.

Dual Fulfillment—First coming of Messiah: He enters history. He enters man's domain. The Second Coming of Messiah: He enters man's domain and brings about the Messianic Age.

Epiphany—A sudden insight into the essential but personalized meaning of an important human truth. Spiritual awakening. Transformation. The unveiling and personal presence of God.

First Coming of Messiah—Jesus came, Jesus died, Jesus rose again. (1 Corinthians 15). He enters history. He enters man's domain, to forgive sins, to grant eternal life, to experience human nature, to empathize with our lot in life. To be our friend. To grant open personal and individual communication between God and man. To become our mediator between God and man. To establish a close and intimate relationship with us. (See Notes 3 for prophesies fulfilled by Jesus 1st coming, identifying him as the true Son of God and our Messiah.)

Geology—The study of the earth, dry land.

Geosphere—See Lithosphere.

Horse Snow—Cocaine.

Hydrosphere—The water portion of earth. The water vapor in the atmosphere and the water on the surface of the earth as opposed to the atmosphere.

Imitation—An extreme and long-lasting form of learning.

Interpretation, Biblical—Exegesis, Hermeneutics. The science that endeavors to discover and explain the true meaning of sacred Scripture by means of a determined set of rules and methods of interpretation, i.e., Literal (see Literal) Allegorical (see allegory).

Liebestaum—Memories from the past.

Literal—The immediate and primary words as conveyed according to the intention of the author. The description of what actually did happen. In the future the millennial kingdom will be a literal reign of Christ on earth (Isaiah 32:1, Matthew 19:28, Ezekiel 21:27, Revelation 12:15). However, the literal sense can also include the use of metaphors (John 21:27).

Lithosphere—The solid portion of the earth as opposed to the atmosphere (air) and the hydrosphere (water); geosphere.

Magnetic field, Electro Magnetic field—Invisible force with fields in the earth, sun and moon.

Mala fide—Good faith. The opposite is rare, i.e., acting in bad faith, with the intention of deceiving or defrauding.

Mendeleev Table—List of Chemical element, periodic table..

Meshumadism—Lable branding Jews who leave Judaism and convert to Christianity.

Messianic Jew—Biological Jew who convert to Christianity but do not call themselves Christian but instead are called Messianic Jews.

Metaphor—A figure of speech. (John 21:17). When Jesus commanded Peter to "feed my sheep," he was speaking of sheep metaphorically. That is to feed not the animals but his followers, not literal food but spiritual food, the Word of God to feed their minds and spirits.

Metaphysics—Vast comprehension of concepts and the energizing picture of reality behind the world of primary perception which transcend higher dimensions of ordinary language and logical reasoning about who God is, where the person is going and what he has to do.

Meteor—Mass of rock or metal that enters earth's atmosphere from outer space.

Meteoroid—What is left from a comet and may detonate into the air.

Meteorite—A meteor that has reached the earth without burning up. Most made up of iron and nickel.

Mole—A spy. A political burglar called doing a Black Bag Job. This term created by former President Nixon.

Mystical Experience—Secret or hidden knowledge of God, The eternal. His light untarnished. "… doctrine that knowledge of God and spiritual truth may be attained intuitively." It is not knowledge about God but God Himself that is apprehended intuitively. Mystical theory is the secret or hidden knowledge of God revealed to a human persons intuition.

Mystical Phenomena—The human ability to enter another reality while still in real tine.

Mysticism—An altered state of consciousness. Is not an occult experience.

Nanosecond—Is one billionth of a second.

Nemesis Theory—Extinction of a dark star.

Negev—or Harvegve, the gateway to the Negev, the desert in Israel, made up of limestone rock, on its borders everywhere and its multicolored sandstones at the Wadi Rum.

Nulli gravida—A woman who has never be pregnant.

Opprobrin—Disgrace, caused by shameful conduct.

Occident—West.

Orient—Oriental, East.

Paradigm Shift—Psychological shift in opinions.

Paleontology—The study of early living.

Parousia—The personal presence of God at the 2nd coming, or presence of Christ which will complete history, the salvation of man, the coming of God's Kingdom to earth and the end of the world (or system of things).

Praxis—Action, practice as an exercise or practicing art, science or skill. Usual or continual conduct, such as habit or custom.

Precognition—The ability in perception to see the future.

Prophesy—The communication of divine revelation written down by inspired men who were God's representatives on earth. History written in advance, as a message or prediction about the future. "God ... spake in times past ... by the prophets. From the start of Jesus Christ's Ministry in A.D. 33 until now he ... has in these last days spoken unto us by his Son" (Hebrews 1:1–3).

Revelation—The uncovering or unveiling. It expresses what God has made known to man that which he could not find out on his own. General revelation—is what god reveals to all men in nature, history and the nature of man himself (Romans 1:19,20). Special revelation—Given by Jesus Christ to his Apostles as found written in the Bible. The Ultimate revelation—Given to everyone on earth at once as to who Jesus Christ is. The visible appearance of Jesus Christ to all mankind all at one and the same time. The Bible Book of Revelation—The last book of the New Testament. The unveiling regarding future events. The end of all Bible Prophesy and revelation fulfilled. It is a record of prophetic visions that Jesus Christ himself gave to the Apostle John, A.D. 98 while he was banished on the Isle of Patmos for his faith in Christ. It was written to bring comfort to the persecuted church in the final days of this world. It depicts the final battle between good and evil. The end of the devil and all cowards and the beginning of the new rule by God (Revelation 1:1–22, 20). And as far as comparing its symbols to current events we have received only the outline along with the missing dimension of time makes it difficult to interpret ahead of time. Or to interpret the final outcome of history, the nature of the world to come in chronological order, or the end of time. We can and must rely on the Holy Spirit to reveal its truth to us in his time and in his way.

Rift Valley—The longest rift on the Earth's surface. It is 4000 miles long and an average width of 30–40 miles. It is very, very deep. The fault line from Jordan to Africa.

Sabra—Natural Born Israeli.

Second Coming—When Jesus returns to earth, man's domain for the 2nd time. It will come at a time of total catastrophe for the actual earth and the possible extinction of man. Prior to earth's shattering events Christ will appear to his people first (Hebrews 9:29, "... and to them who look for him shall he appear a second time ...")

Semantics—Linguistic development. The study of the meanings of language in the use of and true meaning of its words. Some misuse of words and their true meaning that turn out to be false or spurious.

Shangri-la—A non-existent place believed to be a place where you would live in eternal peace and happiness. A place similar to heaven or Nirvana.

Simultaneously—An event or situation that occur together in a split second. Can understand the experience of what is spoken.

Socialism—Government ownership. It is not a share the wealth program. It is really a method to consolidate and control wealth.

Solar System—The macrocosm.

Spiritual—Understanding the supernatural and invisible realities which are non-existent in the world of our sense experience, i.e., the five senses; see, hear, taste, touch and smell and the material world. Instead it involves the invisible world of thought, perception, intuition, insight, apprehension, comprehension, character and love. Using inductive reasoning and seeing invisible realities, i.e., the atom and electricity made visible by the power it provides us with.

Subconscious—It is the barrier of the mind where time and space do not exist. In order to enter it you must still the conscious mind of all thought, silence. Silence is to the mind as sleep is to the body.

Tautology—Needless repetition, i.e., etcetera, etcetera, etc., etc.

Telepathic, Neurogenic transmission—Possibly one of the mediums the Lord Jesus Christ communicates with his people. Conveying one's thoughts without speech or talking and without writing. A non-acoustic medium of transmitting thought by means of the use of radioactive propagation, using alternating currents, done with a vastly greater accuracy.

Thermodynamics, Law of—Energy changes , energy flow. Conversion of heat into other forms of energy. The first law of thermodynamics is the law of conservation of energy. The energy content of the universe is constant. The second law of thermodynamics is spontaneous change from uneven distribution of energy to an even one. The entire content of the universe is steadily increasing.

Type—See Anti-type.

World—Cosmos, system of things. The end of the world is the end of the dimension of time and the system of things now governing and controlling our world.

GLOSSARY
FOREIGN WORDS AND POLITICAL TERMS

AFL—Arab Liberation Front.

Agency—Term used by outsiders to describe the CIA.

Agent—A spy.

Bag Job—Breaking and entering to steal or photograph intelligence material.

Big Daddy—National Security Agency (NSA) in U.S.A.

Black Box—Known as ELINT, an electronic intelligence collecting device.

Black Chamber—Any room used to code or decode intelligence messages.

Bodels (Plural, Bodlim) or Lehavdil—Go between various safe houses, to protect spy agents.

Burn—Reveal the true identity of a spy.

By-Child—A kinder word for Bastard.

Circus—Headquarters of British intelligence.

Daylight—Israel's Highest state of Military alert of the Mossad (Israel's Intelligence Agency.

Delitzsch—Hebrew/English Translation of the New Testament.

Diamonds (Yahalomin)—A Unit in the Mossad that handles intelligence communications to their agents in target countries.
Din—A Jewish term used for the strongest form of judgement against criminals of the state.

Duvshamin—Usually United Nations peacekeeping troops paid to transport messages and packages back and forth across Israeli-Arab borders.

Fansis—Arab word for infidels.

Frames (Misgarot)—Jewish self-protection units set up all over the world.

Gadult—A state off expanded spiritual consciousness.

Hadash—A state of ecstatic devotion and abnegation to a degree of leaning towards the Divine. A high degree of religious enthusiasm towards God. The utter degree and of self-detachment to God.

Hagama—The Mossad. Israel's Secret Service Intelligence.

Hamodia—A daily newspaper published by the Agudat-Israel, the Jewish Orthodox Party of the Knesset (Parliament) which has four member.

Ha Negev—The Gateway to the Negev Dessert.

Hazohf—Being moved. A state in which one is moved by a sense of alteration in perception. A new perception of reality. See also Paradigm Shift.

Hazazo—A state of deep ecstatic devotion to God. A state of abnegation and having turned to the Divine. The utter abandonment to God. Being moved. A stage of emotional transformation in which one is moved and senses an alteration in their mind. See also Abandonment, Abnegation, Perception.

Har Am, Al-Sharif—The Temple Mount. Located on it is Mosque called "The Dome of the Rock." To the Muslim it is second only to Mecca, their holiest Shrine.

Hesed—Benevolent. Kind.

Hibonevt—Contemplation.
Institute—The Formal name of the Mossad. In English known as Israeli intelligence and Special Operations.

Kalashnkov—An Arab rifle.

Kefyeh—Arab Scarf or Arab Head dress.

Kibtznek—Israel's elite Tank Soldiers. The Army that is first to go into combat.

Kidon (Bayonet)—Israel's Operational arm Metsada, responsible for executions and kidnappings.

Kifirs—Arab word for unbelievers.

Lakam—Israel's Prime Ministers Scientific Affairs Liaison Bureau.

Lap—Psychological warfare.

Maulter—Hebrew word meaning simply unplanned. Used to describe unplanned or improvised security route.

Meshumadim—A Jewish expression for a crazy person.

Mozel Tov—Good Luck.

Odessa & SS—Are the same. Hitler's Secret Service of Europe and Germany.

Reconnaissance—An exploratory military survey of enemy territory or preliminary survey to gain information.

Rizadh—Name of Arab Secret Service.

Safabun (Goldfish)—The department within the Mossad that deals with former PLO, Hamas and Hesbulla.

Shaback—The Israeli equivalent of the FBI. Israeli internal intelligence force.

Shalom Alei-khem—Jewish term used to say Good-bye, Peace.

Shicklut—The Israeli department that handles listening Personnel, i.e., Marats.

Shin Bet—Former name of Shaback.

Shuitat-Bidzan—Dessert Police along the Arnon/Bagdad Highway.

Tafrit—Jewish term for Dinner Menu.

The Farm—A training school for the United States Central Intelligence Agency (CIA) in Virgina.

The Company—Another name for the CIA.

Taxi—Monet in Israel.

Tsiach—Annual meeting of military and civilian Israeli Intelligence organizations; also for the next year, listed in descending order.

United Arab Emirates—Arab Organization.

ACRONYMS
Arab, English, and Hebrew (Jewish)

ACHOR: Valley of Achor, located below the cliffs of Qumran

ALF: Arab League Front

AMAN: Israeli Military Intelligence Unit

BCLZ GENE: Stops cellular death of Chondriana. An Army of Cloned men

IDF: Israeli Defense Forces (The Mossad) Israeli Intelligence

IED: Improvised Explosive Device

KIDON: Israeli assassination Unit

LAKAM: Israeli Defense Ministries, Scientific Affairs

LPN: Licensed Practical Nurse

MK: Member of the Knesset who make up Israel's Parliament

NDE: Near Death Experience

O-LAM-HA-BA: Jewish Term for "the World to Come"

RAMBAM: Historic Fourteenth Century Rabbi-Maimonidies

RCN: Reconnaissance—An exploratory military survey or preliminary survey of enemy territory to secretly gain information, using aerial vision.

RIZAD: Arab Secret Service

R.N.: American Registered Medical Nurse

SABRA: A natural born Israeli

SAYRET-MATCAL: Israeli Top Intelligence Reconnaissance Command

SIR: Subterranean Interface Radar-a recently built machine, capable of emitting images of what may rest underground.

U.N.: United Nations

LIST OF CITATIONS

Amiran, D.A. Earthquakes in Jerusalem: Israeli Exploration, Israel Exploration Journal, Vol. I. The Israeli Exploration Society with Assistance of the Hebrew University and the American Fund for Israeli Institutions. 1951.

Archeology. Vol.84, #5. September/October, 1981.

Asimov, Isaac. A Choice of Catastrophes: The Disasters That Threaten the World. Simon & Shuster a Division of Gulf-Western Corp., Rochester Center, 1979.

Atlantis Rising. #17. Livingston Mt. 1998.

Axelrod, Dr. Alan and Phillip, Charles. What Everyone Should Know About the 20th Century: 200 Events that Shaped the World. Adams Media Group, 1995, 1998.

Bass, George. Categories of Archeologists: Natural, Ocean Terrestrial. Omni, 1991.

Bendiner, Elmer. The Rise and Fall of Paradise.

Bernstein, Herman. The Truth About The Protocols of Zion: a Complete Exposure. KTAV Publishing House, 1971.

Bertman, Stephen. America's Future and the Crisis of Memory: Cultural Amnesia. Praeger.

Birnbaum, Philip. Daily Prayer Book. Hebrew Publishing Company, 1977.

Blackstone, William E. Jesus is Coming. 1916.

Boleah, Samuel, Rabbi. The Wolf Shall Lie With the Lamb: The Messiah in Hasidic Thought. Jason Aronson, Inc., 1993.

Brittin, Norman A. A Writing Apprenticeship. Auburn University. Holt Rineb, Ast and Winston. 1977, 1973, 1968, 1963.

Buber, Martin. For The Sake of Heaven. The Jewish Publishing Society, 1930.

Buck, Pearl, S. The Good Earth.

Brunter, Noel and Kenneth. Philosophy, the Power of Ideas. Mayfield Publishing, 1990.

Byers, Gary, Rev. Associates for Biblical Research.

Conde' Conde' Nast. October, 1994.

Carey, John and Catherine Young. From Smart to Brilliant Weapons: Technology, The Military Section. Business Week, October 8, 2001.

Carter, Leslie. The Science of Human Extinction: The End of The World, a View, a Review.

Cayce, Hugh Lynn Eds., and Littler, Glen. Edgar Cayce and The Dead Sea Scrolls.

Charlesworth, James H. The Old Testament Psudepsgraphia, Apocalyptic Literature and Testament. Doubleday Company, Inc. Garden City New York, 1983.

Charlesworth James H. Reinterpreting John. Bible Review, February, 1993, 18–28.

Charlesworth, James H. First Glance. Bible Review, February, 1993, 2.

Cheetham, Nickolas. Keeper of the Keys: a History of Popes from Peter to John Paul II. Charles Schribner's Sons, 1983.

Childe, Gordon V. Prehistoric Archeology. University of Edinburgh.

Christ For the Nations Eds. Messianic Prophesies and Their Fulfillment (The First Coming). Christ For the Nations 1979.

Cohen, Bruce L. Israel, Arabs and the Middle East. Mt. Tabor Publishing, LTD, 1991.

Cooper, David., Th.M.Ph.D., Litt.D The True Nature of the God of Israel. Biblical Research Society.

Davis, Daniel J. Dualistic Dilemma. Gap, March/April 1999.

Davis, Timothy. Middle East—World News & Views. Zion's Fire, 2001.

de Chardin, Teilhard. The Phenomenon of Man Harper Torch Books: The Cloister Library, 1959.

Discover Magazine. Breakthrough Science, Technology and Medicine: Water 400 Miles Below Earth Surface. May, 1998.

Discover Magazine. Earth's Interior and Plate Tectonics. Discover May, 1998.

Discover Magazine. Plate Tectonics. Discover January, 1997, 55.

Discover Magazine. Re-inventing Life. Discover May, 1998.

Drosnin, Michal. Bible Code II: The Countdown. Viking Penguin, a member of Penguin Putnam, Inc., 2002.

Elior, Rachel. The Paradoxical Ascent to God: The Kabbalistic Theosophy of Habad Hasidism. State University of New York, 1993.

Eidelberg, Paul, Professor, ed. Dateline Israel: Arafat and the Koran. Zion's Fire, May/June, 2000.

Encyclopedia.com. Negev: Great Rift Valley. The Concise Columbia Electronic Encyclopedia, Third Edition. Columbia University Press, 1994.

Epstein, Isidor, B.A.,Ph.D.,D.Litt. The Faith of Judaism London, The Soncino Press, 1951.

Evans, Mike. Jerusalem Betrayed: Illusion or Reality. Word Publisher, 1997.

Family Circle. Follow That Bird. Family Circle, August 13, 1985.

Fried, Daniel K. Delitzsh, Hebrew\English New Covenant. Hope of Israel Publications. 2003.

Glaususz, Josie. The Great Gene Escape.

Gribetz. The Atlas of Jewish history: The Timetable of Jewish History: Near End Books, 1948.

Graham, Billy. Why Did Jesus Say, "I Am"? Decision Evangel, September 1991.

Gruber, Daniel. Dual Covenant Theology. Pentecostal Evangel, June 1999.

Hammel, Eric. Six Days in June: How Israel Won the 1967 Israeli War. Charles Schribner's Sons, New York, Maxwell Macmillan, Int'l. Press, 1992.

Hargrove, Lubrett, M.D. Temple, Temple, Where Was the Temple? Gospel Truth, L3, L7, Vol.23 No.8. South Church Radio July, 1983.

Hawking, Steven, Stephen W. A Brief History of Time. Bantam Books, 1988.

Hertzel, Theodore. Introduction to Jewish History. 1898.

Hills, Christopher and Rozman, Deborah. Exploring Inner Space. University of the Trees Press, 1978.

Hook, J.N. The Grand Panjamdrum. MacMillan Publishing Company, 1980, 1991.

Hoyle, Fred P. The Black Cloud. Harper Brothers, 1957.

Huchede, P., Rev. History of the Antichrist. Tan Books & Publishers, Inc.,

Hunter, Brian, Ed. KGB Statesman Yearbook. McMillan Publishing Company, 1977.

Hussein King of Jordan. Valley of Peace. Conde' Nast Travel, October, 1994.

Ironside, H.A. The Lamp of Prophesy. Zondervan Publishers.

Isaac, Ephriam. Is The Ark of the Covenant in Ethiopia? Biblical Archeology Review (BAR) July\Aug 1993.

Isaccs, Ronald, H. The Jewish Information Source Book.

Israel, Steve and Forman Seth. Great Jewish Speakers Throughout History. Aronson, Jason, Inc., Northvale, N.J., 1994.

Jaroff, Leon. A Chip Off of the Doomsday Rock. Time, March 23, 1998.

Jaroff, Leon. Whew. Time, March 23, 1998.

Jeffrey, Grant. Armageddon.

Jones, Vendyl. Will the Real Jesus Please Stand Up or Seven Riddles of Israel and Messiah. Priority Publishers, June 1983.

Jones, Vendyl. What Happened to the Tabernacle and the Ark of the Covenant? Researcher Institute of Judaic Christian Research (IJCR), 1992, 7.

Jones, Vendyl. Agan Gilgal and Emsq Achor. Researcher: IJCR, May, 1993.

Jones, Vendyl. The Copper Scroll and the Excavation at Qumran. Researcher: Vendly Jones Research Institute, December 1995.

Jones, Vendyl. Who Is and Who Was Jesus? Researcher: Vendyl Jones Research Institute, March 1998.

Jones, Vendyl. A Door of Hope. Researcher: Vendyl Jones Research Institute, October 1998.

Jones Vendyl. Location, Valley of Achor. Researcher: Vendyl Jones Research Institute, November 1999.

Jones, Vendyl. Excavation 2002 Targeted for Early Fall. Researcher: Vendyl Jones Research Institute, September 2002.

Kahn, David. The Codebreakers. The Macmillan Company, N.Y. 1967.

Kaufman, Ashers, Dr. Where the Ancient Temple Stood. Biblical Archeology Review (BAR). March/April 1983, 40–60.

Kutter, Hillel. First Sa'ar: 5 missile boat launched. Jerusalem Post, March 27, 1993.

LaHaye, Tim and Jerry Jenkins. Left Behind: A Novel of the Last Days. Tindale House Publishers, Inc., 1995.

Lambdin, Francis X. Pop Trivia: Seven Up. Catholic Digest 1996.

Langer, Jeri. Hasidism Piestic Movement: Nine Gates to the Hasidic Movement. Aronson, Inc., 1937.

Lapide, Pinchas. Israeli's, Jews and Jesus.

Larouch. The Bilderberger Group: The Invisible Power House. Larouch Publications.

Lehman, Manfred, R. The Key to Understanding the Copper Scroll: Where the Temple Was Buried. Biblical Archeology Review, November/December 1993.

Le Shan, Lawrence. The Medium, the Mystic and the Physicist: Toward a General Theory on the Paranormal. The Viking Press/Eastern Institute Book Reading Program.

Leslie, Charles. The Science of human Extinction: The End of the World, a Review.

Liberman, Paul. Anti-missionary Bill in Limbo. Messianic Times, Vol.9 #4, 1999, 11.

Littler, Glen, D. And the Editors of Cayce, Hugh Lynn. Edgar Cayce on the Dead Sea Scrolls.

Luce, Celia. A Small Pebble. Perception/Focus.

Maimonides, Rabbi. Letters of Consolation. The Jewish Quarterly Review, 1890.

Makovsky, David. U.S. Cool on enhanced Strategic Ties. Jerusalem Post, March 27, 1993.

Malgo, William. The Beginning was the end and after the end there is a new beginning. Midnight Call.

Marsden, Victor, E. The Protocols of the meeting of the Learned Elders of Zion. Translated from Russian. The Thunderbolt, Inc, 1934.

Merkle, Gerorge, Dr. New Frontiers in Molecular Biology, Life Crystals, the Sun. Power/Enlaw (Video) Productions, 1993.

Milner, Anthony. The Science of Catastrophes. Prager Publishers, 2000.

Miller, Robert. The Informed Argument: A Multidisciplinary Reader and Guide—Part I : An Introduction to Argument Avoiding Logical Fallacies, 1977.

Minkin, Joseph, S. The Teachings of Maimonides. Aronson, Jacob, Inc., 1993.

Morell, Virginia. A Clone of Our Own.

Morrow, Lance. Has Your Paradigm Shifted? Time, November 19, 2001.

McBride, W.S., Ph.D. Could the Antichrist catch us napping? United Community Church of Glendale, California.

McCarter, Kyle, P. Jr. The Mysterious Copper Scroll. Bible Review. 1990.

McCarter, Kyle P., Jr. The Mysterious Copper Scroll: Clues to Hidden Temple Treasures. Bible Review, 1992, 34.

Newsweek. The Changing World Before Our Eyes. Newsweek May 31, 1999.

The Week. News. This Week, July, 2002, 9.

Oren, Michael, B. Orde Wingate: Friend Under Fire. Azure, Number 10, Winter 5761/2001.

Osirovsky, Victor and Clare Hoy. By Way of Deception. St. Martin's Press, 1990.

Our Daily Bread, ed. Radio Bible Class Ministries. September/October/ November, 1999.

Our Daily Bread, ed. Radio Bible Class Ministries. December/January/ February, 2000.

Payne, Ronald and Dobson, Christopher. "Who's Who in Espionage." St. Martin's Press, 1985.

Premium Resources. Great Rift Valley. Encyclopedia.com. The Concise Columbia Encyclopedia, Third Edition. Columbia University Press, 1994.

Premium Resources. Negev. Encyclopedia.com. The Concise Columbia Encyclopedia, Third Edition. Columbia University Press, 1994.

Price, Randall. Search For Ark of the Covenant Intensifies. Messianic Times, Spring 1993, 11.

Philo. On the Eternity of the World: Yonge's Title, a Treatise on the Incorruptibility of the World,

Portin,Bezalel. Did The Ark Stop at Elephantine? Biblical Archeology Review (BAR) May\June 1993.

Riemer, Jack, Rabbi. The Book of Jewish Custom.

Saphire, Adolph, D.D. Lectures on the Jews.

Schachter, Sholom, Zalman, Reb. Paradigm Shift: From the Jewish Renewal. Jacob Aronson, Inc. 1993.

Schwartz, Stephen, A. The Secret Vaults of Time.

Sevener, Harold A. The Search For The Lost Ark The Chosen People. 1982.

Shapiro, Robert. The Human Blueprint, First Edition. St. Martin's Press. 1991.

Shigon, Norma. Cutting up Israel Again. The Philadelphia Inquirer Letter to the Editor. 1977.

Silverstein, Hermman,. David Ben Guria Smith, Houston, Robert. Pella of the Decapolis. Archeology, Vol. 8, Number 5, September/October, 1981.

Steinberg, Robert R. The Copper Scroll. IJCR. Researcher, May 1993.

Stone, Irving. The Artscroll Series\Stone Edition, The Taanach. Mesorah Publications, Ltd. 2007.

Stone, Nathan, J. An Introduction to a Best Seller. American Association for Jewish Evangelism, Inc. 1988. 4.

Stover, David and Erdman, Erik. Facts Values and the Future. Pager Productions and An imprint of Greenwood Productions Group Inc. www.pager.com. 2000.

Strobel, Lee. The Case for Christ. Zondervan Press, 1998.

Suvidler, Leonard. Jesus and the Jews: Farewell to Christian Dogma, A professor of Catholic Thought and interreligious dialogue. Temple University. Welcomat, April 15–21, 1987.

Tan, Paul, Lee. The Interpretation of Prophesy. Cushing/Malloy, Inc. 1974.

Telchin, Stan. Betrayed. Chosen Books, 1981.

This Week, Eds. News Breaking, Stopping Nuclear Terror. This Week, July, 5, 2002.

Thompson, Mark./Washington. Notebook: Defense Mechanisms— Seper Find Marines Get the Ride of Their Life. Time.

Thordike. Burnhart. Advanced Dictionary, Scott Foresman and Company.

Tofer, Alvin. Future Shock. A Bantam Book, Random House, 1970.

To End All Wars. TV Movie Film.

Trye, Peg. My Generation. Longevity, September/October, 2001.

Velikovsky, Imannuel. Age if Chaos. Doubleday and Company, Inc., 1952

Velikovsky, Immanuel. World's in Collision. Doubleday and Company. 1950.

Vesilinde, Brit, J. Science Writer. National Geographic. Vol. 193, Number 2, February, 1998.

Walvoord, John. F. Armageddon, Oil and the Middle-East Crisis.

Weiner, Herbert. 9½ Mystic—The Kabbala Today. Collier Books, Macmillan Publishing Company, a division of Macmillan, Inc., 1992.

White, Ellen. The Great Controversy Between Christ and Satan. Lishing Assn., 1911, 1916, 1939, 1950.

Wilkenson, Peggy, O.C.D.S. The Mystic in You. Living Flame Press.

Will, George, F. The Last Word, The Gospel From Science. Newsweek, November 9, 1998, 88.

Woodrow, Ray. History Making Day, 1917.

Woodrow, Ralph. His Truth is Marching On. 1977.

Wright, Karen. Human in the Age of Mechanical Reproduction. Discover, 1998.

Wright, Robert. Ideas-Games, Species Play. Time. January 24, 2000.

Wurmbrand, Richard. Christ on The Jewish Road.

Washington, Youn, Catherine, Cary, with Otis Port. World's Smart to Brilliant Weapons Technology: The military. Business Week, October 8, 2001.

Zabbidoff, Marc, ed. Fear and Longing. Discover, May, 1998.

Zalman, Schecter,. Shalomi, Reb. Paradigm Shift: Jewish Renewal Teachings. Jason Aronson, Inc., 1993.

Zlman, Schecter, Shalomi, Rabbi. World's of Jewish Prayer. Jacob Aronson, Inc. 1993.

ABOUT THE AUTHOR

 After thirty years of research and development on her novel, "Eve of Apocalypse," Rita Kelley answered her call to write.

In her secular work as a Registered Nurse, she cared primarily for Jewish patients. She had several opportunities to lead some of them miraculously to Christ, some at literarily the time of their last breath.

Always ready to help others and after seeing many positive results, her heart and mind created an intense passion and desire to bring hope to the nation of Jews, as well as individuals she came in contact with. This is why she gave her novel its sub-title, "The Valley of Achor, a Door of Hope."

In her years of work as an R.N., she also undertook missionary work, taking the leadership and establishing a regional office for the Hospital Christian Fellowship, a national and international, non-profit Para-Church organization.

As Regional leader in the Delaware Valley, she took responsibility for all Communication Media. She made appearances and gave interviews on television, radio, and on the lecture circuit.

Her extraordinary eclectic life experiences and her actual conversion to Christ is revealed in the fictional characters of her novel. This makes her a good candidate to use her novel as a tool to evangelize Jews and even Muslims, both who do not accept Jesus Christ's true identity.

Rita De Masi Kelley, D.D.

P.O. BOX 46

Sicklerville, NJ 08081-2008

Hm.Ph.(856)629-4844

www.eveofapocalypse.com

Cell(856)340-6698

ritakelley@comcast.net

Qty.	Item	Unit Cost	Total
	Eve of Apocalypse	**19.95**	
		Shipping	
		Grand Total	

SHIPPING & HANDLING: *Please add $5.95 shipping per item ordered.*
For orders placed outside of the U.S., add $7.00 shipping per item.

Ship to: Organization:_____

_____ _____ (Mr./Mrs./Ms.)_____
Last Name   First Name

_____
Street Address

_____,_____ _____
City   State   Zip

Phone: (   ) _____ E-mail:_____

THANK YOU FOR PLACING YOUR ORDER.

LaVergne, TN USA
30 July 2010
191549LV00001B/2/P

9 780982 637067